Savage Barbecue

Savage Barbecue

Race, Culture, *and the* Invention of America's First Food

Andrew Warnes

The University of Georgia Press   *Athens & London*

Set in Adobe Garamond by Bookcomp, Inc.
Printed and bound by Thomson-Shore
The paper in this book meets the guidelines for
permanence and durability of the Committee on
Production Guidelines for Book Longevity of the
Council on Library Resources.

Printed in the United States of America
12 11 10 09 08 C 5 4 3 2 1
12 11 10 09 08 P 5 4 3 2 1

Library of Congress Cataloging-in-Publication Data

Warnes, Andrew, 1974–
Savage barbecue : race, culture, and the invention of
America's first food / Andrew Warnes.
        p. cm.
Includes bibliographical references and index.
ISBN-13: 978-0-8203-2896-6 (hardcover : alk. paper)
ISBN-10: 0-8203-2896-0 (hardcover : alk. paper)
ISBN-13: 978-0-8203-3109-6 (pbk. : alk. paper)
ISBN-10: 0-8203-3109-0 (pbk. : alk. paper)
1. Barbecue cookery—United States—History. I. Title.
TX840.B3W3683 2008
641.7'6—dc22   2008004517

British Library Cataloging-in-Publication Data available

The discovery of a new dish

does more for the happiness of mankind

than the discovery of a star.

—Jean Anthelme Brillat-Savarin,

The Physiology of Taste (1825)

CONTENTS

List of Illustrations *ix*

Acknowledgments *xi*

Introduction *1*

1. From *Barbacoa* to *Barbecue*: An Invented Etymology *12*

2. London Broil *50*

3. Pit Barbecue Present and Past *88*

4. Barbecue between the Lines *137*

Notes *173*

Bibliography *185*

Index *201*

ILLUSTRATIONS

1. Fish over an open fire (John White, 1585) *40*

2. Fish over an open fire (Theodor de Bry, 1590) *41*

3. Cannibal feast (Theodor de Bry, 1592) *45*

4. "Bar-BQ" road sign (Marion Post Wolcott, 1940) *97*

5. Pig Stands barbecue stand (John Vachon, 1943) *98*

6. Drive-in barbecue restaurant (Arthur Rothstein, 1942) *99*

7. Galvanized steel barbecue sign (Russell Lee, 1939) *101*

8. Big Chief barbecue (Marion Post Wolcott, 1940) *103*

9. Surveying the pigs at plantation barbecue (John Hemmer, 1944) *125*

10. Guests at annual barbecue (John Hemmer, 1944) *126*

11. Basting the pigs under cover (John Hemmer, 1944) *127*

12. Basting outdoors (John Hemmer, 1944) *128*

13. British view of the White House (Robert Cruikshank, 1841) *168*

14. Barbecuing President Jackson (Jack Downing, 1834) *169*

ACKNOWLEDGMENTS

Almost a decade ago I began to gather material in and around the subject of barbecue, and the debts that I have accumulated since then have grown difficult to count. All mistakes here are my own, but what I get right I get right because I have been so lucky in my friends and colleagues. Over those eight years Bridget Bennett, Martin Butler, Susan Castillo, Rachel Farebrother, Denis Flannery, Robert Jones, Caryl Phillips, Jay Prosser, Julia Reid, David Stirrup, and Sam Wood have all offered timely reminders and even timelier new pieces of information. Early in the project conference audiences at the Universities of Leeds, Lancaster, Oxford, and Prague offered murmurs of agreement, leading me to suspect that these speculations about barbecue and writing might lead to a book. An informal conversation with James Walvin helped confirm this suspicion. With the combined support of Leeds University and the Arts and Humanities Research Council in Britain, each of which funded a semester's leave, I was able to devote an entire calendar year to develop the manuscript. Richard Godden, Richard King, and Doris Witt provided help in the form of references and much besides, while the anonymous reporters for my AHRC application offered heartening, important interventions.

I also owe debts of gratitude to libraries both local and distant. Staff at the British Library, the John Rylands Library at the University of Manchester, and the Special Collections of the Brotherton Library at Leeds University remained patient at all times. Further afield, I am grateful for my happy and productive visits to the New York Public Library and its Schomburg Center for Research in Black Culture, while staff at the Library of Congress, and particularly those in the Prints and Photographs Division, were courteous and helpful. At the North Carolina State Archives Boyd Cathey and Kim Cumber in particular provided wonderful and committed service, not only guiding me to John Hemmer's extraordinary photographs but also trawling the archives for barbecue references on my behalf. Last but not least, colleagues at Leeds University, and my good friend Pam Rhodes in particular, were as fantastic as ever.

Acknowledgments for this kind of book would remain incomplete if I did not also thank the cooks who fed me along the way. From the barbecue I ate at Washington D.C.'s Black Family Reunion Celebration to the pulled-pork sandwich that Wall's served up on the outskirts of Savannah's Historic District, lunch has been an integral part of this project. I will not soon forget eating Ed Balls's southern-style pit barbecue—an art he presumably picked up in D.C. between lessons on fiscal responsibility—while listening to a brass band play "Jerusalem" on a rainy day in Yorkshire. For helping to fuel some cracking conversations with John McLeod, Shabab's restaurant in Leeds also deserves mention, as should all the cooks who have kept my spirits as well as energies up over the course of this research.

I would also like to thank those who read the first draft of the completed manuscript. The responses of John T. Edge and the anonymous readers of the University of Georgia Press were friendly, challenging, and have helped make this a far better book. Everyone at Georgia, and in particular my commissioning editor, Andrew Berzanskis, remained remarkably patient throughout. So did the thoughtful suggestions of David Fairer, a colleague whose prose I have long admired, and who remained at all times supportive of my rather brazen foray into 1700s London. My wife, Sue, and my mum, Jill, gave brilliant suggestions, as ever, while all my family, McManus as well as Warnes, were supportive throughout.

Last but not least I would like to express my gratitude to my former doctoral supervisor, Mick Gidley. I should make space here to thank friends as well as professional colleagues, but Mick is surely both and has done more to set me on the path of an academic career than anyone else. Mick's critical interventions, his eye for detail, and the sheer breadth of his knowledge have been a great boon throughout the project. In recent months Mick's characteristically close and insightful reading of the final manuscript led to some enhancements that, I think, are major. As a token of thanks for his efforts, I dedicate this book to him.

Savage Barbecue

INTRODUCTION

September 2005. The museum café is abuzz. People of every color are taking advantage of its wooden benches, easing feet wearied by the galleries above their heads. School parties commandeer long benches of their own, oblivious to the halo of empty tables developing around them. At a distance from their noisy voices, adults relax. Couples pour drinks, lone diners read the day's newspapers, and scholars speak up to make themselves heard. Foreign tourists, unused to carrying their lunches on plastic trays, scan the hall for somewhere to sit. Together, all eat from the café's award-winning menu. Taste buds jaded by air-conditioning and the humid D.C. atmosphere reawaken as they anticipate dishes from the five regions into which the café has sorted Native American cuisine. Some try the Great Plains option, taking on the fire of buffalo chili, while others pick their way through a quahog clam chowder from the Northern Woodlands. Others choose from the "handheld" possibilities—from the precapitalist fast food of the South American corn pupusa, the Mesoamerican enchilada, or the calorific Plains taco. Others still savor what is perhaps the café's finest dish, lingering over the delicate pink flakes of the "cedar-planked juniper salmon" representing the Northwest Coast.[1]

Hearing again the sound of running water, all from time to time look up to gaze out of the museum's tall window panes. Here and there rainbows appear. Disappearing just as quickly, they come to life elsewhere, leaping about on the waterfall tumbling down the glass outside. Seen from within, these rainbows link the foreground with the background of the scene. Somehow they link the diverse customers eating in the museum café with the prospect of the Capitol, blurred by the waterfall, bulking large on the horizon. An outside view throws a different light on things. From here, the full breadth of the waterfall becomes visible, and the rainbows that shimmer in the September sunshine curve into the building itself, brushing against the honey and tan exterior that in turn makes the neighboring monuments and museums seem whiter than they are. Now these rainbows seem a compass of the Amerindian heritage, a declaration that all that is rich and worthwhile in Native America can be found within the museum. They indicate that this eatery's menu is neither idiosyncratic nor accidental, that it is narrating the recovery, diversity, and vitality of the Native peoples of the Americas, and that one might expect to find within it all leading indigenous foods.

Surprisingly, however, the most popular food said to go by a Native name in the United States today is missing from the café's menu. To come by it, you will need to get up and leave that busy hall behind. You will need to walk past security, to face the sting of the late summer sun, and to drift in among the crowd bustling hither and yon across the Washington Mall. You will need to move past stands representing the National Council of Negro Women and other organizations, past banners promoting Family Values and Economic Empowerment, and past a concert stage whose scaffolding shakes and shivers to a hip-hop beat. The music will shrink back down to its bassline as you walk away, again tracking the scent of the pork butt that is slowly smoking somewhere you have yet to find. Some secret mix of bourbon, cayenne, chili, molasses, paprika, and vinegar will mingle in your nose as you close in on the food outlets at the end of the lawn. Joining the line, you will look up at the menu above the vendor's head. And there you will read, next to Fried Chicken and Gumbo, an acronym almost as famous as USA itself: BBQ.

The moneymaking efforts of the Mitsitam Native Foods café at the National Museum of the American Indian are as discreet as they are at other Smithsonian franchises. The championing of foods native to the Americas is already enacted in its name—*mitsitam* means "let's eat!" in the Piscataway and Delaware tongues—and spills into its menu and information boards, all of which devote more attention to the history of given dishes and ingredients than they do to promoting daily specials. Prices, offered in small and bare fonts, seem incidental, secondary to the café's endeavors to provide an "extension of the cultural experience" of the museum overall.[2]

By contrast, at the national annual Black Family Reunion Celebration taking place in the hot afternoon outside the museum on the mall, few such external or educational pressures apply. No Smithsonian authority directs this annual Washington event. Unembarrassed by the sight of dollars and dimes, its atmosphere remains free: festive, inclusive, and relaxed. Children can play here; families can indeed reunite. And friends can break bread, gathering together to reclaim the Washington Mall for Washington, paying homage to the civil rights victories to which this federal space once played reluctant host. The classic Americana of BBQ as such seems far more suited to the outdoor event, encouraging elders to wax nostalgic about the shacks and joints of old even as it helps vendors turn a profit and keep black dollars in black pockets.[3]

Questions accordingly arise. Evidently the curators of the Smithsonian found the open commercialism of BBQ hard to stomach. No less evidently, however, they also took exception to *barbecue* in general, preventing not only the menu of the basement café but also the galleries above it from mentioning even the full version of this purportedly native Caribbean word. Someone somewhere seems to have realized that the national museum that celebrates the Natives of North, Central, and South America is no suitable venue in which to celebrate such food. Someone somewhere seems to have realized that this is no place from which to correct that apparent historical erasure whereby, in Eve Zibart's words, the native Caribbean's "greatest contribution to the American diet—barbecue—isn't generally recognized as Caribbean at all."[4] For one reason or another, although almost every dictionary of the English language to appear since Samuel Johnson's in 1755 attributes an indigenous American provenance to the word *barbecue*, the managers of the Mitsitam seem reluctant to look beyond the food's famous association with southern cultures black and white.[5] Now the issues before us grow complex, and the questions we must ask urgent. Exactly what historical circumstances, we must ask, allowed this food to leapfrog out of its original Caribbean and into the white and black cultures of a supposedly segregated South? Why is it that, whereas BBQ signs festoon the food stalls of the Black Family Reunion Celebration, even authentic Caribbean *barbacoa* remains absent from the Mitsitam's menu?

In this book I answer these questions by demonstrating that, from the era of conquest onward, barbecue arose less from native cooking practices than from a European gaze that wanted to associate those practices with preexisting ideas of savagery and innocence. I argue that *barbacoa* or *barbicu* or *barbikew* or *barbeque*, however it has been spelled, not only referred to the smoked foods of American Indians, it also enacted Europeans' deep desire to see those foods as barbarous—as the result of a primitive kind of cookery, savage and base, akin to that which their own distant ancestors long ago performed. In fact, one way of seeing this book is as a vindication of the apparent suspicions of the National Museum of the American Indian. It shows that this museum's curators are right—that dictionaries should not be taken at face value, and that we need to look beyond their definitions if we are to grasp the true origins of barbecue. We need to grasp that the story of this most contentious food is necessarily transatlantic—that European ideas of the primitive have shaped it from Day One, and that its native credentials have been somewhat overstated. We need to grasp, in other words, that barbecue is an invented tradition.

The historical concept of the invented tradition first gained ground in the early 1980s, as a result of Eric Hobsbawm and Terence Ranger's studies of transformation and crisis in the national cultures of the industrializing West. In his introduction to *The Invention of Tradition* (1983), Hobsbawm persuasively suggested that the "invented traditions" of the Victorian era offered compensation for the demise of traditional communities (2–5). From the commercialization of Christmas in Victorian Britain to President Lincoln's decision to federalize Thanksgiving, Hobsbawm argued, "invented traditions" helped "provide . . . those social bonds and ties of authority" weakened by the experience of industrialization.[6] Elizabeth Pleck provides a useful summary of such thinking:

> Hobsbawm and Ranger considered an invented tradition a ritual implying continuity with the past, even though that continuity is largely fictitious. . . . They argued that the invented tradition met the needs of people in the present for a sense of connection with the past, and a desire of people in a modern world "to structure at least some parts of social life . . . as unchanging and invariant." Bastille Day, kilt-wearing, and the pledge of allegiance, they noted, were all rituals invented between the end of the eighteenth century and the last third of the nineteenth century. . . . These were entirely new ceremonies, they argued, intended to create the fiction of shared national identity and national unity.[7]

Few historical concepts have weathered so well as this. Numerous studies, from Rebecca Spang's *The Invention of the Restaurant: Paris and Modern Gastronomic Culture* (1992) to Donna Landry's *The Invention of the Countryside: Hunting, Walking, and Ecology in English Literature, 1671–1831* (2001), continue to profit from Hobsbawm and Ranger's insight, using the invented tradition as a prism through which to view an astonishing range of cultural phenomena. If anything, though, this idea has gained most ground in the United States, where it continues to help critics sharpen their understanding of a national culture whose symbols and traditions have too long escaped serious scrutiny. One such critic, Werner Sollors, applauds Hobsbawm and Ranger's "devastating and fruitful" scholarship, borrowing their keyword for the landmark collection *The Invention of Ethnicity* (1989, xiii). Another, Cecilia Elizabeth O'Leary, draws heavily on *The Invention of Tradition* to argue that, during the 1870s and 1880s, the U.S. political elite systematically cultivated patriotic feeling, promoting new national "traditions . . . and holidays" to ameliorate the looming "problem" of mass immigration.[8]

Several precedents thus exist for this book and its central contention that barbecue amounts to an invented tradition. Nonetheless, some new strategies are needed. Simply to speak of barbecue in these terms requires that we revisit *The Invention of Tradition* and challenge some of the assumptions that Hobsbawm and Ranger leave unexamined. For one thing, Hobsbawm and Ranger's original analysis tends to see invented traditions as more or less official entities—as entities, brought about by law, which leave behind trails of evidence that the empirical historian can now track. Barbecue, clearly, presents a different kind of phenomenon. Although it can instill a sense of home and belonging in the manner of Thanksgiving and Christmas—although it too can reconnect people with the more human, more real, worlds of the past—it clearly does so in a less than official way, its status shifting from community to community and context to context. A different kind of approach is thus necessary. We need to recognize that, whereas Thanksgiving and Christmas amount to occasions when everything is supposed to stop and people are meant to spend at least some time pondering the "meaning" of the day, the barbecue is altogether less didactic, altogether less national in scope or beholden to legislation. For many, the Fourth of July and barbecue form a perfect match; but such feasts are not confined to this or any other date on the national calendar. Its simplicity and lack of fussiness are more often than not an article of faith. And, even when its ceremonial importance is declared, the underlying aspects of barbecue tradition—its desire to abandon civilization for a while, its interest in outdoor meat cookery, its yearning to rekindle some flame from the agrarian or frontier past—tend to fade from view, individual practitioners talking much more about the things that set them apart. As a tradition that dislikes its own cultural status, a tradition that wants everywhere to establish itself at a grassroots and instinctual level, barbecue cannot be approached head-on. It will only give up its historical secrets if we are prepared to read adventurously, and between the lines of the colonial and Republican archives. For here, as we will see, is a cultural phenomenon that reveals most about its distinctive mythology—its mythology of savagery and freedom, of pleasure, masculinity, and strength—when the minds of men and women are turned to other things, from the rebellious murmurings of upstart colonials to the unstoppable rise of Restoration London, and from rumors of native violence to the Republican marriage of democracy and drink. Letters rather than laws, jokes rather than speeches, fragments rather than masterpieces, will accordingly fill the archive of this difficult work. Pictures and writing, rather than the more circumscribed fields of fine art and literature, will dominate its considerations.

Hobsbawm and Ranger also seem to regard the invention of tradition as a phenomenon that occurs within given boundaries, and particularly within given national boundaries. From the growing popularity of kilts in 1750s Scotland to the invention of modern Christmas in Victorian Britain, Hobsbawm and Ranger's essay collection approaches the invented tradition as a national rather than an international affair. Again, barbecue presents a substantially different phenomenon. Since its colonial invention, alongside its ability to evoke particular communities of the recent past, barbecue's mythological range has included an additional ability to evoke a much more distant, much more primitive, past that it has then associated, for good or ill, with American Indians or others not fully inducted into the long pageant of European civilization. To put it more simply, barbecue is not just an invented tradition. It is a *very* invented tradition. Not only does it construct a largely fictitious continuity with the frontier or wild world from which it is said to derive. Beyond this it projects its point of origin outward, writing it onto the traditions and bodies of "savage" America. Central to this study, indeed, is my contention that, though we tend to assume that the strong assonance between the words *barbecue* and *barbaric* is an accident of history, it is in fact nothing of the kind. Instead it is a clue to my larger claim: that barbecue mythology arose, neither from actual Arawakan life nor from any other indigenous culture, but from loaded and fraught colonial representations that sought to present those cultures as the barbaric antithesis of European achievement. In this book I argue that, in the original incarnation that lingers to this day, barbecue does little more than naturalize to America an idea of barbarism that European explorers carried with them as part of their transatlantic cargo.

Two snapshots from modern U.S. culture help illustrate the racial factors that even now remain at work in barbecue's mythology. Here is one:

> Barbecue's appeal isn't hard to fathom and may explain why barbecue cookery seems such a Neanderthal corner of modern gastronomy. It elegantly embraces several stereotypically Guy Things: fire building, beast slaughtering, fiddling with grubby mechanical objects, expensive gear fetishes, afternoon-long beer drinking, and, of course, great heaps of greasy meat at the end of the day. Top this off with the frisson of ritual tribal warfare and you've got the mother of all male pastimes.[9]

Journalist David Dudley's funny, fruity comments help explain why barbecue cannot fit into the National Museum of the American Indian's general commitment to "the preservation, study, and exhibition of the life, languages, literature, history, and arts of Native Americans."[10] For Dudley, by installing barbecue as just about the most macho food imaginable, reminds us that transatlantic English cultures have long bent and warped the food into shapes altogether more malignant than the roadside sign BBQ. He reminds us that barbecue, as it is understood today and as it has been understood for centuries in the west, evokes a stereotype of savagery that has nothing to do with Native culture and everything to do with white European need. What this book shows is that, behind Dudley's lighthearted and decidedly nonracist ruminations, is a surprisingly long and hitherto unconsidered history of seeing barbecue as a bestial kind of cookery too close to cannibalism for comfort. *Savage Barbecue* shows that, at least since the publication in 1661 of Edmund Hickeringill's *Jamaica Viewed: with All the Ports, Harbours, and their Several Soundings, Towns, and Settlements*, transatlantic literary culture has placed in circulation an invented paradigm that has seized on a Native Caribbean term for a cooking frame, *barbacoa*, apprehended its affinity with the Latin for those beyond Rome's jurisdiction, and duly insinuated that all *barbarians* must *barbecue* and all who *barbecue* must be *barbaric*. By tracking the journey that led this barbaric stereotype from the first colonial encounters to Jacksonian United States, this book suggests that Dudley, and the general outlook that his remarks embody, remains caught in logic whose racism he would denounce—remains yoked to a racial organization of humanity that can no longer display itself as such.

Rather as other words arising from early European exploration of the Americas quickly became associated with primitivism in general—rather as the Caribbean *canoe* quickly became Europe's favorite word for primitive boats, for example—so seventeenth- and eighteenth-century European references to the word *barbecue* rode roughshod over its nominal Caribbean meaning, forcing it to refer to the "savage" instinct behind the food rather than to the banal framework on which it cooked. From the Afrikaans *brai* to the Punjabi *tandoor*, and from the Mogul *dum* to the English *roast*, different culinary traditions from around the world boast distinct terms to describe distinct ways of preparing meat for ceremonial occasions. Each describes a specific and situated cultural variation on what Nick Fiddes has called the universal instinct to cook meat ceremonially so as to prove "human control of the natural world."[11] Of these traditions, however, *barbacoa* alone has been stripped of its culinary particularity and made to refer to this universal instinct rather than a specific cultural manifestation of it. Barbecue alone has been made primitive, the province of the native everywhere the colonizer has found him.

Here is the second snapshot: the tour de force opening of *The West Wing's* second television season, first aired in 2000.[12] U.S. President Jed Bartlet lies in hospital nursing a gunshot wound, thinking himself lucky to have survived an assassination attempt. Rumors of terrorism, Islamic or otherwise, fizz and crackle down the corridors of power. For a long time only a handful of FBI officers know what viewers of the previous season had already figured out: that, perhaps because the drama appeared after the Oklahoma bombings and before 9/11, this attack was in fact perpetrated by a fictional organization calling itself West Virginia White Pride, and the bullet that lodged itself in Bartlet's back was actually meant for his African American assistant, Charlie Young. Soon we receive more privileged information. Our TV screens go black, then break this darkness open to reveal a neon sign: *Bar B Q.* No other information is necessary. Neither the swastika tattooed on the lone diner's hand nor his skinhead haircut adds much to the signal that Bar B Q alone emits. Neither adds much to our knowledge that this diner is America's Most Wanted, and that the country's greatest threat is thus no Muslim nor alien but his opposite:

the white bigot filled to the brim with pork, beer, and racist bile. Writer Aaron Sorkin, in other words, is quite right. He is right to surmise that anyone acquainted with modern U.S. culture will know straightaway that this particular sign, placed into this particular context, will call the unreconstructed South to mind. He is right that anyone so acquainted will intuit that this food contains a suggestion of savagery appropriate to the modern Ku Klux Klan.

At this juncture, let us pick up the gauntlet recently cast down by Tennessean sociologist John Shelton Reed, and consider the comparison between jazz and pit barbecue tradition.[13] As Reed has intimated, it is possible to compare jazz and pit barbecue, not just because both are children of the U.S. South, but also on a more formal, structural level. Both, after all, seem to result from the collision of radically different preexisting traditions—indigenous, African, and European—on southern grounds. Both now appear quintessential, perhaps even mythical, work of U.S. culture. And both refer to new ways of treating old and unchanged European imports, jazz "smoking" and "marinating" the classical orchestra just as pit barbecue "improvised" and "riffed" on the pig. Perhaps, one might even say, southern jazz musicians' common love of eating and talking about pit barbecue is more significant than it would seem. Perhaps it is a recognition that both of these cultural activities arose from much the same epic encounter, played out in the countryside as well as the cities of the South, between European materials and African and American forms of cultural process.

Certainly this can seem an unlikely comparison. Jazz now occupies a hallowed place in U.S. life. Squeamishness about this "mongrel" music is virtually nonexistent nowadays; attacks on its "irritation of the nerves," familiar enough in the 1920s, now sound antique.[14] But even as jazz completes its impressive rehabilitation—even as its leading cheerleader can now breezily call it a "joyous and sublime celebration" of America's "redemptive future possibilities"—pit barbecue traditions remain, to many outside observers, mired in racial strife, a byword for savageries old and new.[15] After all, simply by showing us a single *Bar B Q* sign, Aaron Sorkin does all he needs to alert us that the net is falling over Charlie Young's would-be killer. Had the TV screen remained blank, the sound of jazz horns instead breaking the silence, our thoughts would surely have taken a completely different turn. No longer would we have braced ourselves for yet another foray into the clichéd world of white southern bigotry. Now we would have awaited another, no less stereotypical, chain of associations, jazz alone prompting a dramatic movement toward some cool refuge from racial strife.

A striking and important contradiction thus exists. On the one hand, Reed, among other writers and critics born and raised in the South, insists on the profound structural affinity between these jazz and pit barbecue traditions. Reed, having eaten approximations of pit barbecue in places as far away as the East End of London, even asserts that both cultural activities suffer a similar deterioration once they leave their "southern birthplace." On the other hand, however, mainstream U.S. culture continues to evince sharply different estimations of pit barbecue and jazz, deriding the former even as it invests the latter with almost infinite reserves of democratic and liberal prestige. Not only *The West Wing* but numerous films and TV programs place these cultural activities into a binary opposition, wedding them to hostile political ideologies that seek nothing less than each other's complete annihilation.

Savage Barbecue argues that this contradiction arises in large part from the fact that no one has yet properly acknowledged the powerful racist connotations bound up in barbecue's name. Continuing feelings of unease about the human body and its functions no doubt help to explain the striking contrast between American culture's low estimation of pit barbecue and its celebration of "ethereal," weightless jazz. But the two snapshots offered here, and my opening critique of the curatorial policies of the National Museum of the American Indian, suggest that something beyond a general sense of ambivalence about food animates barbecue's cultural denigration. They suggest that this food has yet to escape the fraught implications of savagery and cannibalism inbuilt and original to its name. In the longstanding absence of official recognition or interest, barbecue has continued to flourish. Gorgeous and appetizing smells have continued to fill the air outside the museum. But this has also meant that, with the invention and reinvention of different barbecue traditions, the loaded racial meanings bound up and discernible in the word itself have been allowed to pass without notice. And, in certain contexts and under certain circumstances, these loaded meanings have accordingly been able to resurface. Thus, in an age from which racism has been more or less driven from polite society, barbecue remains shaped by an old and all but obsolescent savage mythology. Dirty and cheap, bad for you but good, and culturally promiscuous, barbecue might not sit comfortably in any Smithsonian museum. It might not take kindly to being put on display. But the charged and various meanings of barbecue demand that it be recognized nonetheless. They demand that those of more sophisticated tastes should now take a deep breath, hold their noses, or just look away as we delve into the history of this most American food.

FRANCISCO. They vanished strangely.
SEBASTIAN.   No matter, since they
Have left their viands behind; for we have stomachs.
Wilt please you taste of what is here?
—William Shakespeare, *The Tempest*

I From *Barbacoa* to *Barbecue*
An Invented Etymology

Pretty soon, within a week or so of setting sail, all onboard
would have grown tired of salt cod. Like the new maps of the world that
greatly shrank the distance from Andalusia to the Orient, the increasing
availability of this food throughout Europe over the course of the fifteenth
century was a necessary precondition that brought the impossible within
reach, enabling Columbus to persuade himself and others that the western
ocean could be crossed.[1] Bacon could putrefy, and wine turn to vinegar in
the tropical heat; salt cod alone endured most weathers, outlasting even
salted whale and salted herring to give crewmen a daily dose of protein
long into their exploratory voyages.[2] But in the course of keeping them
alive, the food would have bored these men to distraction. Boiled, accompanied by little more than a cup of unfortified wine and perhaps a little
cheese, its appearance day after day would soon have seemed monotonous,
the pleasure some took from it paling as the thoughts of all drifted to
the foods back home.[3] In hunger the Basques who formed a large part of

Columbus's first crew perhaps dreamed of a kind of *txarriboda*, the ancient tradition of annual pig slaughter out of which a feast of offal and sausage would arise.[4] Men from Palos itself, said by Richard Eden to be unfailingly "gyuen to searchinge of the sea," days after sailing from their Andalusian home sought to augment their dull and tedious diet with whatever fish they could coax from the Atlantic.[5]

Indeed, although the journals of Columbus are famously unreliable, and far more concerned with his personal ennoblement than the welfare of his men, they still evoke the boredom and fear of starvation that built in the minds of every crewmember as the flotilla sailed further and further from the known world. Fifty days into the first voyage, by late September 1492, false sightings of land become frequent, and signs of it spurious: a whale offers hope, "because they always stay close by" the shore, but cannot still the men from their "muttering."[6] Less than two weeks later, Columbus's journal suggests, the threat of outright mutiny has thickened the air: "Here the men could stand it no longer; they complained of the long journey; but the Admiral encouraged them as best he could, holding out good hope of the rewards they could gain" (27). Columbus, his own eyes still fixed on what he increasingly saw as his divine mission, thus knows enough to appeal to his crew's self-interest. He knows enough to promise them that landfall will bring more than glory—that it would herald their entry into a paradise beyond desire, full of good things to eat and to take home to sell.

Babeque

For the able seamen and ship's boys who dominated the crew, of course, such hopes were bound for disappointment. No man but Columbus himself climbed a social rank as a result of the transatlantic mission. Hunger, too, still haunted this paradise: the largely unnamed gifts of food that the Taino of Cuba and elsewhere brought to these inquisitive Europeans were only occasional, while Columbus's habit of dismissing all the evidence of indigenous agriculture before his eyes made it difficult to ascertain which island fruits were good to eat and which not. Moreover, whereas many Taino were accustomed enough to the heat of chili to gain significant quantities of vitamins A and C from it, the same could not be said of those

European colonizers for whom even a taste of this New World food set their mouths ablaze.[7]

It is clear that, to Columbus himself, the thrill of discovering Hispaniola and Cuba was always tempered by frustration. Gold always lay elsewhere, spices always seemed to resist classification, and the gateway to Cipangu (Japan) always remained beyond reach. To his weary crewmen, on the other hand, frustration was perhaps baser and more human. For here they were, the discoverers of paradise, forbidden from its gifts; allowed only to gawk at the naked Taino, and too often deprived of a share of the foods that Native caciques brought in tribute to their white counterpart Columbus. October in these islands was as green as "May in Andalusia," Columbus's journals like to suggest (43); but it seems that his crew still ate biscuit or salt cod most days, and discovery for them certainly proved a banal enterprise, anything but mythical. Indeed, by November that year, such crewmen had as much reason as Columbus to listen hard to Taino references to the island "Babeque." Accounts of this mythical island where "people collect gold by candlelight at night on the beach and afterwards beat it into bars with hammers" surely resonated with them no less powerfully than they did with their ambitious admiral (75). All would have been agog to hear that

> *there is in these lands a huge amount of gold and not without reason do these Indians I have with me say that there are in these islands places where they dig up gold and wear it at the neck and from the ears and in very thick bracelets on their arms and legs. And there are also pearls and precious stones and an infinity of spices.* (77)

In the middle of the Atlantic, Columbus had been quick to quell the rebellious murmurings of his men by tempting them with the promise of future riches. Upon reaching the Caribbean, however, such promises turned against him. Resurfacing, mutinous feelings were now aggravated by the suspicion that Columbus's ambition and egotism would prevent his men from gaining a share of the gold that, certain Taino sources had supposedly said, covered nearby beaches. The captain of the *Pinta*, Martín Alonso Pinzón, a native of Palos who had done much to persuade the men of that fishing village to join the expedition, in November 1492 left the flotilla "without leave and against the Admiral's will" and in the hope of finding "Babeque" by his own lights and for his own gain.[8] By the time the *Pinta* rejoined his flotilla in January 1493, Columbus, dismayed by Pinzón's "arrogance and disloyalty," was perhaps at a loss to digest his news that he had "found no sign of gold" on Babeque but reputedly saw it in Bohío (Hispaniola) itself.[9] Following the expedition's return to Spain, and after Pinzón had died as a result of the tiring Atlantic crossing, Columbus's plans for and during the second voyage certainly seem shaped by this new quest—by this desire, no longer to find a way to Cipangu, but to come by a more literal treasure.[10] Historians often see this second voyage as one of settlement rather than discovery: if anything, however, supplies were poorer than on the first voyage, men hungrier, and the promise sent forth by Native reports of free riches more potent.[11] In most accounts of the expedition, noteworthy geographical discoveries such as that of the vast natural harbor at Guantánamo seem surprisingly incidental to the pursuit of a horizon full of gold:

> [Columbus] proceeded by sea, . . . leaving Tierra Firme on the right hand, as far as a very remarkable harbour, which he named Puerto Grande. In that land the trees and plants bear fruit twice a year; this is known and proved to be true. From them came a very sweet scent which was wafted out to sea in many places. In that harbour there was no settlement, and as they entered it, they saw to the right hand many fires close to the sea and a dog and two beds, but no people. They went on shore and found more than four quintals of fish cooking over the fire, and rabbits, and two serpents, and very near there in many places they were laid at the foot of the trees. In many places there were many serpents, the most disgusting and nauseating things which men ever saw, all with their mouths sewn up. And they were the colour of dry wood, and the skin of the whole body was very wrinkled, especially that of their heads, and it fell down over their eyes. And they were venomous and terrifying, and were all covered with very hard shells, as a fish is covered with scales. From the head to the tip of the tail, down the middle of the back, they had long projections, disgusting, and sharp as the points of diamonds. The admiral ordered the fish to be taken, and with it refreshed his men.
>
> And afterwards, while exploring the harbour in the boat, they saw on the crest of a hill many people, naked according to the custom there, and making signs to them that they should come near, one did so. . . . He gained confidence and called the rest, who were some seventy men in all. They said that they were going hunting by command of their cacique, in preparation for a feast which they were going to make. And the admiral

commanded that hawks' bells and other trifling things should be given to them, and ordered them to be told that they must pardon him, that he had taken the fish and nothing else. And they were greatly rejoiced when they knew that they had not taken the serpents, and replied that all was well, since they would fish again at night.[12]

Based on fleet physician Diego Alvarez Chanca's firsthand journal of the second voyage, and written following conversations with Columbus himself, the myth that chronicler Andrés Bernáldez makes of the landing at Guantánamo Bay is rooted in fact.[13] Just as William Lemos and others have persuasively identified the "serpents" of Bernáldez's account as iguanas—a food the Spanish had not yet grown fond of—so its broad affinities with later eyewitness descriptions of Amerindian smoke cookery suggest that it is mythologizing an actual event in which the crewmen indeed marveled at the slow smoking of Caribbean meat, falling upon its more palatable ingredients, thrilled to find neither cod nor biscuit.[14] This said, even Bernáldez's lyrical extravagance, though limiting what we can say for sure about this ominous encounter, holds historical value. For this extravagance is what raises the actual incident to the level of myth, confirming that it can be considered alongside those other Spanish portrayals of encounter that stage "a debate about the very humanity" of the so-called Indian. For Bernáldez was far from the only colonial propagandist who wanted to find out whether the indigenous American "was human but uncivilized," a "legitimate target . . . for religious conversion and cultural assimilation."[15] Nor was he alone in mixing such questions with an interest in New World riches, avarice and morality sitting awkwardly alongside each other in his writings. Like early reports of Mexico that make much of its "very rich gold and silver mines" while announcing plans to "instruct" its people "in the Christian faith," Bernáldez's description is one of many writings meant to offer crown and elite a twin and necessary assurance: not only can Indians be made Catholic, but their conversion will not upset the smooth establishment of Spanish power.[16]

The world is cleft in two by Bernáldez's version of events. In its course the familiar habit of speaking of the Indian only in the singular finds a perfect shadow in the collective white gaze that he casts upon the strange and savage feast. Differences between the Genoese Columbus and his Spanish crew, like those between Bernáldez and the audience whom he addresses, melt away as all together join in contemplation of a culinary scene of surpassing strangeness. Head to head, the Amerindian cooks and Catholic crewmen of Guantánamo Bay magnify the clash of two worlds, each incarnating and distilling a veritable mass of humanity. But this symmetry by no means places Native Americans on an equal footing with their Catholic conquerors. Rather, it lumps Natives together in order to fix them in place as innocent but heathen, and it lumps their conquerors together in order to fix them in place as the natural judges of the New World.

European cultures have long understood that conversion is not the complete transformation of the soul so much as the hard-won and enduring triumph of the good over the bad impulses within it. Something in the subject is virtuous and something is vicious, and approval and disapproval, acceptance and rejection, are the means by which priests and others strengthen the good and enable it to overcome the bad. Bernáldez's account of the meeting of two worlds at Guantánamo Bay allegorizes this process. The sheer deliciousness of the fish and the sheer hideousness of the "disgusting" serpents not only evoke the temptations and bedevilments of the Garden of Eden. They also indicate that both human and bestial desires lurk within the Indian, and that those representing the Spanish crown thus have something to work with, something to draw out, even as they have a barbaric love of iguana meat to suppress. Bernáldez's logic in this way performs a curious reversal: the theft of the fish comes to seem to him an act of generosity, a minor misdemeanor that the donation of "trifling things" can rectify, because it is more properly a reaching into the Indian soul and a recognition that something of worth resides there.

Other ambiguities become manifest in Bernáldez's account. Just as the foods are at once disgusting and delicious, so the cooking method that produces them is both familiar and strange. Seen from afar, it looks a little like roasting, a little like the technique used in Basque *txarribodas* and other Western European feasts. But it cannot be that, for how then could it be left so long and not spoil? Seen closer up, amid the tropical and "sweet smell" that supposedly filled the seamen's noses offshore, it becomes apparent that the food is not spoiling because it is lifted high above the embers and is slowly warming in their smoke. But how can it be—how can you smoke without a smokehouse, and how can these Indians who know so little know so much as to expose a low fire to the elements without it dying? A fascination with the slow fires of Amerindian cooking that would prove longstanding, arising wherever Europeans saw Natives who needed "a whole day to make ready their fish as they would have it," thus seems heralded at Guantánamo Bay.[17]

So too, though, does the fascination with the apparent inclusiveness, perhaps even the classlessness, of the indigenous feast. In Spain, as throughout Europe, banqueting had long been an aristocratic affair—a way of reinforcing the authority of the elite via the conspicuous consumption of swans, the elaborate molds and statues known as sugar subtleties, and all else that lay beyond ordinary means. Back there, "the populace was firmly excluded from the pleasures of the rich," and you would no more prepare so lavish a feast in the open air, outside the walls of the noble estate, than you would ask a commoner to sit at its august tables.[18] Not only in cooking "serpents" and fish beside each other but also in its social inclusivity, the feast thus seems to place the familiar alongside the strange; the potential for civilization seems wedded to savage instinct. Spanish proselytizers, it is clear, must encourage some Native ways and discourage others, exploiting the potential of these subjects to meet cultural norms that Bernáldez considers prerequisite to God's salvation.

The comfort of this process of conversion is that it restores order. Palatable and abject, smoked but outdoors, prestigious and open, the Amerindian feast begins life as a powerful and liminal affair, able to upset the European social and culinary customs that it evokes. But such power seems quickly undone by the crewmen's intervention. Their dividing of the foods into the acceptable and the unacceptable, their and Bernáldez's disgust at the eating of iguanas, effectively restores Spanish authority, maintaining the fiction that Spanish tastes are governed by God rather than culture. Nausea tells its own story, the chronicle of it by Bernáldez producing a written reminder of savage wildness that will continue to speak regardless of the success or failure of Native conversion in years to come. By the end of Bernáldez's mythic account of the feast at Guantánamo, judges are still judges: however redeemable they now appear, the Amerindians still seem dutybound to thank their thieves for sparing them some food.

Barbacoa

Barbecue in its modern understanding arose from such encounters. It arose in hybridity. From the moment it entered Old World cultures, it referred not only to actual native practices but also to the way such practices were seen by European eyewitnesses and even by those who, like Bernáldez, would never set foot in America. More than a native form of smoke cooking objectively reported by European discoverers, barbecue was then invented in contact itself; and this hybrid status, this marriage of New World practice and Old World myth, is nowhere clearer than in its etymology. For to study the history of the word *barbecue*, as I propose to in the rest of this chapter, is to identify its part in a wider pattern by which those who followed in Columbus's wake ignored, misheard, misconstrued, or otherwise stated their authority over native tongues. *Barbecue*, as we will see, belonged to the general establishment of what Colin G. Calloway calls the "new cartographic and political identities" that were the mark and proof of European authority across those conquered worlds.[19] It belonged to a larger historical process by which Amerindian cultures and languages were conflated, bowdlerized, and generally exploited in order to make America seem more like *America*, the New World that Europe wanted to discover.

Even an objective term like *Taino* played a part in this process. Often seen as the chosen name of Hispaniolan and Cuban Indians, *Taino* in fact meant "good" or "noble," and was used by them to distance themselves from the allegedly bloodthirsty Caribs.[20] Columbus's transformation of this word into the name for all those who said it as such illuminates the way in which European imperialists established their linguistic authority over the New World. It shows that they could do so by subtler means than we appreciate: that, for every European word that they roughly imposed upon America—for every *Hispaniola* or *Jamestown*—others arose from a less noticeable, but no less useful, mimicking of indigenous terms. The particular power of these latter usages was to present Old World ideas as though they already existed in the New; as though Columbus's references to *Tainos* and *Caribs*, for example, merely reported indigenous binary oppositions, making it seem an objective fact that some Caribbean Indians were good while others were as bad and "disgusting" as the iguanas he once found smoking on Guantánamo Bay.

In saying this, though, we should recall that the use of European words to describe American things can itself pass us by unnoticed. If Hispaniola, Jamestown, and similar place-names starkly established imperial command over the Americas, other European imports more subtly massaged Columbus's belief that he had found a gateway to the Orient, or gently blurred Asia and America together to form a single image of the Other against which Europe could enunciate its supreme and distinctive civilization. Sheer habit has made many of us deaf to some such imports. Even now some forget that the practice of calling Native Americans "Indians" sprang from Columbus and his penchant to discover, not only the New World, but also what Valerie Flint has called "the Old World which he carried with him in his head."[21] Other imports remain incognito due to their subtlety. It can take effort to recognize that even the most insignificant act of naming—even decisions like that which named American chili after Asian pepper and exported it, as the Portuguese did, to Goa within years of its discovery—could serve a wider European design, helping to cast the Americas as another Orient and to blur landmasses together to form a single image of civilization's barbaric opposite.[22]

The feast at Guantánamo would seem to present ideal circumstances both for the rough imposition of European names and for the further mimicry and misappropriation of Native words. In the actual encounter, as far as we can tell, the feast began nameless. Columbus's crew at first disdained the iguanas, stole the fish, and drank in the liminal and exotic spectacle with no indigenous name for the meal, and no native cook on hand to give it. But in its alleviation of hunger, its juxtaposition of the palatable and the unpalatable, and indeed in all its joyous abandon—in its ability to allow Basque and Andalusian crewmen subordinate to Columbus to lord it over the Amerindian for a while—this was without question a memorable meal, savage and free, abject, demanding the distinction of a name. Neither Columbus nor his transcriber Bernáldez meets this demand; Columbus's writings never include *barbecue* or any word like it. But it is conceivable that his crewmen, in conversation, did. It is conceivable that, in their hunger and happiness for once to diverge from their ship's rations, they spoke something close to the term, carving it from the confusing dialogues that they held both with each other and with the Native people who would in time return to the scene. Indeed, I would suggest that modern English and north European usages of the word *barbecue* likely originated, not at Guantánamo Bay in particular, but in the kinds of confusing and intercultural conversations to which it here seems to have played host. Specifically I would argue that, alongside *babeque* and other Native American words, other reference points, no less suggestive, existed. For these European sailors at the vanguard of discovery arrived in America with what Ania Loomba has called "abiding templates" of civilization and wildness in mind (105). Encouraged to discover "barbarians" wherever they looked, predisposed to wonder at the "*barbe*" sound that seemed to crop up everywhere on these islands, they were likely to have paid particular attention to the Native word for the framework of sticks that raised these fish and iguana above the fire—*barbacoa*—and to attach particular meanings, meanings of savagery and abjection, to it.

The editors of dictionaries and encyclopedias would perhaps view the inferential character of this argument with some suspicion. Speculations about the conversations of the past certainly have no place in current editions of *Webster's* or the *Oxford English Dictionary* (*OED*). Weightier sources, reputable, Victorian, and academic, dominate their attempts to distil barbecue history into paragraph form. Thus—in a definition that differs little from those offered by almost every U.S. dictionary published since H. L. Mencken's *The American Language* in 1919—the *OED* offers the following:

> **barbecue** . . . *sb.* Forms: 7 barbecu, 7–8 borbecu, 8 barbicue, 7–9 barbacue, 8- barbecue, (9 babracot). [ad. Sp. *barbacoa*, a. Haitian *barbacoa* (E. B. Tylor) 'a framework of sticks set upon posts'; evidently the same as *babracot* (? A French spelling) of the Indians of Guiana, mentioned by Im Thurn. (The alleged Fr. *barbe à queue* 'beard to tail,' is an absurd conjecture suggested merely by the sound of the word.)]
>
> 1. A rude wooden framework, used in America for sleeping on, and for supporting above a fire meat that is to be smoked or fired.
>
> 1697 DAMPIER *Voy.* (1699) I. 20 And lay there all night, upon our Borbecu's, or frames of Sticks, raised about 3 foot from the Ground. *Ibid.* I. 86 His Couch or Barbecu of Sticks . . .
>
> **barbecue** . . . *v.* . . .
>
> 1. To dry or cure (flesh, etc.) by exposure upon a barbecue; see the sb. (senses 1 and 5)
>
> 1661 HICKERINGILL *Jamaica* 76 Some are slain, And their flesh forthwith Barbacu'd and Eat. (1:947)

The patrician tone of these definitions suggests that, like the U.S. dictionaries that concur with its assessment, the *OED* could well label my remarks so far another "absurd conjecture." It suggests that these authorities would want to insist on the simple truth of the matter: that the word *barbecue* bore no relation to barbarism, and that its perpetual association with savagery and violent death, if at all explicable in etymological terms, must have arisen from the Caribbean sources identified by Victorian anthropologist E. B. Tylor. And yet, when we reread its attack on the *barbe à queue* etymology, it is hard not to feel that the OED has here grown unusually vociferous. It is hard not to feel that, as Jeffrey Steingarten has put it, the denigration of this etymology as an "absurd conjecture" amounts to fighting words for a dictionary.[23] Something in its sheer ferocity, in its fire and heat, should perhaps give us pause here; perhaps we should consider matters awhile before we defer to the OED's account.

The definitions certainly grow more curious following such consideration. For one thing, the OED's citations seem as though they are the wrong way round. Edmund Hickeringill's *Jamaica Viewed: with All the Ports, Harbours, and their Several Soundings, Towns, and Settlements* (1661) treats the word as a commonplace, weaving it without fanfare into doggerel about savage cannibalism (59), while thirty-seven years later William Dampier's *New Voyage round the World* (1698) approaches it as an entirely new English word requiring explanation (20). Already, then, in some of its earliest appearances in English writing, *barbecue* appears to encompass radically divergent meanings, and seems curiously familiar in some English circles but utterly unknown in others. No less odd is the fact that E. B. Tylor's *Researches into the Early History of Mankind and the Development of Civilization* (1878), a work that the OED still accords authoritative status, should uncharacteristically fail to provide evidence to support the Hispaniolan provenance it advances.[24]

The earliest known written reference to the word *barbacoa* further muddies the waters. Although Gonzalo Fernández de Oviedo y Valdés's *Historia general y natural de las indias* (1526) devotes much attention to Hispaniola and other Caribbean islands, it refers to *barbacoa* in connection with "Tierra Firme," or the Panamanian isthmus, using the word to describe the raised frames by which the indigenous peoples of that region were said to store grain (2:161). Oviedo's references to the food suggest that the OED has been quick to accept Hispaniolan provenance. Before we turn to Oviedo as a more authoritative source, however, a few points must be considered. The primary motive of Oviedo's encyclopedia, after all, is the need "to impress upon King Ferdinand and Queen Isabella the wealth, value, and beauty" that America had to offer.[25] Accordingly, the fact that Oviedo only vaguely associates *barbacoa* with Panamanian culture, never offering an explicit attribution, suggests that his encyclopedia, while casting doubt on the confident certainties of Tylor's Hispaniolan account, is itself less than trustworthy. It suggests that Oviedo is in fact pioneering a rhetorical strategy that we will encounter time and again throughout this book, his encyclopedia caring less about the actual roots of *barbacoa* than its ability to evoke the exotic wondrousness of the New World.

On one level, then, the prevailing wisdom of modern dictionaries—their broad acceptance of E. B. Tylor's rather specific attribution of *barbecue* to the Arawaks of Hispaniola—is more or less disproved by its appearance in a Panamanian context in Oviedo's 1526 encyclopedia. But on another level, even as Oviedo helps us to contest the *OED*'s version of events, his encyclopedia could lure us into new error. For Oviedo could conceivably send us back to Dampier's *New Voyage* and its reports of the Nicaraguan Gulf Coast and of the Moskito word *barbecu*, thus producing a field of evidence that would seem irresistibly to suggest that the word originated, not in Hispaniola, but in the native settlements hugging the Central American coastline. But although the weight of written evidence would seem to be behind it, such a conclusion would be as partial as the *OED*'s account. Oviedo, after all, never actually says that *barbacoa* was "the word that the cooks themselves used to describe the proceedings," while Dampier proves no less reluctant to tell us that his Moskito hosts in fact spoke the word.[26] Our faith in books needs to be held in check here; the actual origins of *barbacoa* remain cloudier than these writings would have us believe.

This mystery only deepens as subsequent references, arising from later transatlantic encounters, either remain as vague as Dampier and Oviedo or else rely on their works to fill the vacuum of primary evidence. In 1557, for example, Nikolas Federmann's *Belle et agréable narration du premier voyage* would follow the example of Oviedo's encyclopedia, failing to offer a direct attribution as it generally associates *barbacoa* with the people living deep in the rain forest, in the heart of what is now Colombia (192). Caution is thus called for. References by Federmann, Oviedo, and others certainly suggest that many different Caribbean peoples used *barbacoa* or some word similar to it. Even this etymology, however, requires a caveat or two and should only be forwarded with care. Probably the most we can say is that, in a number of Amerindian languages before colonial settlement, *barbacoa* seems to have been an objective noun, the practical referent of which—cooking frames and other kinds of raised bed—was banal and devoid of the savage implications that now cluster around the English noun and verb *barbecue*.

And so, even as it condemns the blatant Eurocentrism that gave rise to *barbe à queue*, the OED allows an altogether subtler and more insidious Eurocentrism to pass unchallenged. To some extent it still succumbs to that old colonial vanity whereby the American territories that European explorers first stumbled across were magically, inevitably transformed into the mainsprings of transcontinental native culture. The weight that it gives to Tylor's unsupported attribution lures it into a familiar trap. For this inclusion is a kind of acceptance of the way in which, for Tylor, the simple, unsupported claim that colonists first heard a word like *barbacoa* in Hispaniola results in its sole and exclusive attribution to the Arawaks, the people of that island. Effectively, the OED here reinscribes Tylor's tendency thus to tidy Amerindian cultures—to identify single indigenous peoples with single islands, and to downplay wherever possible the existence of travel and dialogue around the region before 1492.

Other Victorians liked to put butterflies in glass cabinets. Tylor, though, pins the idea of *barbacoa* down, his influential etymology preventing it from leaving Hispaniola's shores. Indeed, although the OED's modern account puts this old Hispaniolan exhibit back on display, it allows other members of the same species to fly free, disturbing the air all around it. But even as they surface here, there, and everywhere throughout the Caribbean, these diffuse references to *barbacoa* remain unexamined. Even though they confirm that Hispaniola's primacy for Tylor more or less resulted from its primacy in the sequence of colonial discovery, these references remain powerless to challenge the authority of the Victorian anthropologist. Uncomfortably juxtaposed, Tylor's confident Hispaniolan etymology and these complicating colonial references in fact reveal that, here, the OED is staging an etymological puzzle that it is refusing to acknowledge, let alone resolve. The need for a written history, for a chain of references that will lead it neatly from book to book, is here discouraging the OED from talking of likelihoods or probabilities. Force of habit is inhibiting it from grasping that, in this situation, "conjecture" might not be absurd—might, in fact, be necessary if we are to recognize that the word *barbacoa* probably roamed far and wide around the Caribbean, remaining free of *barbecue*'s savage connotations everywhere it surfaced.

New light is thus cast on the genesis of the English *barbecue*. The journey that runs from these diverse references to Caribbean *barbacoas* to the European notion of "savage" *barbecue* now seems neither innocent nor trivial, but an important part of colonialism's establishment of cultural power. It seems akin to the moment *chili* became *pepper*, indigenous Cubans became *Tainos*, and diverse other American things became fundamentally changed by the linguistic commands of those at the vanguard of discovery. Indeed, as Peter Hulme has suggested of its definition of *cannibalism*, the OED's account of *barbecue's* etymology now seems another "ideological account that . . . repress[es] important historical questions about the *use of the term*."[27] It too remains caught up in the "absurd" Eurocentric politics from which it seeks redemption.

It seems likely, then, that, throughout the Caribbean before Columbus, *barbacoa* was known and understood to mean nothing more sinister than a framework of wood on which one might sleep, store maize, or suspend foods high enough above fire that they could be left smoking with little risk of spoiling. *Barbacoa's* transformation into *barbecue* and all that it connotes, its new association with what the journalist David Dudley called "ritual tribal warfare," would thus seem to belong to a later stage in its etymological development—a stage that followed 1492.

The first steps in this later stage can be identified in Richard Hakluyt's *The Worthy and Famouse History of the Travailes, Discouery & Conquest, of that great Continent of Terra Florida, being liuely Paraleled, by that of our Inhabited Virginia* (1611). Also included in Hakluyt's protégé Samuel Purchas's famous compendium of colonial writings, this is a translation of a 1557 work in which the Portuguese writer known to us only as the Gentleman of Elvas chronicled the Spaniard Hernando de Soto's much-noted exploration of Florida.[28] It is important to us for the simple fact that it establishes that the first English writer to refer to *barbecue* or *barbacoa* was neither Edmund Hickeringill (as the OED suggests) nor William Dampier (as Diana and Michael Preston maintain in their biography of Dampier [60]) but Hakluyt. Yet it is also important for the less determinable, more interpretive reason that it exhibits signs of that colonial process by which *barbacoa* came to acquire new associations of savagery and violence. It is important because, I want to suggest, it initiates a discourse of barbarism around the barbacoa, turning this simple and decidedly innocuous framework into a scaffold on which spectacular colonial violence could occur.

From its opening description of de Soto's landing at the harbor of the

Little Manatee River, near present-day Tampa, Hakluyt's translation is never less than ominous. Soon it is telling us how this white "Governor" detained the Natives of Uriutina and Napituca (near Alachua, see Hudson, 79) and kept a friendly cacique in "safeguard," marching him in chains deep into Florida's interior:

> After hee had travelled three daies, there came Indians peaceably, to visit their lord, and every day met us on the way playing upon flutes: which is a token that they use, that men may know that they come in peace. . . . They desired the Governor that he would loose the cacique. But he would not, fearing that they would rise, and would not give him any guides, and sent them away from day to day with good words. . . . He travelled five daies. . . . Thither came fourteen or fifteen Indians, and besought the governor to let loose the cacique of Caliquen their land. He answered them that he held him not in prison, but that hee would have to accompanie him to Uzachil. The Governor had notice . . . that an Indian told him how they determined to gather themselves together, and come upon him, and give him battell. . . . The Governor commanded his men to be in a readiness. . . . There came foure hundred Indians in sight of the campe with their bowes and arrows, and placed themselves in a wood, and sent two Indians to bid the Governor to deliver them the cacique. The governour, . . . seeing a fit time, commanded to sound a trumpet: and presently those that were in the towne in the houses, both horse and foot, set upon the Indians, which were so suddenly assaulted that the greatest care they had was which way they should flee. . . . He that could get any weapons at hand, or the handle wherewith he did grind the maiz, sought to kill his master, or the first hee met before him: and hee that could get a lance or sword at hand, bestirred himselfe in such sort with it, as though he had used it all his life time. One Indian in the market-place, enclosed betweene fifteen or twenty footemen, made away like a bull, with a sword in his hand, till certaine halbardiers of the Governour came, which killed him: another got up with a lance to a loft made of canes, which they build to keepe their maiz in, which they call a barbacoa, and there hee made such a noise, as though tenne men had been there defending the doore; they slew him with a partisan. The Indians were in all about two hundred men. They were all subdued.[29]

In their silences, paradoxes, and occasional ability to see things from a Native point of view, early colonial writings like these can sometimes give the impression that they share our modern sense that such acts of colonial terror heralded a dreadful and permanent turn for the worse in human history. As with Las Casas's descriptions of atrocities committed during Columbus's expeditions, the Gentleman of Elvas, here watching the belligerent acts of his Spanish "Governor," depicts the ensuing confrontation as though violence could be like gunfire: another invention Europe was introducing to America's shores. Reading Hakluyt's translation, it seems that each massacred Native here heralds another Fall, each blow of the partisan blade bringing closer to reality a future America of genocide, slavery, and inflicted disease.

There are good political reasons for this. Aghast at de Soto's provocations, the Gentleman of Elvas doubtless had every reason to run out of sympathy with the expedition. Hakluyt, writing his translation fifty years later, could have identified with his source in this regard. After all, in England those fifty years had witnessed the rise of a new imperial potential, the inspirational repulsion of the Armada, and an upsurge in public hostility toward the Spanish. So it is far from surprising to find that, for all their differences, a mid-sixteenth-century Portuguese chronicler and his early seventeenth-century English translator should here share much in common, both offering an implicit but unmistakable condemnation of de Soto's confrontational tactics. The surprise, rather, is to find this condemnation is in any way blunted. It is to find that, even as these writings at one level decry colonial violence, at another they seem to understand it: to comprehend it as necessary to the establishment of European power in America.

These Indians, after all, change shape. In the space of a few sentences, writer and translator alike conspire to have it both ways, no sooner casting these Native soldiers as noble victims than demonizing them into savage combatants. These Amerindians talk and negotiate, they endure de Soto's provocations with great forbearance, and they regard the move toward violence with reluctance and in the clear knowledge that the odds are stacked against them. In the course of being slain, however, they gain a curious strength—and now we find ourselves in paradox, caught in a nonsensical situation where, in the world of the text, a handful of Spanish soldiers overwhelm hundreds of Natives by isolating them one by one, outnumbering the enemy that outnumbers them.

Peacemakers and warmongers alike in this way adhere to colonialism's logic. Hakluyt and the Gentleman of Elvas allow the Indian to adorn a series of identities on the understanding that he will eventually slip back on the savage mask that is all de Soto seems to see. Even de Soto's critical observers at one level thus seem to recognize that the Indian, for all his diplomacy, must eventually revert back to a stereotype that has little to do with his actual behavior. They allow that he must eventually revert back to being a savant, a terrifying student able to surpass his teachers with lightning speed and brandish a Spanish sword "as though he had used it all his life." And they allow that he must eventually revert back to his animal essence, turning when cornered and charging at his European adversaries "like a bull." Given that bullfights were held to mark marriages, graduations, and even the canonization of saints in early modern Spain, we might even say that de Soto and his critics are here like the more or less squeamish observers of an acclaimed toreador.[30] Even those who pity the bull, wincing at each spear thrust into its black body, largely agree that it, and the terrifying natural forces it embodies, must be destroyed if civilization is to be upheld.

So it is unsurprising to find that a third native soldier should hoist himself up and meet his death on "a loft made of canes, which they build to keepe their maiz in, which they call a barbacoa." For even though this impressive structure provides irrefutable evidence of Amerindian intelligence—even though it protects grain from insects on the ground and is evidently substantial enough to support the weight of several men—to de Soto's chroniclers its name warrants mention for the fact that it suggests civilization's opposite, conveniently evoking an idea of barbarism and naturalizing it to America. Assonance here condemns the word *barbacoa*, suggesting to these masters of the colonial gaze that this agricultural, rather banal structure is in fact a meet and fated venue on which to commit the kind of barbarism vital to the subjugation of the barbarian. An accident of history, a coincidence of language, here drags a plain and neutral term familiar across the native Caribbean into the path of European racial discourse. And as we next see, in the decades following the appearance of Hakluyt's translation in 1611, several northern European writers and artists would more obviously disrupt the original meaning of *barbacoa*, trampling it to ensure the word's enduring association with the cannibal savageries said to be part of American life.

This phenomenon drew on the colonial tendency to play the moment of discovery over and over again—to reenact it periodically, allowing each new traveler to cast himself as a pioneer and the indigenous cultures that he encountered as new worlds never before seen by civilized eyes. Perhaps the easiest way to explain this phenomenon is in personal terms. Having risked life and limb in their various transatlantic endeavors, individual adventurers were not about to talk up the discoveries of their white forerunners, still less undersell the wildness of the wilderness they had explored. Sheer egotism, not to mention the simple need to hold the attention of European readers and investors, instead persuaded them to dissemble and exaggerate, even to lie outright about all they had seen in an America whose newness they wished to hold in stasis.

Political factors, however, also lay behind this tendency. No imperial power liked to think it was exploring a secondhand America. National prestige alone made it likely that each new transatlantic mission would be presented as every bit as astonishing, intrepid, and glorious as those undertaken theretofore. Every new arrival, in Derek Walcott's words, necessarily "set . . . a shod foot on virgin sand," reclaiming the "elemental privilege of naming the New World." The "myth of the noble savage . . . has always been the nostalgia of the Old World, its longing for innocence"; original encounters are thus destined to recur.[31]

It is in the field of writing that the personal and political factors behind this colonial desire to preserve the virginity of America intersect. There, in the founding myths of empire, America appears frozen in newness, its innocence forever lost and replaceable, its wildness somehow open to negotiation. Daniel Defoe's rambling and expansive *Robinson Crusoe* (1719), for example, here and there acknowledges Spain's prior presence in the Caribbean but otherwise pays it scant regard. Defoe seems to find this prior presence inconvenient, as though it were complicating the story he wants to tell. Crusoe, clearly, is meant to be civilization's herald, the first Christian run aground on the savage and inviolate island. Indeed, *Robinson Crusoe* prefers to emphasize that "the orange, and lemon, and citron trees" carpeting the island are "wild" than to admit that they result from any prior imperial intervention (117). As I have argued elsewhere, Defoe, like Captain John Smith, among others, finds it is easier to forget about the Spanish ships that actually carried these fruits to the New World; it is easier to indigenize citrus, to preserve the wilderness in feel if not in fact.[32]

The invention of barbecue arose from a similar dislocation, a similar dissociation from the colonial cultures that generated it. If English narratives of Western discovery exhibited a desire to Americanize the orange, then colonial writers of diverse nationalities, writing in the wake of Oviedo's *Historia* (1526) and other early transatlantic accounts, likewise assumed that *barbacoa* and *barbecue* were native terms pure and simple, innocent of all colonial filtration. But *barbacoa*'s inclusion among the handful of native words cited by the Gentleman of Elvas and in Richard Hakluyt's translation, as well as its recurrent presence in subsequent English accounts of native life, calls this assumed objectivity into question. These colonial references suggest that the connotations of this American word soon began to outpace its banal and practical denotation.

As it happens, between Nikolas Federmann's 1557 account of Colombia and William Dampier's 1698 account of Nicaragua, *barbacoa* or *barbecue* proliferates so rapidly that its appearance in colonial writings starts to feel almost inevitable. Colonial after colonial starts to reach for *barbacoa* or *barbecue* a little too quickly, each appearing grateful to discover an umbrella term fit for every spit and cooking frame, every savage breed of smoke cookery, that America can muster. By the late eighteenth century, *barbecue*'s ascent to emblematize a savagery general to America seems complete. James Adair's *History of the American Indians: Particularly those Nations adjoining to the Mississippi, East and West Florida, Georgia, South and North Carolina, and Virginia* (1775) treats the term as generic (408). Sometimes cited as proof of *barbecue*'s native origins, John Gabriel Stedman's 1780s journal entries about Surinamese life likewise follow Oviedo and Dampier's lead, offering no direct attribution to native culture whatsoever. In fact, as though to confirm the curious deracination of our subject, Stedman seems as keen to associate *barbecue* with fugitive Africans as with the few Amerindians still living in the environs of that British colony.[33]

Even when more insistent on its indigenous provenance, colonial writings seem to greet *barbecue* with some relief, conveying a suspicious delight to discover such an exotic and authentically "barbarous" term. Even as Robert Beverley attributes *barbacue* to the Algonquian—his *History and Present State of Virginia* (1705) details their custom "of laying meat upon Sticks rais'd upon Forks at some distance above the live Coals," insisting that this is a technique that "they, and we also from them, call Barbacue-ing" (178)—the attribution remains dubious and impossible to trust. Like many other commentators of various nationalities, Beverley's account appears just a little too quick to claim a native provenance for *barbacue*, just a little too slow to tell us about the actual encounter or evidence on which this claim is based.

Barbacoa, beginning life as a Caribbean noun for cooking and other frames, thus morphed into the English *barbecue* as a result of a complex and confusing etymology. Put at its simplest, this etymology involved a twofold process. On its first level, it involved a kind of linguistic generalization reminiscent of that which plucked *canoe* from its Taino context and made it refer to all primitive boats around the world. The second level then boosted this generalization, opportunistically seizing on *barbacoa*'s coincidental resonances in order to reveal that it spanned all America because all America was barbaric. Both processes thus involved a kind of racialization. Out of both the Indian transpires as a known and knowable racial subject. Even those, like Dampier or Beverley, who acknowledged the existence of native humanity ultimately essentialized it inasmuch as their works refer to diverse Caribbean incidences of *barbecue* as though they sprang pure and spontaneous from a common tribal unconscious and had nothing to do with the high levels of commerce and traffic occurring across the Americas before 1492. The fact that such positive commentaries present native individuals as exemplary subjects, walking proxies for every Caribbean who ever drew breath, prepares the ground for the wholesale denigration of the Americas as Europe's barbaric opposite.

The racializing dynamic thus at work bears reiteration. *Barbacoa*, I am contending, acquired its savage and bloody connotations as a result of its entry into emerging European racial discourses. Only after its transatlantic encounter with the European idea of barbarism did it begin to outpace its banal and practical origins and acquire the bloody meanings even today associated with it. But this process no sooner occurred than it disguised itself from view, the misunderstandings endemic to colonial discourse making barbecue seem, from Day One, unmediated by empire. From Day One its cannibalistic implication acquired the status of an incontestable and anthropological truth. Obeying a dynamic that Werner Sollors identifies in other invented traditions, from Day One the word *barbecue* seemed ancient, emanating "from time immemorial."[34]

Even the most lurid European fantasies could thus remain utterly sincere and earnest in their belief that these savage feasts presented an actual American phenomenon. Even the ludicrous tone of Edmund Hickeringill's *Jamaica Viewed: with All the Ports, Harbours, and their Several Soundings, Towns, and Settlements* (1661), for example, cannot assuage the deadly implications of its cannibal violence. In one of *Jamaica Viewed*'s more lurid forays into savage territory, Roundhead soldier and religious iconoclast Hickeringill writes:

> But usually their Slaves, when captive ta'ne,
> Are to the *English* sold; and some are slain,
> And their flesh forthwith Barbacu'd and eat
> By them, their Wives and Children as Choice Meat
> Then are they called *Caribs*, or *Cannibals*;
> The very fame that we *Man-Eaters* call. (59)

Recent scholarly works showing that the Caribs were much less cannibalistic than many colonials alleged should make us doubtful of such verse. Only one "ethnohistoric account" of cannibal violence stands up to historical scrutiny, after all. According to James B. Petersen, the Caribs' continuing demonization as the preeminent anthropophagi of world history results "largely [from] . . . a myth promulgated by the Spanish and others as a justification for" colonial dispossession.[35] What is more, no evidence would suggest that the Caribs should be counted among the numerous Caribbean peoples who used the word *barbacoa* or some approximation of it. That is to say, other colonial reports might have suffered much the same problems of transcription, misunderstanding *barbacoa* or quickly losing sight of its apparent banality. But it still seems interesting that the more sober and objective among these reports never associate *barbacoa* with Carib cultural life. No even faintly reliable contemporary reports vindicate the marriage of *barbacu* and cannibalism that we find in *Jamaica Viewed*. Here, it would seem, Hickeringill performs this wedding for no better reason than that some Native Americans are known to make "a fire under their *Hammocks*" to ward off the cool night air.[36]

The evidence in fact suggests that, if anyone in the early modern Caribbean was going around yoking barbecue and violence together, it was the English. Already, with only the vaguest recourse to its murky Amerindian origins, *barbecue* had entered England's dismal repertoire of torture and punishment, giving its name to a particularly agonizing and visible form of execution. Not long before *Jamaica Viewed* appeared on the streets of London in 1661, English soldiers stationed in the restless colony of Guyana had been ordered to set a thwarted assassin onto a "Barbicue" and to "dry-barbicu" his body in the "Indian" fashion before reverting to the more familiar and homegrown practice of beheading and quartering his body; the resulting sections were put on display in "the most eminent places of the colony."[37] We can be fairly sure that, in and around its new Caribbean colonies, England's authorities were making similar connections and perpetrating similar depredations.

Such were the influences on *Jamaica Viewed*'s savage doggerel. And yet, as the jolly tone of this verse makes clear, Hickeringill is not too worried about such facts. What Caribs actually do or say is the least of his concerns. What they might be said to do or say, the kinds of savage punishments that they might concoct and that Englishmen might then imitate without surrendering their souls, matter far more to this transatlantic writer. Actually, for someone meant to be so moral and devout, Hickeringill is having a surprisingly good time here, no sooner conjuring cannibal "barbecues" than taking a kind of voyeuristic pleasure in this orgy he has dreamed up.

In the process *Jamaica Viewed* reminds us that, alongside *hammock* and *canoe*, *cannibal* presents another word borne up out of conquest—another word that the early colonists plucked from its Caribbean context, mangled almost beyond recognition, and made into a key element of an invented savagery now held to inhabit every dark corner of the world. Interestingly, however, whereas Hickeringill flaunts this linguistic generalization, glossing "*Cannibals*" and singing its praises as a more authentic alternative to "*Man-Eaters*," his treatment of *barbacu* remains something of a secret, too furtive for italics. Happy as he is to play a game of association with *cannibal*, Hickeringill, confronted with another supposed indigenous term—*barbacu*—falls strangely silent, becoming reluctant to disturb the myth now unfurled before him. Comedy lapses, suspended temporarily, as *Jamaica Viewed* backpedals to preserve the incontestable and anthropological status of its keyword. Like Oviedo before him, Hickeringill thus seems determined that this keyword "behave . . . as though we knew it already."[38] A curious and necessary authority must envelop it. Hickeringill, one suspects, feels dutybound to resist the urge to delve into *barbacu*'s etymology as he does that of *cannibal*. Deep down, it would seem, he knows what we know: that such elucidation would deal a fatal blow to *barbacu*'s pristine savage aura, laying bare European interventions buried deep within it.

That this myth of cannibal barbecue should find such forceful expression in the pages of *Jamaica Viewed* is no surprise. After all, unlike Dampier or Oviedo, Hickeringill arrived in the Caribbean as a military captain, an "absolute tarpaulin" who knew a thing or two about death and destruction.[39] Civil war sieges and battles that Hickeringill saw in his native Yorkshire and beyond seemingly spelled crisis to this man of the Bible. His cannibal fantasies suggest that the "odor memory" of burning flesh remained, savage and unresolved, a roadblock on the path to a fair and Christian England.[40] The fact that, by the time he reached Jamaica in 1659, only eighteen of Hickeringill's 125 men remained alive seems only to have strengthened a singular religious view in which anticlerical values could mix with an old Puritan fear of the Devil. Throughout his life, indeed, Hickeringill's numerous references to the Antichrist usually took a familiar form—as late as 1682 he was writing of the "two horned Warriors" of the "*Devil-vicar*"—and yet, under the new pressures and guilt of colonial Jamaica, he evidently had it in him to envision different kinds of monsters.[41] Naked Indians who ate serpents and remained deaf to the true Protestant faith certainly presented this prolific writer with likely candidates for the age-old work of sin. Rather as his near contemporary Cotton Mather "knew every disguise in the Devil's wardrobe," Hickeringill thus slipped easily into this racializing field of imagery, *Jamaica Viewed* happily and with some relief projecting colonialism's litany of crimes onto the bodies of its victims.[42]

Hickeringill, though, was far from alone in understanding this set of associations. Not a few Englishmen had been full participants in the atrocious fallout of the civil war, burning Royalist transgressors or setting fire to villages and churches across Catholic Ireland. Plenty more had acquired the "odor memory" of burning flesh from witnessing public executions, battles, and fires. The "savage cruelty" of Cromwell's men, as cataloged in Bruno Ryves's notorious *Mercurius Rusticus, or, The countries complaint of the barbarous outrages committed by the sectaries of this late flourishing kingdom . . .* (1646), should perhaps "be handled with great suspicion," but it is true enough that the civil war had made parts of the country a killing field.[43] Nor could anyone deny that the desperate acts of white cannibalism perpetrated in Virginia at the start of the century remained a raw and collective national memory. Captain John Smith's *Generall Historiee of Virginia, New-England, and the Summer Isles* (1624) remained in circulation, and its lurid reports of the depredations committed during the "Starving Time" at Jamestown—its description of one settler who ate "salvages . . . boyled and stewed with roots and herbs" and of another "amongst the rest [who] did kill his wife, powdered her, and had eaten part of her before it was knowne"—could still shatter any requisite sense that England's imperial authority was at all natural or God given (232–33).

Jamaica Viewed's cold and inappropriate amusement at the terrifying butchery that it dreams up needs to be considered against this dismal domestic backdrop. Its savage doggerel would certainly indicate that, despite actually making it as far as Jamaica, Hickeringill felt little interest in Native life, spurning eyewitness accounts in order to keep the Carib pinned in place as an empty screen onto which he can displace the vicious sadism that was part of colonial torture and execution. By these means *Jamaica Viewed* hangs onto a number of necessary fictions. Uncertainties about the viability of the new and emergent doctrine of white supremacy, the knowledge that some Englishmen were falling spectacularly short of their supposed vocation as moral custodians of the world, ebb away as Hickeringill discovers, in the figure of the barbecuing cannibal, a new yardstick against which to measure all human savagery. Every massacre that Englishmen perpetrated in the name of Protestant authority, every crime they committed to quell dissent or to curb pagan encroachments, pales in comparison to the supreme depravities thus made incarnate. Here, it would seem, is America's new and unsurpassable epitome for the barbarism that once dwelt within us all. Englishmen need no longer worry quite so much that their conduct has placed them on the wrong side of the looming eschatological battle between God and the Devil.

Barbarous

And yet, urgent as it could seem in Interregnum England, this Americanization of barbarism is also apparent in other European traditions. Several of the copper engravings that Theodor de Bry's workshop in Frankfurt produced as part of the *Great Voyages* series (1590–1634) provide striking visual forerunners for Hickeringill's savage poetic vision. Although they never mention *barbecue* by name, and although they remain to some extent innocent of the pseudoscientific racial categories that would attend slavery's industrialization, de Bry's engravings are still pioneering insofar as they present smoke cookery as a custom quintessential to an underlying savagery that is everywhere the same and that everywhere contains within it a potential for cannibalistic violence. Their yoking together in *Jamaica Viewed* and other later works was, for reasons I will now outline, all but guaranteed by this juxtaposition.

The fact that de Bry, like Bernáldez and Hakluyt, never crossed the Atlantic Ocean reminds us that the popularization of Europe's first myths about America could be a rather bookish affair, as dependent on second-hand accounts as the nineteenth-century German Orientalists who, Edward Said suggests, rarely left the library, let alone Europe. However, whereas Goethe's *Westöstlicher Diwan* (1819), among other German writings, took it upon themselves to "refine" their particular archive, introducing greater sophistication to the Orientalist "myths" that they inherited from "imperial Britain and France," de Bry's cultural work, if anything, butchers its iconographic sources, cutting away at their complex and matted surface to reveal the mythic muscle beneath. In part this simplification was a function of de Bry's chosen genre. Engraving, as a reproducible form, boosted intellectual activity in early modern Europe, helping to circulate de Bry's repertoire of New World scenes far and wide around Europe and among what Bucher's *Icon and Conquest* (1981) calls its rising "*petite bourgeoisie*" (11). But it also involved certain kinds of loss. The mechanical processes overseen by de Bry and others eradicated much from original paintings and even from original woodcuts, shrinking the color palette of the former to fit a monochromatic mode, and simplifying the intricate details of both into uniform ribbons and dots of ink. Long print runs, if anything, exacerbated this pictorial simplification. Engravers, as Bucher suggests, knew that their prints would end up as advertisements for themselves, being put on display in the street or touted around at fairs by peddlers vying for book sales (12). Myth and sensation as such became their stock in trade. None could afford to produce prints that failed to catch or command the attention of their far from captive audience.

De Bry responded to these demands with stunning skill. Straightaway he seemed to grasp that the genre of the engraving and the new conditions of publication that it opened up required him to ride roughshod over his various American sources and to produce out of them a single, composite image fit to grip the European imagination. Continuing *Icon and Conquest*, Bucher observes that, in pursuit of this image, de Bry

> scorned no evidence or document and did not scruple to interpret or plagiarize every illustration [of the New World] he encountered whether it concerned the subject of his book directly or had only a distant relation to it. . . . No attempt is made to distinguish among the different tribal or cultural groups, indiscriminately grouped together in the category "Indians." . . . Old materials going back fifty years and more are . . . separated from their original settings and turn up again in new arrangements. We are, then, confronted with a sort of Tower of Babel of the Amerindian peoples. Physical types, articles of ornamentation, and hairstyles, all borrowed from different cultures appear together, quite incongruously in a single plate. (15–18)

And yet, it must be said that the real arrogance of de Bry's *Great Voyages* series is not to be found in its "incongruous" mix of different indigenous sources, nor even in its attempts to mask this incongruity, but in the fact that these attempts are so few and far between, so haphazard and half-hearted. Brazenly *Great Voyages* skips around the colonial archive, its panoramas mixing myriad unconnected details. Aspects of Incan civilization surface in Tupinambá life, Algonquian elements spill into Arawakan scenes, and numerous other mismatches occur as de Bry pays only intermittent attention to native particularity. But the fact that these mismatches are so easy to spot alone suggests that, to him, they are not errors at all, still less the building blocks of some new American Babel. Their blatancy alone suggests that de Bry, instead, sincerely believes that Incan, Tupinambán, Algonquian, and Arawakan peoples all share a profound and underlying kinship, that all are at root savage or otherwise prehistoric, and that it is therefore legitimate to assume that what holds true for one must, in most instances, hold true for all. Of utmost importance to de Bry is the discovery of what those underlying and unifying truths might be. Some sacrifice of detail or accuracy has thus been deemed necessary in his pursuit of a bigger prize: the knowledge of barbarism itself.

De Bry's incorporation of John White's watercolors of Algonquian life into the grand sequence of his *Great Voyages* series offers us a glimpse into how this pursuit of a barbaric template worked in practice. As the official cartographer to Richard Grenville's expedition to the Carolinas and Virginia in the late 1580s, White produced a series of watercolors of Algonquians as well as of their cooking and other cultural practices, and these paintings are today widely admired, not only for their beauty, but also for their attention to detail. Some today are perhaps prone to overstate their accuracy, however. It is arguable that Edmund S. Morgan's recommendation of White's "drawings of the American Indians . . . [as] the best executed in the whole colonial period" tends to accept that the watercolorist is a reliable guide to native life, downplaying his more outlandish visions.[44] Portraits of fictitious Uzbeks, like the images of Picts by which White reminded English audiences of the savagery of their own ancestors, reveal that his work was only sometimes straightforwardly ethnographic or representational. Mindful of such caveats, however, it remains undeniable that White made his name from those paintings in which his aptitude for patient observation and careful brushwork is paramount; and that his more outlandish artworks exist in a kind of secondary relationship to, in the sense that they derive their distinctive form *from*, watercolors made in quiet contemplation of his Algonquian subjects. In short, White and de Bry shared certain impulses in common. Both were inclined to make generalizations about "the" Indian. Both took pleasure in imaginatively portraying the savages of prehistoric Europe, an exercise that Paul Hulton notes was "fashionable at the time," and both drew heavily on tropes that White first forged in Virginia as they did so.[45] Both accordingly identify savagery or something close to it as humankind's default condition—a condition that looks the same and *is* the same wherever it surfaces in the world, and which is now revealing its elemental character to civilized Europeans in the course of their exploration of the Americas. And yet, for all these similarities, it remains clear that de Bry's reproduction of White's watercolors engineers a shift of considerable magnitude. It remains clear that de Bry is dragging these images out of one visual tradition and dumping them into another, lifting them out of an intimate paradigm and depositing them into one in which machinery begins to generalize and shrink the possibilities of the aesthetic. The journey that these images undergo, as we will now see, is from a careful watercolorist whose most outlandish images still seem haunted by the need for observation, to a commercial mythmaker interested only in the bare bones of the story he wants to tell.

Icon and Conquest focuses on the straightforward reproductions in

Great Voyages. It fixes its attention on the engravings that seem to replicate White's originals, or at least the subject matter at their core, faithfully and with little intervention or embellishment on de Bry's part. Immediately Bucher warns us that this appearance of transparency is misleading. Numerous ideological readjustments, readjustments that we cannot simply attribute to the engraving process, are in fact afoot. For example, whereas White's watercolors "attempt to express anatomical differences," capturing "the high cheekbones" and "arched nose" among other "features of the Algonquian face, . . . de Bry mutes or entirely omits these differences: he rounds out the women's flat faces and makes them chubby and even corrects the shapes of the body here and there, giving the men an athletic musculature and the women shapely legs, thus sacrificing to contemporary taste" (33).

Icon and Conquest as well as critical responses to it can seem unsure as to whether these adjustments Europeanize the Algonquian or, conversely, fix them in place as racial Others. In reproducing these watercolors, Bucher contends, de Bry has forced some of the features of White's original subjects to conform to a classical model, and at the same time he has omitted others entirely. The question thus arises as to which of these two strategies is paramount. For Jennifer Morgan—and, sometimes, for Bucher herself—the answer is clear: de Bry depicts the Algonquian "as classical Europeans," contorting their bodies to mirror "Greek and Roman statuary." Morgan goes so far as to suggest that these bodies are not savage at all, noting that this label was not yet "uniformly applied to Amerindian people." *Great Voyages,* she maintains, instead allows these figures to remain within the fold of virtue or Christian goodness even as it casts the Tupinambá of the Brazilian rainforest as a demonic race beyond hope of redemption. For her, a cleavage between civilization and barbarism thus becomes apparent even within *Great Voyages'* gallery of native subjects. On one side stand the Algonquian: "modest" and virginal, natural friends to Christianity. Opposite them loom the Tupinambá: "aggressive" and "monstrous," savages bedeviled by cannibal thirst.[46]

The different uses that de Bry made of John White's watercolor of Algonquian fish cookery (see fig. 1) tell another story. These uses reveal that Jennifer Morgan's argument—effectively, that *Great Voyages* grants European features to the noble Algonquian but withholds them from the demonic Tupinambá—simplifies its position on race and representation. For

I. John White, "The Broyling of Their Fish over the Flame of Fier," 1585. Reprinted with kind permission of the British Museum. © The Trustees of the British Museum.

Morgan's argument, although shedding light on *Great Voyages'* depiction of Algonquian physique, cannot explain de Bry's enthusiasm for White's broiling frame. Nor can it accommodate his decision to make of this frame a template to depict all savage cookery, both noble and ignoble, throughout the world.

The great beauty of White's original watercolor stems from the harmony it sustains between the Algonquian frame and the manner of its presentation. Patient and economic, White's painterly style finds a perfect subject in this culinary apparatus, his clean and simple brushstrokes echoing the hands of the Algonquian and the movements that have whittled and honed the wood into the smooth legs of the frame and slats of the grill. Empty, devoid of any human subject, the canvas concentrates attention on this apparatus. Quickly fish broil upon it. Perhaps freshwater herring, perhaps Virginian shad, their blue skins shimmer above the woodsmoke,

Ann ſie eine groſſe menge Fiſche haben gefangen/begeben ſie ſich auff einen dãrzu ver-
ordneten Platz/welcher die Speiß zu bereiten bequeme iſt/ daſelbſt ſtecken ſie vier Ga-
beln auff einem vierecketen Platz in die Erden hinein/ auff dieſe legen ſie vier Hõltzer/
vnd auff dieſelbigen andere zwerchsweiſe/ alſo/ daß es einem Rooſt/ der da hoch gnugſam ſey/ gleichfõrmig werde. Wann ſie die Fiſche auff den Rooſt gelegt/machen ſie ein
Fewer darunter/doch nicht nach der weiſe der Võlcker von Florida/welche die Fiſch al-
lein beſengen/ vmnd im Rauch außtrücknen/die ſie den gantzen Winter vber behalten.
Dieſe Võlcker aber braten alles/verzehrens/vñ behalten nichts in vorraht/ darnach/ wann ſie deſſen dõrff-
tig ſind/braten oder ſieden ſie friſche/ wie wir hernach ſehen werden. Wann aber der Rooſt ſo groß nicht
iſt/daß die Fiſch alle mõchten darauff gelegt werden/ſtecken ſie kleine ſtecklein am Fewer in die Erden/ vmnd
hencken die vbrigen Fiſche durch die Ohren auff/vnd braten ſie vollendt ſo lang es gnug ſey. Sie ſehen aber
mit fleiß zu/ daß ſie nicht verbrennt werden. Wann die erſten gebraten ſind/ legen ſie andere/
ſo ſie friſch herzu gebracht/auff den Rooſt. Vnd alſo widerholen ſie diß braten
ſo lange/ biß ſie der Speiſe gnugſam zu haben
vermeynen.

2. Theodor de Bry, "Native Men Cooking Fish on a Wooden Frame over a Fire," 1590.
Courtesy of Library of Congress, Prints and Photographs Division, reproduction number
LC-USZ62-53339.

their scales apparent in a series of hatched lines parallel and perpendicular to the slats on which they rest. A curious reversal therefore occurs. Symmetry and order no longer appear a hallmark of civilization. Echoing the slats of the grill, the scales of the fish instead bequeath symmetry to nature, rendering it to convey the Algonquian's symbiotic relationship with their American habitat. And, at the same time, out of the billows of smoke and the tongues of flame that try to lick the fish, another cluster of surprising associations beckons. Each arc, it would seem, echoes the flamboyant serifs and calligraphic loops of White's title beneath the grill. Quite what these echoes signify is hard to say. But we might venture that White's handwriting is here figured not only as natural but also as potentially destructive, as though it could eat its subject as fire can eat fish. Something within the watercolor itself, we might feel, already envisions, not so far on its horizon, the approaching demise of the harmony it stages between Amerindian subject and European art.

If so, then de Bry's engraving (fig. 2) heralds the beginnings of this dismal journey. Harmony is shattered, ripped apart as de Bry submits White's original watercolor to a mechanical process that sacrifices the luminous blue shimmer of the shad or herring and much besides to generate duplicate copies for circulation around bourgeois Europe. This alienation of art and subject, moreover, results from far more than the technicalities of the engraving process. Numerous ideological readjustments are again afoot. Quite obviously, de Bry's placement of Native figures on either side of the broiling frame transforms the image. Likely these are just the kind of figures that Morgan had in mind when advancing her thesis. Their gymnastic poses as well as their impressive musculature confirm that, in adapting his iconographic sources, de Bry has leaned heavily on Renaissance or classical convention. If only because White's original broiling frame remains fresh in our minds, however, it is clear that de Bry's use here of these classical conventions is isolated to the human element of the engraving, and that even within these boundaries they are far from simple in effect. Keeping White's original watercolor in mind, it becomes hard to agree with Jennifer Morgan's contention that de Bry is straightforwardly seeking to Europeanize the Algonquian. De Bry is instead raiding Europe's archive of classical conventions, not for its fund of physical norms, nor even especially for its configuration of the ideal human form, but as a kind of storehouse of myth, a storehouse of legend from which he can access all manner of quick and readymade ways to portray the American saga now unfolding before him. Far from just Europeanizing their subject, *Great Voyages'* classical embellishment of dress and physique seems a symptom of the fact that de Bry, who never set eyes on an Algonquian, wants to portray this mysterious tribe according to tropes by which European art has, since time immemorial, depicted its classic monsters.

No other details in de Bry's engraving suggest that he is that much interested in promoting empathy between the Algonquian and his European audience. The absence of background scenery reveals that de Bry is in fact at pains to keep his panorama free of anything that might make the Algonquian at all knowable as fellow humans. The distance between the empty canvas of John White's original watercolor and the empty landscape of de Bry's engraving is a great deal further than it looks. Mutual cultural respect is never less than apparent as White omits humans and other distractions from his canvas in order to concentrate exclusively on the Algonquian broiling frame. Simply by paying such close and careful attention to its arrangement of poles and slats, White's brushstrokes pay tribute to the considerable labor and expertise invested in this indigenous structure. His canvas margins accordingly shine forth as space in which the hunters and artisans of the Algonquian village may dwell; his decontextualization of the apparatus indicates that such a context exists. In de Bry, by contrast, emptiness empties. It heralds a casting out, an expulsion of some kind. It catapults the Algonquian onto a hostile and barren landscape. To use Bethany Schneider's phrase, it keeps them "in the air."[47]

This landscape, its desolation at odds with the lush and verdant Virginia envisioned by most colonial reports, thus exposes de Bry's mythologizing intentions. Its treelessness, like the lack of any waterway to interrupt its desolation, reveals that his project is to arrest narrative and suspend explanation. Now the apparatus appears, not as the result of indigenous manipulation of the natural habitat, but out of nowhere. It exists and it always existed because it exists and it always existed. It is mythic, beyond the pale. Fish appear on it, conjured not from any river but thin air. And yet, amid the throes of this mythologization, the broiling frame continues to look right. It continues to look real. Because everything about White's original, down to the slightly skewed angle of its horizontal slats, is here present and correct, de Bry's blurring of native particularity, his Europeanizing of Algonquian physique, indeed all his many embellishments appear under cover of authenticity. Myth masquerades as fact, harnessing White's original texture and detail to preserve an ethnographic air.

Only with the publication of the third volume of *Great Voyages* do the full implications of this adaptation become clear. Commissioned to produce illustrations to accompany Hans Stade's sensational narrative of captivity and cannibalism among the Tupinambá, de Bry perhaps inevitably returned to the image of savage cookery that he had fashioned when adapting John White's watercolors. Expediency alone no doubt encouraged him to reach for this template. Equally, however, a deep ideological belief in the common savagery of all Americans likely legitimized such corner cutting. A belief that savagery lurked in the breast of even the gentlest Amerindian, a belief that not only the Tupinambá but even the Algonquian could potentially force Stade into his legendary cry—"'I, your food, have come'"—certainly seems apparent in the brazen transformation that we witness in de Bry's "Tupinambán Cannibal Feast" (1592, fig. 3).[48] Here—cast again on a barren landscape that can remind us that "desert" was at the time as common a description of the Americas as "wilderness"—Tupinambá dance and celebrate, eagerly anticipating what *Jamaica Viewed* calls "Choice Meat."[49] Nudity, not to mention a certain sagging of the body, admittedly distinguishes these Tupinambá from the muscular and loin-clothed Algonquian depicted elsewhere in *Great Voyages*. Little else, however, differentiates the two groups. No tattoos or body paint, no particular styling of the hair or dress, separates them. Difference is instead concentrated on the broiling frame itself, a frame that once again replicates White's original. On this grill broil neither fish nor even the "serpents" of Guantánamo Bay. Humanity instead, human arms and legs, smoke to perfection, drawing the Tupinambá around the fire. The luminous blue shad or herring that sat on White's original broiling frame are thus discarded. Alongside them, consigned to a similar oblivion, is de Bry's earlier pretense that white Christians might befriend Amerindians or consider them their equals. A savagery not limited to the Tupinambá is in this way unmasked. Cannibalism stands revealed as the impulse that lurks within even the kindest native breast.

Type the word *barbecue* into Google Images today, scroll through the family photographs and pit joint advertisements, and soon de Bry's engravings will begin to appear onscreen, each scanned and grainy reproduction looming arcane and sinister among the colorful bitmaps. Some links

3. Theodor de Bry, "A Tupinambán Cannibal Feast," 1592. Courtesy of Library of Congress, Prints and Photographs Division, reproduction number LC-USZ62-45105.

are to academic and even governmental sites. Others lead to the weird and wonderful Web pages that many consider the main business of the Internet. But all these Web sites, whatever their tone, subscribe to the received wisdom that "A Tupinambán Cannibal Feast" and other engravings describe not only barbarism but *barbecues*—actual, verifiable, indigenous barbecues. Even those that point out that not all barbecues were so cannibalistic, or which limit themselves to de Bry's engravings of Algonquian fish cookery, pay lip service to the continuing credibility and even anthropological status of the *Great Voyages* series. Nor is this failure to call attention to the manipulations and plagiarisms of de Bry's engravings exclusive to the Internet. Popular, serious histories like Daniel Diehl and Mark P. Donnelly's *Eat Thy Neighbour: A History of Cannibalism* (2006) describe these engravings as portrayals of actual barbecues, legitimizing them as they fail even to mention their creator de Bry by name. Even the respected *Food: A History* (2002), by Felipe Fernández-Armesto, while acknowledging de Bry's historical inaccuracies, perpetuates their deeper legacy by referring to his Tupinambán engraving as a "barbecue" without interrogating the term (26–27). Thus the cannibalistic implications of *barbecue* retain their American mask, their origin in European culture even now eluding detection. Thus a long tradition of conflating barbecue and cannibalism flourishes across English-speaking cultures. When Joel Chandler Harris has Brer Fox threaten to "bobbycue" Brer Rabbit; when Herman Melville has an unnamed sailor tell Ishmael about the human "barbecues" of Queequeg's Polynesian home; when Robert Louis Stevenson, not long after a tour of California, nicknames his dubious cook Long John Silver "Barbecue"—in short, whenever English-speaking culture has turned to a favorite verb to evoke the cannibal act, de Bry's legacy is once again accepted, its invisibility once again renewed.[50] Once again the colonial invention of *barbecue*—an invention that reduced diverse practices down to a single "barbaric" essence—is allowed to pass by unnoticed. Once again its savage camouflage is left intact.

Barbecue

In his masterful contribution to the collection *First Images of America: The Impact of the New World on the Old* (1976), Harold Jantz solves a famous puzzle, shedding light on the curious fact that America took its name from Amerigo Vespucci even though the Florentine was "just one of many explorers who journeyed across the Atlantic shortly after Christopher Columbus," as Gordon Sayre puts it.[51] Jantz puts flesh on standard dictionary explanations, showing that Vespucci acquired a fame beyond his unexceptional if remarkable career, not because derivatives of Columbus like *Columbia* and *Christophoria* sounded wrong, but because *America*, the Latinized version of the Florentine's first name, resonated with many native Caribbean place-names even as it met rhetorical conventions key to the German Renaissance. Jantz's contribution is to direct attention to the "young humanist poet" Matthias Ringmann and his associates, and to show that the name of the western continents derived from their publication in 1507 of a translation of Vespucci's writings and a poem in tribute to his achievements.[52] For Jantz shows that the puns and allusions of these writings, though dismissed as "so much vexatious literary flourish" by many a historian, in fact helped develop a new concatenation of words that led straight to America's designation. Jantz's own "plain translation" of this extraordinary text reads as follows:

> Now truly these parts [Europe, Africa, Asia] have been more widely explored, and another, fourth part has been discovered by Americus Vesputius (as will be heard in what follows), and I do not see why anyone should rightly forbid naming it Amerige, land of Americus as it were, after its discoverer Americus, a man of acute genius, or America, inasmuch as both Europe and Asia have received their names from women. Its position and the customs of its people may be clearly learned from the twice two voyages of Americus that follow.

Jantz then comments that, in Ringmann's "poetic freewheeling with the sacred Greek language," we receive

> the pretty broad hint that, however much these young men revered Amerigo and were taken in by his claims, they were under no illusion that the continent was really being named after him. They were simply delighted [to discover] . . . that the name of the discoverer corresponds so closely to the most prevalent continuity of place names along the newly explored continental shore.
>
> In modern studies the phenomena have been misrepresented, as though they were only an isolated Indian place name or two in Central or South America that was analogous in sound to *America*. As a matter of fact, the name occurs in many variants as a series of aboriginal place names along great stretches of Brazil, the Guianas, and Venezuela—precisely that part of the continental coast that was first extensively explored. . . . Among the dozens of variants that could be mentioned are such striking ones as Amaracao, Maraca, Marica, Maracaibo, Marahuaca. . . . With this as background, it is easier to explain why the proposal to name the new continent "America" was so readily accepted by so many and contested so ineffectively by so few. If it had burst on the world as a total novelty without precedent, the reception would probably have been quite different.[53]

In this chapter I have suggested that modern English and other northern European usages of *barbecue* originated in a similar pun, a similar transatlantic marriage between a set of Amerindian words and an unrelated European concept. Admittedly, the history that we have explored in these pages is in many ways very different from that which designated America as *America*. No single written work inaugurated *barbecue*. Whereas the naming of a continent was clearly the work of a single poet, the naming of its first food just as clearly presented a far messier business involving books, pamphlets, and engravings as well as the unknown dialogues that early colonials held with islanders, one another, and those awaiting their return back home. Murkier than Martin Ringmann's rhetorical "freewheeling," the historical process by which *barbecue* entered northern European languages and English in particular nonetheless shares certain key features with those uncovered by Jantz. For one thing, for every native word Jantz's essay offers as a potential cognate of *America*, another is "analogous in sound" to *barbecue*. References to *barbacoa* seemingly noted by European discoverers throughout the Gulf of Mexico region, town names like Barbacoas and island names like Barbados, colonial French references to frames called *babracot*, and whispered reports of the elusive island of Babeque are all unreliable, unclear in meaning, and the work of only approximate transcription. But each such incidence reveals another "prevalent continuity of . . . names," adding, to the variations on *America* that Jantz catalogs, another body of evidence that suggests that an impressively high degree of cultural traffic took place in and around the Caribbean before Columbus.

Barbecue, then, was America's first food; and it was so because it entered European consciousness at roughly the same time and from roughly the same rhetorical circumstances as those that gave America its name. We can readily extend the comparison. Not only the etymology of both words but also the myths that they expressed arose from a similar, almost opportunistic intervention by which key cultural commentators, some still known to us and others lost in the mists of time, seized upon and magnified those details of New World life that most closely correlated to Europe's preexisting image of it. Each word added up to a kind of bowdlerization of the dispossessed by the arrogant—a bowdlerization that paid no heed to the richness of Native life, that derided its particularities but that could somehow still "sound" or "feel" faithful to it. *America.* Ensuring that the names of all the known continents would continue to begin and end with a vowel but that only Europe would do so with an E, Ringmann's naming of the western continent rather brilliantly brought to completion an image of the world that satisfied Renaissance desires for symmetry and pattern even as it met the growing imperial demand for signs of Christendom's supremacy. *Barbecue.* On Guantánamo Bay and the Moskito coast, in the Florida panhandle and Panamanian isthmus, soldiers, crewmen, missionaries, and other individuals not so erudite or visible as Ringmann could still indulge in speculation about the meaning of Native life and the sounds of their curious words. Poets were far from America's only unacknowledged legislators. Commoners, too, could remark on the coincidental assonance between *barbarians* and *barbecue*: white Europe's "usual term for New World peoples" and dark America's "usual term" for wooden frameworks.[54] Even those touring America itself could make of it that locus of savagery for which Old World cultures had long yearned.

So it can seem surprising to find that, only a few decades after Hakluyt's death, Europeans began to hold barbecues of their own. It can seem surprising that, even as de Bry's engravings and Hickeringill's verse continued to circulate, some white and Christian men decided to hold their own versions of these lurid fantasies, reveling in their savage—not to say cannibalistic—aura even as they retained a foothold in civilized life. Looked at another way, however, this phenomenon is not that surprising. For the civilizing process that paved roads, spread light, enclosed land, popularized cutlery, and endeavored to banish ribald and vulgar behavior from sight also offered people poor outlet for their sensual and libidinal desires. Implicit and essential to civilization was the understanding that its subjects would from time to time need to seek relief from it, entering bedrooms or brothels, taverns or carnivals, to escape its expectations of purity and restraint. The discovery of America, like the colonization of Asia, proved a godsend to this European dynamic. It made available a whole continent for the displacement of the hungers and taboos on which civilization preferred not to dwell. It made available a new field on which men and women could continue to hold an old kind of feast—the kind of simple and rugged feast now being rendered beyond the pale, outcast from the dining halls of civilized Europe. Those tired of such chambers, like those never admitted entry to them, could find in the idea of America solace and relief. Barbecue, savage and free, could appeal to them as it can to us today: as a chance to relax and spend an hour or ten in flight from the pressures of civilized life.

The true Cockney has never traveled beyond the purlieus of the metropolis. . . . The world turns round, and his head with it, like a roundabout at a fair, till he becomes stunned and giddy with the motion. Figures glide by as in a *camera obscura*. There is a glare, a perpetual hubbub, a noise, a crowd about him; he sees and hears a vast number of things, and knows nothing. . . . "Beyond Hyde Park all is a desert to him." . . . He is, in short, a great man by proxy, and comes so often in contact with fine persons and things, that he rubs off a little of the gilding, and is surcharged with a sort of secondhand, vapid, tingling, troublesome self-importance.
—William Hazlitt, "On Londoners and Country People"

2 London Broil

Like many landmark novels of the African diaspora, Ralph Ellison's *Invisible Man* (1952) rejects linear narrative, telling its story from end to beginning and back again. No obvious plotline links its celebrated set pieces. No distinct thread links its southern protagonist's attempt to ward homesickness off by buying a yam from a Harlem vendor with his earlier involvement in a boxing match held to please a white crowd (214). Eventually, though, it grows clear that these diverse episodes belong together because all share a concern with visibility and with the shifting gaze that U.S. culture casts upon its black subjects. All share a concern with the black quarters of American life—with their status as a repository for the smut and squalor that this national culture has dreamed up, and with the various ways in which their denizens have handled such denigration. Like the white supremacists of Sterling A. Brown's "Strong Men" (1931) who "shunt dirt" onto their black chattel (57), like the dolls and rhymes that present beauty as a white affair in Toni Morrison's *The Bluest Eye* (1970), all of these set pieces thus draw attention to the racial meanings that purity and pollution have come to acquire in U.S. cultural life. Taken together, all comment on the way in which, in this cultural life, the abiding prestige of whiteness—its lingering reputation for "cleanliness and goodness," for beauty and freedom from adulteration—has arisen out of its comparison with blackness's far more negative battery of connotations.[1]

Of all *Invisible Man*'s uncanny set pieces, perhaps the most uncanny occurs in the factory of a company that Ellison knowingly names *Liberty Paints*. Grateful for the work, our unnamed protagonist receives some unlikely directions from his white boss:

> "The idea is to open each bucket and put in ten drops of this stuff," he said. "Then you stir it 'til it disappears . . . You understand?"
>
> "Yes, sir." But when I looked into the white graduate I hesitated; the liquid inside was dead black. Was he trying to kid me?
>
> "What's wrong?"
>
> "I don't know, sir . . . I mean. Well, I don't want to start by asking a lot of stupid questions, but do you know what's in this graduate?"
>
> His eyes snapped. "You damn right I know," he said. "You just do what you're told!" . . .
>
> I worked fast but carefully. With a man like this . . . the least thing done incorrectly would cause trouble. . . .
>
> "How's it coming?" he said, standing with hands on hips.
>
> "All right, sir."
>
> "Let's see," he said, selecting a sample and running his thumb across the board. "That's it, as white as George Washington's Sunday-go-to-meetin' wig and as sound as the all-mighty dollar! That's paint! That's paint that'll cover just about anything! . . . White! It's the purest white that can be found. Nobody makes a paint any whiter. This batch right here is heading for a national monument." (163–64)

In the immediate wake of *Invisible Man*'s publication, few paid much attention to this paint factory scene and the curious white mixture at its core. Only after 1990 did critics start to grasp that this magic paint could allegorize the way in which U.S. culture's fund of pure white images arises and has arisen, in Harryette Mullen's words, from "the operation of marginalizing blackness."[2] Read as a sign of what Ellison elsewhere called "the true interrelatedness of blackness and whiteness" in U.S. life, this magic paint has since come to seem nothing short of prophetic, anticipating Toni

Morrison's *Playing in the Dark* (1992) and Richard Godden's *Fictions of Labor* (1997) among other intellectual studies of racial interdependence published toward the end of the twentieth century.[3] Folklorist John Roberts, even while branding its symbolism "heavy-handed," helps explain how *Invisible Man*'s paint episode belatedly acquired this appeal. For him the allegory exposes that

> the "pure" whiteness of the United States is . . . an optical illusion created by the ability of the economic and sociopolitical establishment to render invisible the contributions of the roughly 10% of the African Americans in the population. The betrayal of this illusion [later in the novel] is effected accidentally when the protagonist inadvertently adds the paint thinner, thus reversing the process. His actions in revealing the cover-up cannot be tolerated, for they expose the truth about whiteness, its source of economic and sociopolitical dominance, and, on a deeper level, the true nature of the relations between Black and white in a society in which blackness is revealed not as an alienated other but, rather, the condition of possibility for "the whiteness of whiteness."[4]

Oddly, although he can sound a little tired of *Invisible Man*'s allegory, Roberts here reveals its profounder cultural resonance, unearthing the "deeper level" at which it reveals the epistemological origins of race itself. Even as his logic stumbles, Roberts gets to the heart of the matter. For, while it is hard to see how this black element is neither "alienated" nor "other," even this phrase is of value insofar as it propels Roberts toward the discovery that such droplets are "the condition of possibility for 'the whiteness of whiteness.'" The resonance of *Invisible Man*'s paint allegory widens terrifically as a result of this discovery. No longer can it be presented solely in political terms, as a parable on white America's longstanding dependence on and denial of slave labor. Now a bigger truth is revealed: that *Invisible Man* is allegorizing the racial philosophy responsible for such horrific legacies. It is showing that, in the long history of empire, race grew out of encounter: that the European begot the Indian, the white begot the black; and that the most insular racial fantasy, including the Nazi fantasy of purging Germany of Jews, found its basis in an ongoing experience of difference rather than in any real or original loss of unity. Roberts, in describing this magic black element, might well seem too quick to jettison "alien" and "other"; but a third noun, *stranger*, does seem preferable to the other two, referring as it can to someone or something that exists *within* a given social system and that gives it life even while bearing the brunt of its lies and slanders.[5] Now *Invisible Man*'s droplets of black paint start to disclose their symbolic potential. Now they start to look like strangers in the strange land of the dazzling white paint. Now they appear to the white skin of the U.S. monument as the ghetto is to the city or the quarters are to the plantation: that immiserated minority element within the overall system, from which the majority element draws its energy and, by a process of binary projection, its myths of superiority.

Throughout its discussion, this chapter will remain mindful of the implications of *Invisible Man*'s memorable set piece, here and there invoking it to maintain a realistic attitude toward the new interracial foods and dining experiences that emerged in London in the first few years of the eighteenth century. The story of barbecue's assimilation into the expanding repertoire of 1700s and '10s London dining certainly requires such realism. For the rapid and revolutionary journey that led this invented food from *Jamaica Viewed*'s lurid pages and dropped it, by 1707 at least, into the mouths of ordinary Londoners in many ways amounts to a disheartening tale about the rise of racial consciousness in English life. Here is a tale that, in many ways, contradicts the high and enthusiastic account that postcolonialists and other critics now give of such interracial, hybrid culture. Far from exemplifying Homi K. Bhabha's *The Location of Culture* (1994) and its exaltation of the "borderline experience[s] . . . *in-between* colonizer and colonized"—far from presenting a historical precedent for the hybrid "chapatti" in which Bhabha seems to glimpse a future beyond race (206)— barbecue's popularization in 1700s and '10s London appears wedded to the ascent of new notions of racial exoticism and mastery. Even among those who ate it, as we will see, barbecue in these years seems to have retained its full complement of savage and cannibal meanings, if anything strengthening the racist mythology enshrined in Hickeringill's vicious doggerel.

Postcolonial critics are right to suggest that there is something hypocritical about those who hold racist attitudes even as they continue to harbor interracial desires. Vron Ware and Les Back are right, in their coauthored *Out of Whiteness* (2002), to express surprise at the Luftwaffe jazz buff "who switched on the bbc, hoping to catch a few bars of Glenn Miller before bombing the antennae" (187). Only as it goes on to assume that such interracial pleasures must be guilty, or must prove that racism is always unstable, does this postcolonial way of thinking grow problematic, revealing its naive and somewhat idealistic foundations. For, contrary to what this postcolonial logic can imply, those who think racially do not go about their day in a bubble that spontaneous and isolated brushes with exotic cultures can burst. Chapatis no more trouble the stomachs of British racists than jazz lessened the extent of Nazi terror. Indeed, the value of Ellison's *Invisible Man* is to reinstate the more pessimistic appraisal of human behavior necessary to a realistic account of the rise of racial attitudes. Intercultural encounter, it is true, helps dismantle existing forms of racial authority. Exchange helps create new and complicating lines of affiliation. But such encounters often prove no less crucial to the production of race thinking in the first place. Only when Europe and the Americas met, after all, did these oppositional identities come into being. And it seems clear that, at Guantánamo Bay in 1494, in Kingston, Jamaica, in 1661, and outside London in 1707, the negative aspects of encounter—its capacity to obliterate shades of difference, to collapse regional or religious variations into a single binary opposition continental in scale—easily outweighed any more democratic or humanist possibilities that it could muster.

In short, it is all but impossible to see the barbecues of 1700s and '10s London as a historical precedent for Bhabha's "postracial" chapati. If anything, these "Jamaican" and "Creole" feasts are more reminiscent of those drops of black paint whose magic evaporation, in *Invisible Man*, produces the dazzling whiteness of the Washington Mall. Alongside other American reports in 1700s London—alongside the growing popularity of Indian exhibits at the raucous Bartholomew Fair, the four Iroquoian kings who were presented to Queen Anne's court in 1710 amid great public interest, and the gang of "Mohocks" whose supposed forays after dark fuelled speculation in *The Spectator* and other pages—these barbecues thus seem linked to the growing consciousness that England's writers were beginning to display about whiteness and the social meanings it might carry. The fact that the earliest named and detailed account of a barbecue—Edward Ward's *The Barbacue Feast: or, the Three Pigs of Peckham*—should appear in 1707, the year of union between England and Scotland, strengthens the impression that such feasts could already help to call new and unifying notions about whiteness into action. *Invisible Man's* paint allegory in fact tends to suggest that Londoners' mimicry of Jamaican barbecue not only coincided with but was also connected to the cultural work of British union, at some level presenting a new dark field against which the "lack of a color difference between Celts and Anglo-Saxons" could be made increasingly apparent.[6] Years before some American revolutionaries began to "play Indian," dressing in native garb to demonstrate their cultural distance from Westminster, a similarly ludic notion of "savage" barbecue thus seems wedded to the genesis of imperial ideas in the heart of London itself.[7] By eating barbecue if not "dressing in feathers," some Londoners were beginning to find ways of hitching mastery to skin, in the process developing a less religious and more racial identity that could in time cut through Hadrian's Wall and draw Scots and English together.

Numerous British scholars still seem reluctant to acknowledge the full imperial history of their country.[8] Even today many give the impression that the British Empire only really began to have a significant effect on the economic and cultural life of their nation as the eighteenth century wore on and profits from India and other colonies piled up. Only a few have fully absorbed Christopher Hill's important recognition that the "capture of Jamaica in 1655 provided the base" for England to industrialize transatlantic slavery, thus enabling its merchants to "wax rich."[9] By far the most prominent study on this subject to date strongly implies that Britain only became a full-blown imperial state after its victory in the Seven Years' War. Linda Colley's *Britons: Forging the Nation 1707–1837* (1992) asserts that only after 1763 did Britain find itself in command of territories "neither Christian nor white" (102), as though Barbados and Jamaica among its other American colonies were all-white and slave-free societies. Although she mentions that Britain's control over the transatlantic slave trade long predated this point, Colley seems keen to curb any sense that such mass enslavement clarified and boosted the new talk of English freedoms back home (351).

Many others who take the "long" eighteenth century as their subject go along with Colley's decision to associate empire with the later decades of the period. Others, working in more specific areas, ignore racial matters altogether. Very often, in historical writings that deal with England's first successful American colonists, a curious cleavage opens; the lives of such men seem to fall into separate spheres, their religious work and city dealings appearing distinct from the hotter life that they spent among slaves on the plantation or in war. Even as it draws attention to the older Hickeringill's penchant for yoking blackness and evil together, *The Oxford Dictionary of*

National Biography chooses not to relate this habit to *Jamaica Viewed* and its fearful account of the "hellish Visage of the grim *Negroes* and *Molettoes*, beyond all imagination" (74).[10] As reticent is *The Culture of Commerce in England, 1660–1720* (2006), in which Natasha Glaisyer refers to Jamaican planter Thomas Lynch's attempts to keep his "Name Whyte" no matter "how black soever" others paint it without even tipping her hat to the loaded nature of such words (39). Too many mainstream British historians share this blind spot, failing to absorb the fact that, as Sidney Mintz puts it, England's imperial role as well as its taste for transatlantic commodities was actually "welded in the seventeenth century."[11] Too little consideration has been given to the impact of the economic transformations evocatively described in James Walvin's *Fruits of Empire* (1997):

> The British appetite for those staples which were disgorged by returning ships in ever greater profusion did more than simply transform the tastes of the western world. In cultivating those crops, vast regions of the world were brought under careful, regulated cultivation. The wilderness was won over and converted. . . . It was the plantation, above all . . . that left an indelible mark on huge expanses of the world. By the seventeenth century wherever Europeans settled they turned to the plantation as a means of settlement . . . It was the plantations' labour forces that created the wealth and life-styles of their owners, the planters, and shaped the European taste for those distant fruits of empire. . . . It was the instrument which had brought the wilderness to heel, had cowed and disciplined millions of Africans and, as if all that were not enough, had been the source of apparently limitless wealth to Europeans on both sides of the Atlantic. (132–39)

And yet, if mainstream British history still seems reluctant to admit that this transatlantic culture dates back to the 1660s, the same cannot be said of contemporary English writing. Restoration English poets and playwrights were beginning to exhibit an obsession with furthering their acquaintance with this new imperial zone. Novels, travel journals, satires, and other publications soon thereafter brim over with castaways and cannibals, with slaves and squaws, and with savages both noble and monstrous. Skin color begins to undergo a profound reorientation as a result of this overseas interest. Time and again, whiteness and Christianity are yoked together; and time and again, as these fields of identity start to bleed into each other, we find them thrust against a dark and savage field now global in scope. Neither Aphra Behn nor Ned Ward, the writers we turn to now, seems quite as innocent of racial considerations as some critics might imply. Already, in their work, London seems a city where the mention of *whiteness* and *blackness* in the same breath could raise the specter of transatlantic slavery. Behn's brief reference to "barbicu" and Ward's very early report of a "white" version of the feast in fact amount to powerful evidence that this new and "savage" food, like other signs of curiosity in American things, might be helping to construct a new, less partisan and less religious, model of national identity. This chapter, then, interrogates the invention of London barbecue interested in its relationship to a new identity under whose white banner, to quote James MacPherson's *The Highlander* (1758), "Scot and Saxons [could] coalesc." The following pages enquire whether this new imperial identity—an identity forged under a "common crown," that could help Britain put its old "native storms" to one side and begin to rule "o'er the trembling nations" abroad—was analogous to the whiteness that rises magically out of *Invisible Man*'s dirty gray paint (64). Was barbecue integral, even by dint of its erasure, to the emergence of this new national identity? Was there even just a little black in the Union Jack?

Barbicu: The View from Above

Amid the turmoil of London in 1688, as William of Orange and his supporters put together plans for what Christopher Hill famously called the "last successful invasion of England," Aphra Behn, feeling her age, racked with arthritis, and living alone in a garret that would be her final home, continued work on her last play.[12] Elsewhere in the city, at the Houses of Parliament and the taverns fronting onto the main thoroughfares, in the grander squares and terraces built since the Great Fire of 1666, men of influence were on tenterhooks, the thoughts of loyal Tories and disloyal Whigs alike rarely drifting from James II and his faltering hold on power. But Behn, in seeking a subject for this play that she would not live to see performed, turned her back on the crisis thus engulfing the city around her, her mind turning to the Atlantic and American world she had known as a young woman. In a tense and agitated England—an England scarred by anti-Catholic violence and soon to be abandoned by its king—*The Widdow Ranter*'s Virginian setting stood out, suggesting a hankering on her part to escape London.

Or so it seemed. Looked at another way, the Virginian setting of Behn's final play was a necessary conceit, the American mask it needed to wear if its attacks on the mob and "the middling sort" others called the lower gentry were to avoid violent recrimination. Persecution not only of open Catholics but of anyone suspected of Popish inclinations was becoming a common part of London life, and rabble-rousers could easily lump Behn into the latter, looser camp. Her detailed knowledge of Catholic theology, her provocative decision to set *The Feign'd Curtizans* (1679) in Rome at a time of heightened antipapal feeling, and her continuing loyalty to James II when others were branding him a traitor to the Reformation had already earned her the contempt of Protestant stalwarts. And anti-Rome sentiments never grew more poisonous than when directed against women, this rising Protestant establishment never crueler than when condemning Charles II's wife, Henrietta Maria; his mistress, the Duchess of Portsmouth; and other leading Catholics it branded "Whores of Babylon." No doubt Behn also knew of the notorious London apprentices, seeing or hearing these young men in action as they went about burning effigies of the pope, stopping coaches to demand "money for alcohol and bonfires," and breaking the windows of some Catholics while beating up others in the street.[13] By 1688, as London glowed with "bonfires made by the rabble" to celebrate James's outmaneuvering by the Protestant courts, Behn surely saw that she could ill afford to voice her disgust at these mobs openly and, as it were, to their face.[14]

Virginia thus gave imaginative shelter, allowing Behn to state *The Widdow Ranter*'s political critique allegorically and in a code intelligible to likeminded theatergoers but too subtle for the mob. Behn could insist that her play turned a blind eye to domestic matters, assuring critics that it merely dramatized Bacon's Rebellion in 1670s Virginia rather as Joseph Addison could, if necessary, maintain that his play *Cato* (1713) had everything to do with the history of the Roman senator and only accidentally chimed with the republican and libertarian attitudes then growing strong in London. At a deeper level, though, *The Widdow Ranter* also wants to draw attention to this allegoric mode that it is employing. Again like *Cato*, it also wants its parallels between colonial America and the immediate crisis to become known, to grow here and there apparent to reveal the desperate but resurgent measures that art must take in an age of mounting tyranny and fear. Just as Alexander Pope and other luminaries introduced editions of *Cato* with verse calculated to make its British parallels even more explicit, so Behn wove into *The Widdow Ranter* several English references that, though on their own insignificant, together reveal that it is not set in Virginia but "dispersed across an imperial horizon," drifting back and forth across the Atlantic Ocean.[15]

Virginia certainly seems to swing between Englishness and the exotic as Behn simultaneously flees from and engages with the events leading up to what became known as the Glorious Revolution. Masks slip and reappear, Anglicisms and shoehorned Americanisms rub shoulders, as characters light up pipefuls of homegrown "mundungus" before consuming a "cagg of cider" among other products available in the colony but still more closely associated with England.[16] The seventeenth-century English penchant for seeing the American colonies as a kind of laboratory for homegrown ideas thus grows apparent here. Behn employs a multilayered approach, reveling in some surface mysteries of Virginian life, Anglicizing others, and shaping and sculpting the deeper social formations of the colony to fit the world outside her window.

Bacon's Rebellion, *The Widdow Ranter*'s main subject, bears the brunt of this manipulation. Slaveholding Nathaniel Bacon becomes a man of honor, and his revolt against the Virginia Council for its inaction in the face of the Susquehanna threat a righteous act aimed at restoring class and order to the colony. Two transformations more jarring and of graver consequence than the play's references to quintessential English drinks then follow. In the first, military-minded Bacon becomes a friend to the American Indian. His stated desire to wage war "against all Indians in generall" evaporates, his noble status propelling him into the arms of the no less eminent Queen Semernia.[17] And in the second, this bond between Bacon and indigenous nobles strengthens as both recoil from the true villains of the piece, the Virginia Council, whose members *The Widdow Ranter* now denigrates as Johnny-come-latelys, as Roundheads in all but name, and as a *nouveau riche* lower gentry one would "sooner take . . . for hogherds" (258).

This misidentification is perhaps the most outlandish of all committed by the play. It contradicts the facts of the matter, turning a blind eye to the wealth of the council as well as its noted lack of religious zealotry. Nor can we reconcile Behn's portrayal with the fact that, even when England's revolutions had started to come thick and fast, the council had managed to remain more or less loyal to whoever happened to be in power. But still

Behn risks this mischaracterization, and she does so because it forms a critical link in her allegoric chain. For by misidentifying the Virginia Council as revolutionary Protestant agitators she can send Bacon before it and have him say things that would have made no sense at all in America in 1676 but all the sense in the world in London a dozen years later. This is what permits her to have Bacon burst into an eloquent defense of a monarchy not then facing any grave threat.

BACON   Pardon, for what? . . . Should I stand by and see my country ruined, my king dishonoured, and his subjects murdered, hear the sad cries of widows and of orphans. You heard it loud, but gave no pitying care to it. And till the war and massacre was brought to my door, my flocks and herds surprised, I bore it all with patience. Is it unlawful to defend myself against a thief that breaks into my doors? . . .

WELLMAN   And call you this defending of yourself? . . . We every day expect fresh force from England, till then, we of ourselves shall be sufficient to make defence, against a sturdy traitor.

BACON   Traitor, 'sdeath; traitor—I defy ye, but that my honour's yet above my anger, I'd make you answer me that traitor dearly.
[*Rises.*]

WELLMAN   Hah—am I threatened—guards, secure the rebel.

BACON   Is this your honourable invitation? Go—triumph in your short-lived victory, the next turn shall be mine.
[*Exeunt Guards with* Bacon]
A noise of fighting—enter Bacon, Wellman, *his Guards beat[en] back by the table,* Bacon *snatches a sword from one, and keeps back the rabble* . . .

RABBLE   We'll have our general, and knock that fellow's brains out, and hang up Colonel Wellman.

ALL   Aye, aye, hang up Wellman.
The rabble seize Wellman, *and* Dullman, *and the rest.*

DULLMAN   Hold, hold, gentlemen, I was always for the general.

RABBLE   Let's barbicu this fat rogue.

BACON   Begone, and know your distance to the council.
[*The rabble let them go.*]

WELLMAN   I'd rather perish by the meanest hand than owe my safety poorly thus to Bacon.

BACON   If you persist still in that mind I'll leave you, and conquering, make you happy 'gainst your will.
[*Exeunt* Bacon *and rabble, hollowing "A Bacon, a Bacon."*]

Bacon's heroism here derives, not out of any recognizable American situation, but from his very English ability to prevent power from devolving further into the hands of the lower gentry. He is masterful because he is the only character in the play who understands the consequences of domestic social change, alone grasping that, whenever Englishmen get ideas above their station, violence will soon follow. Bacon alone sees that, as this lower gentry fails to heed this natural law, climbing up regardless to invade the corridors of power, onlookers among the "rabble" will soon dream of their own uplift, and will brandish the considerable muscle power at their disposal as they do so. And Bacon alone nips this situation in the bud, enforcing his noble authority over the upstart council even as he brings to heel this "rabble" that, at least still knowing its natural station in life, falls naturally to his command.

Our interest, then, lies in the way in which the idea of barbicu helps Aphra Behn visualize English vulgarity. If taken overall, this dramatic confrontation would seem to indicate that *The Widdow Ranter* is here following the apparent example of her narrative *Oroonoko* (1688) and seeking to disavow the importance of race as a category of difference. Because it flows from his ability to restore the natural social order, Bacon's heroism implies that Virginia's real problems derive neither from its slaves nor from its Amerindians but from its vulgar and overambitious white commonfolk. But if only because the word carried such a forceful racial baggage at the time, *barbicu*'s infiltration into this dramatic confrontation begins to understand this English vulgarity and commonness as a kind of savagery incarnate. *Barbicu*'s surprising appearance in *The Widdow Ranter* seems to reinstate the racial philosophy from which Behn seeks escape, yielding to its authority in order to restate the central question of English rank.

The Widdow Ranter's reference to barbicu certainly stands as a remarkable development. Even allowing that Behn's subtitle *The History of Bacon in Virginia* simplifies matters, failing to declare her allegoric interest in English affairs, we can still draw certain historical insights from her use of the word. Upon encountering it we can say that as early as 1688 London audiences could keep pace with Behn's punning reference to this quintessentially savage food. Exactly how this was so is difficult to say. Copies of *Jamaica Viewed* (1661) no doubt remained in circulation, keeping at least some Londoners acquainted with Hickeringill's spurious cannibal vision. Just as likely, the *Great Voyages* engravings and the pastiches and parodies that they inspired remained familiar to many. Certainly it is possible that the aforementioned tendency to see de Bry's cut-and-paste engravings as authentic images of actual barbecues took hold in this colonial period. And yet what distinguishes *The Widdow Ranter* is that it invokes barbecue's existing status as a savage and cannibal act only to mix into this brew a new association with pork. The pun that Behn weaves around the word *barbicu* not only invokes Bacon himself but also, by extension, the pigs that de Soto first brought to the North American mainland in 1539, and which had so flourished in Virginia that its English settlers were by now enjoying "pork . . . as good as any in the world."[18] Already, then, in this pun a reversal characteristic of barbecue culture becomes evident. No sooner is it condemned as savage, branded somehow anthropophagous, than it enters the mainstream. It is becoming associable as something that white and Christian men might do whenever the ties of polite and civil life, for one reason or another, slacken.

Certain caveats need to be stated here. Every time Behn drags events back toward England, having Bacon pontificate on king and country or bringing characters together to share a "cagg of cider," we remember that little is straightforward about this play, and that its subtitle, *The History of Bacon in Virginia*, only hints at the bigger picture that it paints. *Barbicu's* status as an element within this bigger picture—and its marriage in the script to *rabble*, a word then evocative of metropolitan English life—accordingly reveals that Behn is here hoping that her audience will associate this "barbaric" form of cookery not only with Virginia and pork but also, and perhaps less consciously, with the mobs that appeared a new and outrageous force on London's streets.

Like Bacon's anachronistic defense of an unmenaced crown, then, Behn's vision of a rabble threatening to "barbicu" a social superior can be considered another unexpectedly English moment of the play. After all, although contemporary social attitudes could often take on exaggerated forms, *The Widdow Ranter's* belief that Virginia teetered on the brink of mob rule, taken at face value, appears downright paranoid. Here ruled the hardest of civilized men, a draconian colonial regime determined to subdue plantation labor and to keep its African chattel terrified and apart from the indentured white "Servants" whom Daniel Defoe's *Moll Flanders* (1722) would "more properly call . . . Slaves" (133). In this territory, for all that Bacon managed to assemble "a ragtag army," the threat of a full-blown mobocracy of the order imagined by *The Widdow Ranter* was remote to say the least.[19] Fear of the "rabble" was a London fear, a fear forged in the sight of the Protestant and "middling sort" of that city turning a blind eye to the anti-Catholic antics of young roughs in the street. *The Widdow Ranter's* overall allegoric design, its tendency to dress homegrown fears in American clothes, as such seems epitomized here: the Virginian rabble's threat to "barbicu" a detested politician, it would seem, provides an American mask for Behn's fear of the bonfires that London's mobs lit across the city to mark James II's fall from grace.

Behind this American mask, beyond its convenient ability to assure hostile critics that the play takes place in Virginia, thus lurks a new political idea: that the real Native people who frightened the real Bacon in fact pose less of a threat to civilization than the vulgar hordes to be found within its fold. Taken together, the bond between Bacon and Queen Semernia, the fact that neither she nor her fellow Indian nobles ever mention *barbicu*, and the subsequent implication that the white rabble have learned the word from an indigenous peasantry whom Behn has banished offstage add up to powerful evidence of *The Widdow Ranter's* surface and conscious desire to prioritize rank over race. Together, these complicated transatlantic maneuvers make the play's political message difficult to avoid: wherever you are in the world, it would seem, cream is always cream and scum is always scum.

Modern readers, wrestling with Behn's oeuvre, sometimes seem relieved to stumble across such repudiations of white supremacy. For many, Behn's snobbery and slavish devotion to the Stuart crown are bad enough; the discovery of her racial ambivalence could condemn her work outright. Relief as such seems to greet those moments where Behn's dramas seek to declare themselves innocent of race thinking. Little effort is devoted to the examination of such claims. Still less goes into asking whether, as *The Widdow Ranter* all but beatifies its Indians, all the while grinding its poor white characters in the dirt, Behn might, in fact, be protesting too much.

For all that Behn is keen to parade her freedom from racialism, *The Widdow Ranter's* intertwining of *rabble* and *barbicu* certainly suggests a more complicated situation. This intertwining, after all, marks the moment when the questions of race that Behn exorcises from her surface narrative creep back in. Single-handedly it reveals that, even as *The Widdow Ranter* yearns for raceless colonial encounters, it remains trapped in an epistemology in which color has already completed much of its inexorable voyage from what David Wallace has called "an accidental trait of person-hood" to "an absolute determinant of freedom."[20] Because, although it is true that the main purpose of this cannibal threat is to condemn an English rabble, it is also true that the reference achieves this in a fashion de Bry would recognize: by calling upon America to deliver an image of supreme and essential savagery—in this case, barbecue—and by lining these vulgar whites up against it. Homegrown white vulgarity, in other words, acquires an unmistakable racial tinge here. Even as it ushers Queen Semernia on-stage, parading her as a kind and noble Algonquian, *The Widdow Ranter* seems to force someone or something like one of de Bry's Tupinambán savages behind the scenes, demanding that this unseen monster furnish a new and clarifying epitome for white barbarity. Rather as Behn's *Oroonoko* (1688) cannot quite reconcile the nobility of its eponymous African king with his failure to escape transatlantic slavery, *The Widdow Ranter* thus comes to seem powerless to consummate its desire to escape race. Reliant on the American "savage" as its new yardstick for savagery of all types, Behn's last play instead offers a glimpse into a new epistemological world in which the dialectic between whiteness and blackness can occlude all others. Bacon's virtue, it would now seem, arises from his ability to master and tame a white barbarism now shown to be savage in origin.

Barbacue: The View from Fleet Ditch

Historians often present the years between the Glorious Revolution of 1688 and the Act of Union of 1707 as a period of improvement in English life—as a period in which the country lay aside its old zealotry, restored stability to its constitutional affairs, and established *modesty* and *accomplishment* as the watchwords in a new civil attitude that would in time lead it to global dominance. Evidence for this view is not hard to find. In the period after Aphra Behn's death, the commodities necessary to polite life began to fall within reach of more and more English subjects. Up and down the country, as Christopher Hill pointed out in *The Century of Revolution* (1961), forks and spoons grew increasingly familiar on dining tables, as did looking glasses on a certain kind of drawing-room wall (23, 251). Even the simple fact that, in these years, slavery helped reduce the price of refined, white sugar illustrates that ordinary Englishmen and -women were now beginning to enjoy a lifestyle that had only lately been the preserve of their aristocratic masters.[21] This evidence, however, encourages the suspicion that rude and uncouth behavior was now finding itself on the wrong side of history, a remnant of an earlier and unenlightened way of life that England's rulers would now, sooner or later, legislate out of existence. The possibility that such rudeness was itself new, a sign that many had felt and were coming to reject the social anxieties that such new civil forces could produce, disappears from this empirical account. So does the likelihood that the first barbecues to go by that name—outdoor events held just outside London in the first years of the eighteenth century—amounted to a new kind of rebellion against the orderly and "ideal meals" growing ever more familiar in that city.[22]

This tendency to sideline the less-than-splendid aspects of eighteenth-century life, or to see them as aberrations or anachronisms that barely belong to its polite and progressive culture, also becomes evident in the critical reception of Ned Ward—or, rather, in the lack of it. Only a handful of literary historians, after all, have sought to challenge Alexander Pope's flat dismissal of Ward as a mere "ale house keeper."[23] And, of the few who mention him, this chronicler of London life is first and foremost one of the "dunces" of Pope's *Dunciad Variorum* (1729), a common peddler of drink-fazed doggerel.

A glance at some of Ward's titles, from *Sot's Paradise* (1698) to *The Delights of the Bottle* (1720), reveals that this boozy reputation was well deserved. But the titles also remind us that many other writers fond of drink have not made it so prominent in their work. Similar observations can be made of other key elements in Ward's low reputation. For Pope and his friend Jonathan Swift, Ward could be dismissed as a doyen of Grub Street, a district outside the city walls that had long carried "overtones of refuse-disposal," thus suiting the "satirists' . . . aim of connecting vice and squalor with the sewerage of the town."[24] Etymologically and geographically, Ward's Grub Street neighborhood linked up with the city's "main artery of disease," Fleet Ditch, whose effluent outpourings "crept sluggishly to the Thames."[25] Not only the pariahs but also the excrement and other waste of the city thus tarnished Ward's reputation; the most casual observer could identify his work with the nauseating climax of Swift's "Description of a City Shower" (1710):

Filth of all hues and odours seem to tell
What street they sail'd from, by their sight and smell.
They, as each torrent drives with rapid force,
From Smithfield, or St. 'Pulchre's shape their course,
And in huge confluent join'd at Snow Hill ridge,
Fall from the Conduit prone to Holborn-bridge.
Sweepings from butchers' stalls, dung, guts, and blood,
Drown'd puppies, stinking sprats, all drench'd in mud,
Dead cats, and turnip-tops, come tumbling down the flood. (257)

Here, admittedly, Swift's loyalties are divided. Like the subject of "A Meditation upon a Broom-stick" (1701), this noxious torrent can be seen as a metaphor for "satire itself," the energies of which bring "hidden corruptions to light," raising a "mighty dust" as they do so (60).[26] What is more, the "beau" who Swift shows us, "box'd in a chair" and trembling at the prodigious filth of the city outside, suggests that the accomplished and polite cannot yet claim all of London as their own, and must still harden their skin and brace themselves against its seedier sights and smells. And yet, although this is a telling image, it is clear that Swift's view of such things differs greatly from that of Grub Street hack Ned Ward. For even as "A Description of a City Shower" and other writings evoke the moral capacities of satire, Swift continues to invest in the filth of filth, the dirt of dirt, inviting us to shudder at its necessary work. Nothing in his oeuvre seems as ambivalent about dirt's intrinsic qualities as *The London Spy* (1698–1700), a chronicle of the city in which, more often than not, Ward embraces its seedier aspects just as his smaller writings embrace drink.

After all, as anyone with a taste for soul food knows, the "turnip-tops" that tumble down Fleet Ditch can inspire delight as well as disgust; their status is open to negotiation.[27] And though he does not yet profess love of such rejected food, Ward, throughout *The London Spy*, valorizes its equivalents in urban space, seeking out those "lowlife haunts" into which Pope pens his dunces and celebrating their boisterousness and vim.[28] Again and again, *The London Spy* hurries through the polite thoroughfares, more eagerly pursuing some skuzzy and insalubrious encounter. Occasionally Ward stops to salute London's uplift, at one point paying homage to St. Paul's "Towering Pinnacle" (106). Even in such dutiful moments, however, *The London Spy* seems keen to return to earth—to crash-land into some tawdry fair or "uncooth" brothel, some backstreet tavern hidden from the rich replacement city (375).

Even at the start of his career, Ward's celebration of such forgotten enclaves carried a certain racial baggage. One of the tawdrier districts with which Ward could be identified, St. Giles, was already noted for its population of "blackbirds," and these African beggars were far from the only sign that this poet of the seedy and dirty could reflect the new importance that race was starting to assume in English life. Another was Ward's 1700 description of a "Negro" who *views* his *Loathsome Colour in the Glass*," an image that neatly but nastily touched on the proliferation of mirrors in London's smarter houses and the proliferation of black beggars on its seedier streets, mixing both to produce a new absurdity: a barbaric reflection in civilized glass.[29] As it happens, Ward's ability to assimilate such fraught racial images into his interest in London's dirtier energies suggests there was some truth to the old rumor that he wrote his *A Trip to Jamaica, with a True Character of the People and Island* (1698) without leaving dry land. *A Trip to Jamaica* certainly seems short on new insights into colonial life, long on accounts of waste and contagion that make the island sound like little more than a warmer version of Fleet Ditch. "Without *Malice* or *Partiality*," Ward summarizes the "*Character of* JAMAICA" thus:

> The Dunghill of the Universe, the Refuge of the whole Creation, the Clippings of the Elements, a shameless Pile of Rubbish, confus'dly jumbled into an Emblem of the Chaos, neglected by Omnipotence when he form'd the World into its admirable Order. The Nursery of Heavens Judgments, where the Malignant Seeds of all Pestilence were first gather'd and scatter'd. . . . As Sickly as an Hospital; as Dangerous as the Plague, as Hot as Hell, and as Wicked as the Devil. Subject to Turnado's, Hurricans and Earthquakes, as if the Island, like the People, were troubled with the Dry-Belly-Ach.[30]

Over the course of *A Trip to Jamaica*, whatever the truth of its production, two things become clear enough. One is that its catalog of the immoralities and contagions of Jamaican life in the first and last instance concerns the conduct of the colonials; slaves appear only inasmuch as they "suffer" at their masters' hands. Alexander Pope's laughing reference, in *The Dunciad Variorum*, to Ward's foray into "ape and monkey lands" thus masks and belittles the latter's complex identifications, spiriting attention away from the possibility that this laureate of booze might also, under certain circumstances, empathize with the black subjects whose color he could elsewhere call "loathsome."[31] The other thing that *A Trip to Jamaica* makes clear is that, whether or not he actually set foot in the island, Ward remained, at the dawn of the eighteenth century, oblivious to a word that he would fairly soon be spelling, with a certain authoritative flourish, *barbacue*. It reveals that, in order to hear of and see such a feast, Ward needed neither to cross the Atlantic nor to tell people that he had. He just needed to walk across London Bridge.

At least since Elizabethan times, Londoners had been able to escape the rigors of civilized life in one of two ways: by going along to Bartholomew or some other raucous fair, or by traveling across the river to frequent that southern part of the city that had always been seen, in Peter Ackroyd's phrase, "as a poor and disreputable appendage."[32] Fairs held all around London at particular times of the year and the rough taverns and playhouses of Southwark provided perfect opportunities for coarse behavior. And a fair like Horn Fair—a fair on the "disreputable" south side of the river—amounted to an opportunity Ward could ill afford to miss. His chronicle of the event, *A frolick to Horn-fair with a walk from Cuckold's-point thro' Deptford and Greenwich* (1700), duly showcases his trademark espionage, eavesdropping on macho behavior wherever he finds it, and generally suggesting that these seafaring settlements to the south of London lie beyond its civilizing powers.

Even Greenwich, for all its royal privileges, palace, and observatory, emerges in Ward's report as a rough sort of place. Right near the High Street, in the churchyard itself, Ward has an army of ghosts from England's recent past gate-crash its civilized present. Climbing from their shallow graves they peep, like Tom Sawyer and Huck Finn, "in at the Church Window, on a *Sunday*, and frighten the whole Congregation" (7). Nor are death and carnage the only subjects of repression that, in Ward's reckoning of things, are better able to haunt civilization in Greenwich than in London. Barbarism, too, stalks the gentler quarters of this parochial world. For if Ward makes these dead spies look a little like gargoyles—if they seem somehow to restore signs of medieval superstition to the light and air of the English church—then another kind of degeneration seems apparent in the mean and scattered huts that, Ward tells us, look down upon the burial grounds. In a phrase linking old European notions of the grotesque to a new American repertoire, Ward says that these huts are "no bigger than *Indian Wig-wams*" and claims that they stare directly out at the "Good Houses . . . fit for Christians" that stand opposite the churchyard (7). But Ward seems surprisingly indifferent to this apocalypse he has conjured. Having intimated that civilization and savagery are about to do battle for the soul of the English church, he blithely moves on to other things. In Deptford, he seems unperturbed to discover that civilization has fallen into further retreat. It is almost as though he senses that both belong to a single social system—as though he is pleased to discover that the town's New Dock, an impressive engineering achievement not long open, has been colonized by "a parcel of *West-Indian-Creolians*," white men born in the Caribbean, who now stand around

> cooking in the open Air, an English Porker after the Indian manner. . . .
> They drove Sticks in the Ground, and Fenc'd in a square place with Old
> Tarpaulins, leaving one side open for the Wind to Fan the Fire which was
> made in the middle with Charcole, directly over which lay the Grunter on
> a Grid-Iron, made of Spits; which were laid Cross, from side to side; the
> part that lay uppermost, being cover'd with the Dripping-Pan, to preserve
> it from Cooling, and the Fat droping into the Fire, cast up . . . savoury
> Fumes from the burning Grease . . . ; and about Six or Eight foot distance,
> from the main-Fire, was another Fire, to the Windward of the Pig, most
> Cunningly Contriv'd to Warm the Air, as it pass'd, lest its Coldness other-
> ways might be some Impediment to the Grilliading, or beastly Cooking of
> their Ill favour'd Beast, whose Eyes were Roasted in his Head according to
> the Negroes Cookery, that he star'd like a Dead Pig; and that side that lay
> next to the Fire, with the Smoak of the Driping was almost as black as the
> Charcole beneath it; that I question not but by the Time it was Ready, it
> stunk like a piece of Cheshire-Cheese, Toasted in the Flame of a Candle,
> and look'd all over as black as the Rind of a Flitch of Bacon, that has hung
> Six months in a Country Chimney. (8)

Something about the feast at the New Dock clearly caught Ward's fancy. Something about its savagery, something about its ability to offer outlet to the masculine desires that the civilizing process had started to drive from London life, apparently captivated Ward, drawing him to visit further ex-amples of this scene that happenstance had put before him on the road to Horn Fair. From the transition between *A frolick to Horn-fair* (1700) and *The Barbacue Feast* (1707), then, we can deduce that Ward learned to refer to this "Savage Piece of Cookery" as *barbacue* only some years after his alleged Caribbean sojourn. But we can also start to see that Ward, throughout *The Barbacue Feast*, is trying to cover up this inconvenient fact. Here, then, is a maneuver akin to the way in which *Jamaica Viewed* withholds italics from this word, presenting it as a commonplace and silencing any etymological speculation. A similar emptying out occurs: *The Barbacue Feast* bears witness to another commodity that we are asked to accept as American, but which seems strangely bare of any evidence to confirm this authentic status. Now the Americanness of barbacue transpires as it does in *Jamaica Viewed* or de Bry's engravings, namely, out of the sheer necessity to believe in the existence of savagery and its foods. The word and the idea that it conveys can once more "behave . . . as though we knew it already." No provenance needs to be given, no attribution offered, to support this impulse to know that savagery resides and is perfected in the world abroad.

Not least because it is the first work to name and report a barbacue as we know and eat it today, *The Barbacue Feast* is thus of major importance to this book, of major importance to the invention of this more or less "American" food. Indeed, while Ward has often earned the disapproval of critics for embroidering reality—*A Trip of Jamaica* is not his only work that plays fast and loose with the facts—the historical importance of *The Barbacue Feast* can be gauged from the striking resemblance between its account and feasts more lately associated with the Americas.[33] Mindful of such considerations, let us consider this work further. Let us look at several long passages from Ward's report, offering numerous explanatory endnotes as we go. *The Barbacue Feast* begins:

> About a Month after *Midsummer* Moon when the Brains of the *Rotherhitheans*, in a sultry Day, happen'd to be over-heated with that *West-India-Diapente*, call'd *Kill-Devil-Punch* . . . made of that odoriferous evil Spirit, according to the Language of the Small-coal-colour'd Heathen most learnedly distinguished by the name of Rum; which infernal Juice has so great an Affinity with *Train Oil*, both in Taste and Smell that it causes a Man's Mouth, after a plentiful Dose, to become as fragrant to his Nostrils, as a Leather Dresser's Work-house, or the Snuff of a Play-house Lamp, burnt into the Socket.[34] . . .
>
> By the powerful Ascendancy of the *American* tipple, their Natures were so wonderfully chang'd, and their *English* Appetites so deprav'd and

vitiated, that nothing would satisfy the squeamish Stomacks of the fanciful Society, but a Litter of Pigs most nicely cook'd after the *West-India*
Manner; a Solemn festival, which had *usually* been celebrated amongst the
neighbouring Tarpaulins, but now agreed upon to be kept with as much
Splendour and Decorum, as the Porculent Projectors could well con-
trive.[35] (2–4)

Somehow the men remain under the spell of the Kill-Devil long enough
not only to form a committee but also to "sign and seal Tickets" for the
event, "provide Bagpipes for the Bears," and generally see that "all Things
were in Order for the Entertainment" (4). They even mull over the best
venue for the feast, eventually agreeing to hold it in

> *Peckham*, for what Cause I know not, except for the Reason of Pig and
> *Peckham* beginning both with a Letter.[36] When the leading Dons of
> the grand Solemnity, had thus far proceeded with very joyful Success, a
> Hoggard coming by with a Drove of young Shoats, whipping along his
> untowardly Companions with as much Severity as . . . a *Jamaica* Planter
> a stubborn *Negre . . . Where are you driving your Hogs, Brother?* says a
> Steward to the Swineherd.[37] *To a fair Market I hope, Brother*, says the
> Swineherd to the Steward. *I want three of thy Shoats, if thou'lt sell 'em me*,
> crys the Buyer to the Seller. *You may be sure I won't give 'em you*, replies
> the Hog-man. . . . *Thou answerest like a cross-grain'd Fellow*, says another
> of the Fraternity.[38] *Dost not see my Hogs are so*, says the Country-man;
> *and how the Devil should I be otherwise, that drive 'em?* However, in the
> Conclusion of their Dialogue, a Bargain was struck up for a Leash of
> Porkers; which, as soon as paid for, were separated from the Herd; and
> to improve their Flesh against their Day of Execution, were sent to be
> nurs'd up in a neighbouring Yard, and strict Orders given, that no Pease
> should be wanting, that might enrich the Flesh to the utmost Delicacy, so
> that . . . every Day they liv'd, they gormondiz'd on more Variety of Frit-
> ters, than a *London-'*Prentice upon a *Shrove-Tuesday* . . .; [and] in a little
> Time they became such delicious Meat, that no *Smithfield* Porker against
> St. *Bartholomew's* Revels, . . . was ever such incomparable Food for a nice
> Appetite.[39] (5–6)

Questions of rank return to Ward's description of the preparation of the
event. Different classes of tickets are sold, a superior kind being "deliver'd
out to the better Sort, at Three and Six-pence," while those "of lower Rank
and Quality" pay "Half a Crown" and think " 'em full dear enough at that

Price" (6). Further signs of class disquiet arise as the society determines that the pigs,

> for the little Remainder of their Lives, [should] . . . be fed with nothing but Pudding-Meat, that is, Blood, Grits, and sweet Herbs, that when they were kill'd, and cut open, ready for Barbacuing, they might have nothing to do . . . but by cutting and tying, to make the Guts into Hogs Puddings, which thro' their wonderful Hospitality, were to be given to the Poor of *Peckham* Parish, that they might lift up their Hands and their Eyes, and pray loudly for their Benefactors, and bless the bountiful good Christians that had distributed amongst 'em such a charitable Entertainment.[40] (6)

At last the day of the barbecue dawns. Advance tickets display rules and regulations whose purpose is to guarantee that the event will appear as unruly and unregulated as possible. Purchasers, assumed to be men, are asked to "bring along . . . a whetted Knife, a sharp Stomack, a nimble Pair of Jaws, and good Grinders, in order to take Part of three *Barbacu'd* Pigs, nicely cook'd after the *Indian* Manner" (7). The tickets further caution participants to "come within a Quarter of an Hour of the time specify'd, or to leave your appetite behind you" (7). No standing on ceremony, no saying of grace or other flimflam, can get in the way of this savage and manly feast.

And so our barbecue feast begins: upon arriving at the scene of this macho event, Ward reports, ticket-holders could see for themselves "the Hogs . . . dress'd, also split for *Barbacuing*, like so many Pidgeons for the Grid-Iron." Considerable attention is devoted to this cooking apparatus. In contrast to that used in *A Frolick to Horn Fair*, it soon transpires that the gridiron itself is not iron at all but the handiwork of a

> dexterous Bull-Calf of a Carpenter, who had [undertaken] . . ., by the Assistance of Hatchet and Hand-saw, to build a Wooden Range, that in Contempt of all Blacksmiths, should endure the Fire, and completely do the Office of a Kitchen-Grate, 'till the Litter of Pigs should be sufficiently broil'd, and by the penetrating Heat of lighted Charcoal, be made incomparable Food, fit for the Table of a *Sagamoor*.[41] (8)

But the carpenter is not the only member of the community whose contribution to the feast attracts this level of esteem. Soon there comes along "a cunning Apothecary" who "humbly petition'd the Stewards, in an eloquent

Speech, stuff'd . . . full of hard Words . . . that the Superintendency of the Cookery might be wholly resigned to his discretionary Management" (8). He wins the society over with his knowledge; they listen intently as he insists that, if this barbecue is to be a proper barbecue, then the pork, "*being very guttulous, should, when under a Dissolution, by the igniferous Particles that have their Ascendancy from the Charcoal, cause a fumiferous Effluvia, to add an unsavory Gust to the three Porculent Creatures*; so that in plain *English*, their Dinner should be smoak'd by the Fats falling into the Fire" (8). He is made "Cook in ordinary to the *Barbacue* Society" for his trouble (9). And now a "Stoaker" goes to work; "by the Help of Breath and Bellows," he blows "up as rare a Charcoal Fire as ever was kindl'd" (9). Ward continues:

Every Thing being now in a Readiness for the culinary Galenist to exert his Talent, the Pig-hogs (for so I call 'em, being between both) were hoisted upon the Range by the understrapping Scullions, and after some Difficulty, being rightly plac'd, by the Cook's Direction, in that nice Order that was thought necessary, there they lay with the Fire under 'em, an Apple-Tree over 'em, and the Company round 'em, expressing as much Joy in their Looks and Actions, as a Gang of wild Canibals, who, when they have taken a Stranger, first dance round him, and afterwards devour him.[42]

According to the *Indian* Fashion, they had made no Diminution of the Creatures, but in taking out their Intrails, for broiling, they lay, with their Heads, Tails, Pettitoes, and Hoofs on, to the Amazement of the Crowd, and the Honour of the Cook.[43] (9)

Soon the smell of barbecuing meat begins to offend those who live in the vicinity of Peckham but who would seem unwelcome at the feast. Dismissing religious prohibitions on pork as a "*Jewish* superstition," Ward celebrates this food's ability to repel a "stigmatized Infidel, or a freckly Pedlar, who hate Swines-flesh as the Devil does Holy-Water" (9–10). Ward continues, warming to his hateful theme:

No sooner were the sweating Carrot-mongers pretty well warm'd thro', but they began to prick up their magnificent Lugs, as an Ass does his Ears, when he meets a Brother on the Road; and their uncircumciz'd Tails being left the whole Length, so pluck'd up their Courage, by Virtue of the Fire, and curl'd so like a Bottle-Screw at the Tip, that every

Stiffrump, as it stood cock'd with the Heat, look'd like the venomous Tail of St. *George's* Dragon, with an ugly Sting at the End on't.[44] In short, they made such monst'rous Figures with their Heads and Hoofs on, that I was almost ready to think them some of the gaddaret Swine which the Devil had pickled in Salt Water, and that his infernal Worship had brought them hither to be cook'd after a *Jamaica* Fashion, for his own proper Eating; for the broil'd and hiss'd, and so perfum'd the Air with their frowsy Effluvia's, that the very Steam of their dissolving Grease, drove three Families of *Jews* out of the Town of *Peckham*, for fear of being poyson'd, or at least polluted by the *Anti-Mosaical* Smell of those Dung-hill-raking Vermin, which the Devil, in a frantick Humour, once took Possession of.[45] (10)

And now the pigs begin

to change their Colour, and look as brown on the Scabboard side, as the tawny Belly of an *Indian* Squaw, just painted over with yellow oker and Bears-grease, so that warm Disputes arose amongst the crowding Specta-tors, whether it was, or was not, high time to take 'em by the Hocks, and give 'em a Turn upon the Grid-Iron, 'till at last the head Controuler of the Cookery was over-rul'd in his Judgment, after so sawcy a manner, that ev-ery blundering Tarpaulin, that had but cross'd the Tropick of *Cancer*, and taken a *Negro* wench by the short Wool, was ready to wrest his Office out of Hand, and would, in spite of all Disswasion, have a busy Finger in the Cook's Mess; that at last, in the mighty Hurly Burley, . . . the unfortunate food, for want of due Management, tumbled in the Fire.[46] (11)

The food is now served in ramshackle fashion, on tables assembled from "old Butts, Hogsheads, and Tressels," and on linen consisting "of more Variety . . . than an old Beggar-Woman's patch'd Smock" (12–13). "Nap-kins" are "thought useless . . . Finger and Thumb was to do the Office of Fork" (13). Gathered together at this improvised table, the "whole Com-pany gave a joyful Shout, like a Protestant Rabble burning Popish Trin-kets" (14). Each member is "so greedily intent upon the delicious Rarity, that whilst he was feeding himself with one Hand, he had another upon the Brim of the Platter, that their Fingers standing so close together . . . look'd like a Fence of Pails round a Noble-man's Park. Their Stomacks were a little too sharp to admit of time enough to crave a Blessing on their Food." Instead of observing such civilized conventions, the "whole Society"—the General Rendezvous gathered together on the commons of Peckham Rye—eat their savage dinner "as if it was for a Wager" (16).

All that is left, it would seem, is for Ward's narrator to offer some humble words of appreciation:

> *Gentlemen, we are here employ'd and maintain'd by her Majesty Queen*
> *Ann and our Country, to do our Endeavours to keep this Coast from Pyracy*
> *and Robbers, and her Majesty's Enemies,. . . . Therefore I desire you, in her*
> *Majesty's Name, and for the sake of our Country, and the honour of Our*
> *English Nation, and our selves, for every Man to behave himself courageously,*
> *and like* English-Men. (25)

Ward's is a rich and rambunctious report, its sentences jagged and labyrinthine, and it is a rare thing to see him pass up an opportunity for circumlocution or other wordplay. As we navigate this dense imagery, however, we need to keep these final words of *The Barbacue Feast* in mind. For this closing paean to royal authority offers a secular alternative for the "explication of biblical text" that, only ten or twenty years earlier, concluded most if not all English feasts.[47] Why, then, does it seem so natural and necessary that the Barbacue Society should address its members, collectively, as *Gentlemen*? How and why does this savage feast elevate its members to full participants, in Jorge Arditi's words, "in the government of the commonwealth"?[48] To what extent does this barbecue confirm what I suggest throughout this chapter: that such savagery functioned in 1700s and '10s England as so many drops of black paint, its absorption producing an identity based a little more on race and a little less on religion or rank?

This Common Meat

Following Charles I's beheading in January 1649, as Englishmen fought one another for a stake in the new Republican regime, Gerrard Winstanley embarked on a different course of action. Turning his back on London and its internecine violence, the Digger spokesman led a crew of like-minded men and women to open land near Cobham, a Surrey village barely ten miles from Peckham, and invoking scripture proclaimed it a "Common Treasury"; "for Man had Domination given to him, over the Beasts, Birds, and Fishes; but not one word was spoken in the beginning, That one branch of mankind should rule over another."[49] On these Surrey commons still unappropriated by "enslaving lords of manors," the Digger commune set up camp, sowing seed to raise crops that, as they kept telling outsiders, were for the nourishment of all.[50]

Beyond the fact that both took place on common land in Surrey, little seems to connect Winstanley's Cobham commune and the Peckham barbecue of Ward's extravagant report. Generally speaking, *The Barbacue Feast* suggests that the savage meal's architects would have had no more truck with Winstanley's idea of a "Common Treasury" than they would his dabbling with vegetarianism. Not only Digger ideology but also modern academic notions yoking the carnivalesque with democratic freedom would have held little relevance for Ward's Barbacue Society and its vision of a feast in which everyone can get drunk but none so much so as to forget his place. Class steals deep into the heart of this feast—deep into the hearts of the pigs themselves, which, as Ward has told us, the barbecue's "chief Rulers" ordain will be filled with "Blood, Grits, and sweet Herbs" and passed among "the Poor of *Peckham* Parish, that they might lift up their Hands and their Eyes, and pray loudly for their Benefactors, and bless the bountiful good Christians that had distributed amongst 'em such a charitable Entertainment." Sarcastic as it is, the image is worth pondering. Its realization that the rich can qualify as "bountiful good Christians" simply by passing unwanted pig innards to the poor conveys a political disquiet rarely found in Ward's work. A whiff of anger arises from it. Beyond its sarcasm, Ward's religious skepticism is for a moment tempered by his dismay to discover how completely the revolutionary ideals of Diggers and their ilk have been defeated by a civilizing process whose goal is to lift London up and sweep the poor underneath it. The appearance of this satiric anger in a report manifestly hoping not to take anything too seriously reflects new and revealing light on the attention Ward accords to the fact that the barbecue is ticketed. As he tells us, the quality pay "Three and Six-pence" while those "of lower Rank," who earn "their Money by the Sweat of their Brows," pay half a crown and consider this "dear enough." Even for those not reliant on handouts of offal, different classes of barbecue are thus being held. The buying and selling of the pig carry it far from the idyllic English orchard where it began, far from the money-free savage wilderness where it seems destined to end up, escorting it into a new and metropolitan universe in which every cut has its designated purchaser and every mouthful of meat its price. Politics again penetrates the frivolous scene. Ward is suggesting that class has strengthened beyond reasonable measure, growing less vulnerable to dreams of social equality, powerful enough to stalk ceremonies wild and savage in design.

Egalitarianism, however, though in substance expelled from the carnival scene, leaves its residue behind. Its rhetoric persists, its afterglow surviving in a notion of fraternal kinship that sits strangely alongside the fact that some of these "brothers" give orders while others take them. At one level, then, this barbecue consolidates the hierarchy of the wider society, admitting distinctions of rank and class into its savage spaces and so understanding them as more or less natural in character. Even having abandoned London—even having stepped into an orchard where Englishmen can revert to a savagery they would otherwise displace to America and the past—drudges still drudge; "scullions" still lift the heavy pubescent pigs "upon the Range" without complaint. Yet, somehow, in the promotional verse that he includes on the frontispiece of his pamphlet, Ward can still call this a barbecue where

> The Cooks were Numberless;
> The Company Masterless;
> The Meat Carv'd with Hatchets;
> And Punch drank by Pail-fulls.

Here, then, the paradox crystallizes. From its frontispiece onward, *The Barbacue Feast* keeps telling us that it is reporting an egalitarian event— keeps telling us that this report, to lift a word from this promotional verse, will be "Masterless." But Ward soon reveals that the feast is anything but equal, drawing attention to the discrimination of the tickets, the beggars awaiting their barbecued dole, and the scullions who remain under the heels of the company's "chief Rulers." The fact that Ward keeps flaunting this paradox suggests that his use of the word *Masterless* is somewhat knowing and attuned to a new international context. Another kind of mastery is starting to loom over this world, after all. The rabble antics, papist controversies, regicide, and coup d'etats referred to over the course of this chapter hardly interrupted or inhibited England's imperial rise to dominance during the second half of the seventeenth century. By 1700, the England that Aphra Behn and Gerrard Winstanley had known, an England riven by sectarian discord and revolutionary violence, had all but vanished, replaced by a society learning to set its religious differences aside, place profit above principle, and gather together under a single flag. Two new laws, the

Act of Toleration and the Act of Union, amounted to official and obvious measures by which the ruling elite after the Glorious Revolution sought to consolidate this new cohesion. Just as important were actions undertaken to persuade middling Britons as well as the working poor that they were indispensable to, and could take pride in, their country's expanding empire overseas. Needless to say, these ordinary Britons remained voteless. But their continuing political subordination made their growing access to positions of mastery and command within the armed forces among other public organizations appear all the more remarkable. Of course, class prejudices remained firmly entrenched in such institutions. But the need for efficient military forces to protect empire's trading posts and naval bases did lead to significant efforts "to limit the purchase of commissions and to assure the promotion of men of experience and merit."[51] Empire did fulfill some of the promises that had arisen from, but been left frustrated by, the foregoing century of revolution. Equality between white men, or at least an official semblance of it, blossomed in the muck of imperial endeavor.

Other foot soldiers of the empire wore no particular uniform. The sugar plantations of Barbados and the tobacco plantations of Virginia, the saltpeter and rubber farms belonging to the rich doyens of the East India Company, the slave ships and slaving fortresses of West Africa, and the estates of colonial Ireland could all present individual Britons with new means by which to claw their way out of their low beginnings. No one really thought that such work was virtuous or gentlemanly. While discharging their inglorious duties, however, appointees could often experience a remarkable reversal, their lifetimes of social subordination coming to a sudden end as they found themselves made masters of slaves or other colonized peoples.

Squalid as it could seem, this experience of individual mastery mirrored the rise to mastery of Britain overall. It mirrored the fact that, after union, Britain came increasingly to look beyond its shores, toward an outside world it came to see as ripe for the taking, thereby initiating what Edward Said's *Orientalism* (1978) calls the country's "long tradition of executive responsibility towards the colored races" (226). It mirrored the fact that race was in this way starting to matter throughout the British Empire—that, in England itself, lessons could be learned from the Virginia Council's attempts to "subdue class conflict by racism," and particularly from its success in inculcating white feelings of superiority over the "uncivil, unchristian, and, above all, unwhite."[52] It mirrored the fact that slavery and empire brought down the price of once-aristocratic commodities, drawing sugar and other desirable goods within the reach of ordinary Britons and making each such seem, at least in certain cultural contexts, like a natural-born global leader. And it mirrored the fact that, early in *The Barbacue Feast*, "a Hoggard [comes] by with a Drove of young Shoats, whipping along his untowardly Companions with as much Severity as . . . a *Jamaica* Planter a stubborn *Negre* . . . *Where are you driving your Hogs, Brother?* says a Steward to the Swineherd. *To a fair Market I hope, Brother*, says the Swineherd."

To conclude our reading, we need to give this encounter and the vicious comparison it inspires serious thought. It is not enough to condemn such moments from *The Barbacue Feast* as mere elements of white supremacist fantasy. The symmetry Ward here constructs between pigs and Africans, not to mention the stereotypical inevitability of his "stubborn Negre," are indeed classically racist, familiar to the point of cliché. But this discovery should mark the start rather than the end of our discussion. We need to think about *The Barbacue Feast's* violence—about the physical violence of its whip and the animalizing violence it enacts on the bodies of Africans and American Indians alike. We need to think about how this safe violence, and the taboos it purports to break, leads directly to resurgent notions of white brotherhood that can then cut across profound social differences. For it is true that, just as the accounts of Andrés Bernáldez and the Gentleman of Elvas intimated that divisions between European crewmen could melt away in the shared contemplation of the barbarous and barbecuing Indian, so *The Barbacue Feast's* violent and racist fantasies bind a motley crew together, cutting across divisions of class, occupation, and faith to develop a new Barbacue Society out of a white male identity common to all. Until Ward closes in on a point where, much like these colonial chroniclers, he puts abroad an American equivalent to Edward Said's Orientalism, presenting the alien territory of the Americas as a uniform and blanket space, and imagining that the Natives and Africans who live there are everywhere the same and are everywhere different in the same way to the Britons who stand back in innate mastery of them.

In this American exoticism, taboos again flow outward. Indeed, Ward's *Three Pigs of Peckham* can be placed alongside the Iroquoian kings who visited Queen Anne's court in 1710, like them presenting walking American counterparts to the Turkish seraglios and Persian bazaars of the Orientalist imagination.[53] They function as such feted Orientalist signs function: as a screen on which Europeans can project their forbidden desires, a depository for their taboos. Cannibalism, sadomasochism, and other fantasies are no sooner linked to the pigs than they make these animals seem exotic, impostors to the Surrey commons. *The Barbacue Feast*'s oddly lustful attitude toward its three pigs, the lechery that leads it to compare them to a "Negro wench" one moment and an "Indian squaw" the next, typifies this double move, Ward characteristically raising the vexing idea that sexual desire bestializes men only to dispatch it far from English civilization, far from Peckham Rye's common land, plunging it deep into the heart of the savage forest. A similar fate awaits nightmares spawned amid England's recent sectarian strife. Papal effigies spewing live cats, William Wallace's dismemberment at Smithfield, the Calvinist vision of the gridirons of Hell: memories of England's recent violence and disunity seem likewise inscribed on the skin of these pigs, so carved as to exoticize their flesh and send them across the ocean, far from civilization.

Even as he narrates this process, however, Ward seems to retain at least some sympathy for all thus being swept aside in London's rise to ascent. Throughout *The Barbacue Feast*, he seems unable to shake off his premonition that Amerindian and African figures are human; continuously he makes what Mick Gidley, in another context, has called "hedged acknowledgements of the full humanity" of these colonial subjects.[54] To an even greater extent than the Europeans whom Said imagines touring the Orient, Ward's objectification of the alien and foreign mingles with buried doubts and longings, with a tacit sense that Britain's rise to imperial ascendancy entails loss as well as gain, decay as well as progress. Over the course of *The Barbacue Feast*, the taboos of English life are displaced outward, onto savage fields that white men alone can master and control. Even as his writing embodies this process, however, still Ward looks upon it ambivalently. Still he looks upon it with regret. For the savage forest in which barbaric desires are now said to dwell is also being wed, throughout *The Barbacue Feast*, to the free woodland of England's recent past. The impulse that led John White to use identical archetypes to portray the Algonquian of America's living present and the Ancient Celts of England's mythic ancestry again seems operative here, *The Barbacue Feast* in some way associating the vanishing Amerindian with a vanishing pastoral ideal, the face of both being set against the city that lurks sinister and enormous on the near horizon.

The hoggard's impending journey to Smithfield as such seems regrettable, disempowering. This iconic figure—once the bane of genteel London, running amok through its thoroughfares and china shops—now seems passive, lost, able only to "hope" and not expect to find a "fair market" in the all-too-dominant city. Images in *The Barbacue Feast* strongly suggest, moreover, that this yesterday's man can only regain his lost power if he agrees to switch occupations, taking up his whip against the unwilling agents of empire. Here we have, then, been brought far from Winstanley's efforts to defy "enslaving lords of manors" and sow seed for the nourishment of all. We have been brought far from dreams of a "Common Treasury." Empire now beckons, and men like the hoggard, it would seem, can regain their lost status only by agreeing to use their strength in the subjugation of others. In *The Barbacue Feast*, the whipping of slaves goes hand in hand with the savage barbecuing of meat. Both belong to the production of a new imperial supremacy that can corrupt those it empowers.

Mohocks, Turnip Tops, and Blackface Thieves

Between *The Widdow Ranter* (1688) and Ned Ward's *The Barbacue Feast: or, the Three Pigs of Peckham* (1707), then, a remarkable journey occurs. Having appeared to Behn a species of savage violence, barbecue, in the year of the Act of Union, could already seem to some Londoners a fitting and pleasurable pursuit. In less than half a generation this smoking technique thus began and all but completed a stunning mutation. In less than a lifetime, and without shedding any of its savage or cannibalistic skin, it has slivered its way into England's culinary repertoire. Not long after *The Barbacue Feast*, and thanks to the kind of ritual reported there, this way of cooking would have established a firm foothold in national life. By the 1720s and '30s, this cannibal verb would have grown so familiar as to appear alongside *fricassees* and *ragouts* among other exotic words in the emergent genre of the British cookbook.

Even in its most banal aspects, even in those aspects that seem a matter of historical fact, the barbecue that thus entered English culinary life was far from authentic. Even barbecue's status as a form of slow charcoal or wood cookery, a status that Ward helped fix in place, arose less from any isolated Amerindian smoking technique than from the fact that English observers had grown interested in the sheer fact of these techniques and wanted to compare them to their own methods of roasting and spit-cooking meat. As readers grew familiar with the native forms of cooking being reported by Robert Beverly, among others, most almost certainly began to see barbecue not as a practice unique to any particular tribe but as a generic and brilliantly obvious form of smoke cookery for which all American Indians possessed a certain instinctual flair. Even these generalizing terms, however, could hide the fact that this marriage of the Amerindian and smoke cookery resulted to a large degree from the English culinary repertoire's relative deficiency in such techniques. If only because it encouraged cooks and proprietors to find slower and more frugal ways of cooking, the rising price of firewood in 1690s and 1700s London probably mattered as much to barbecue's popularization in England at this time as any specific transatlantic connection.[55]

These domestic factors were important because, throughout its history, barbecue has been about the familiar as much as the exotic. As a matter of fact, if read metaphorically, the fish and "serpents" that Columbus's men found at Guantánamo Bay amount to a sign of the way in which such feasts could combine the utterly unknown with ingredients drawn from everyday life. Originating in colonial encounter, barbecue has rarely lost sight of this underlying desire to root out knowable ways of eating the unknown. Almost always, over the course of its invention in European life, barbecue presented not just an exotic food but a particularly negotiable and open kind of food whose exoticism could be made palatable to ordinary folk. American factors alone thus cannot explain *The Barbacue Feast*. Neither the doubling of Virginia's population between 1674 and 1699 nor the fact that, all across North America in these years, wild pigs likewise went forth and multiplied can fully explain the background to Ward's Peckham report.[56] As the decision to hold the feast in such an unlikely venue suggests, the impact of such American developments in English social life was equally important. Virginia's rising slave and free population mattered to the extent that it increased the prominence of that colony within London's new and increasingly racialized culture. And, as for the long and unbroken marriage of barbecue and pork, likely this owed even more to the pig's ancient ubiquity in England than to its new and emerging ubiquity in North America. Barbecue's specific importance was as a part of New World life that the English could try for themselves back home; on the old side of the

Atlantic, after all, "it was a very poor household indeed that did not own a pig."[57]

The Widdow Ranter's violent pun also makes it clear, though, that barbecue was never just another new culinary technique. It was never just another of the "exotic foreign recipes" that, at least since the appearance of John Murrell's *A New Booke of Cookerie* in 1621, English cookbooks had been offering as a crucial "selling point."[58] Ned Ward's journalism alone indicates that barbecue surfaced in the 1700s because Londoners were starting to get a taste for the odd drop of black paint. *The Barbacue Feast*'s propensity to compare its pigs to the bodies of black and Native women offers compelling evidence that this food belonged to a striking cultural tendency whereby Londoners, from 1700 if not even earlier, started to associate the exciting and the illicit with the exotic realms beyond Europe: Africa, Asia, and America.

Even the few historians who "explore the creation of a culture of empire generally date its emergence later than the visit of the four Indian Kings" to Queen Anne's court in 1710, for one reason or another smoothing down the sensation that this encounter caused.[59] But they are not always successful: as Eric Hinderaker shows, the repercussions of that visit range far and wide, touching everyone from Alexander Pope to the composer of "Rule Britannia," Thomas Arne.[60] Memories of these 1710 visitors, two of whom were feted as Mohawks, are also a likely inspiration for the London gang the Mohocks, who Richard Steele would brand "a sort of *Cannibals* in *India*," and whose nocturnal antics would agitate *The Spectator* throughout 1712.[61] Daniel Defoe, as it happened, was quick to correct Steele's mistake.[62] But the fact that Steele's original description had gone on to imagine that the gang's "President is stiled *Emperor of the Mohocks*; and his Arms are a *Turkish* Crescent" suggests that he was not unduly concerned about the fidelity of his description, and that the imperative behind it was instead to stake out a generalized savage field against which a new notion of white gentility might be called into action.[63] Rather as Defoe worked hard to hammer out of history a confrontation between savage Friday and civilized Crusoe, *The Spectator*'s condemnation of the "Barbarities" that the Mohocks perpetrated "on the good people of *England*" thus mythologized to simplify, simplified to mythologize, waxing polemic in order to cast a white gaze out upon a blackness now global in scope.[64] Out of such maneuvers, in a seminal moment akin to Crusoe's discovery of Friday's footprints, new imperatives are born. Now Steele can tell us that "the Manners of *Indian* Savages are no becoming Accomplishments to an *English* fine Gentleman," both identities sharpening in the course of his injunction.[65] Everywhere on London's streets from about 1700, this generalized savage field started to loom. Advertisements referring to individual servants as "a Black Indian Boy" or an "East-Indian Tawny Black" would become a familiar sight in the pages of the city's periodicals.[66] Blackness, as in *Black Boy* or *Black-amoor's Head*, now rose to become one of the "commonest motifs" of pub signs and other forms of street publicity.[67] Nor, indeed, was this development of a new racial opposition between England and elsewhere limited to London. Even though it is possible to read pages and pages of historical commentary about the Black Act of 1723 without coming across a single reference to race, the idea that the blackface poachers targeted by this law were utter racial innocents seems impossible to credit.

Invented and exaggerated, held tight in perennial repulsion, *barbecue* belonged to this new cultural compulsion to pit English gentlemen against the barbaric world beyond Europe. It was to roast pork what the "President of the Mohocks" was to Steele's "fine Englishman." It was to the sylvan realm of village feasting what Ward's "*Negro* wench" was to the ladylike ladies who *The London Spy* would envisage strolling down the city's gentler thoroughfares. Thus *The Barbacue Feast* suggests that white Londoners could swallow these drops of savage meat, thrill to their subaltern taste, and out of this culinary tourism they could generate and refine their understanding of civilization and barbarism and of their relationship to them. Like British imperialists craving the curries of the Raj, like white slaveholders hankering after the African and indigenous flavors of down-home plantation cooking, they could experience hybrid culture as a form of racial optimization. Thus they acquainted themselves with race, working out how to position themselves in relationship to it.

"Stir It 'til It Disappears"

The revolutionary decades between the English Civil War and the Act of Union in 1707 draw scant interest from U.S. historians. Christopher Hill's tantalizing suggestion that we should regard England's sectarian controversies and its subsequent reconstruction as a dress rehearsal for later U.S.

developments stands almost alone in our postwar discourse.[68] Instead of reckoning with David Cannadine's assertion that, during the eighteenth century, the American colonies became "more like England in their social structures and cultural aspirations, rather than less," historians seem happy to accept the popular assumption that the American Revolution in fact marked a break as much from England's culture as from its crown.[69] In Nathaniel Philbrick's *Mayflower: A Voyage to War* (2006) and other bestselling works of recent years, England's influence can duly seem limited to its curious penchant for persecuting its great men, for no sooner producing a William Bradford or Thomas Paine than hounding him into the arms of lucky, less intolerant America (183–85).[70] For the simple reason that they want to talk about England less rather than more, histories intended to combat Eurocentrism often leave this popular aspect of U.S. history intact, allowing its obfuscation of key English precedents to pass unchallenged.

This tendency has limited our knowledge of important and illuminating English precedents to the kinds of racial concerns that grow acute in the early years of the American Republic. Throughout this chapter I have used *Invisible Man*'s paint episode as a kind of torchlight, holding it forth to find a way through what we might call the origins of British imperial culture. Always implicit in *Invisible Man*'s periodic reappearances, however, has been the knowledge that this cross-cultural comparison works both ways, and that this early British imperial culture can likewise illuminate our view of what Ellison called "the true interrelatedness of blackness and whiteness" in the American Republic.[71] After all, the imperial culture that emerged in 1700s Britain erected its own temples to national cohesion, funding its own white structures from the fruits of unpaid or underpaid labor. Even the most modest reflections of its new and unifying national identity can appear to contain and disguise within their structure some necessary black element. Even its cookbooks conform to this dynamic.

The growing popularity of cookbooks in the 1710s and '20s indicates that wealthier Britons were beginning to conduct their domestic affairs in a more centralized and metropolitan manner. Looking to London and Edinburgh for new trends and protocols, cookbook subscribers were included in a metropolitan culture, and part of this outlook was the cultivation of mastery over even the most exotic foods of the world. Foreign tastes were now stitched within the covers of these domestic guides. And, at least in the case of Nathan Bailey's influential *Dictionarium Domesticum: being a new and compleat houshold dictionary* (1726), foods that others still seemed to consider cannibalistic could be digested, broken down by the culinary Enlightenment:

> To Barbecue a Hog
> Kill a hog about five or six months old, take out the innards, clearing it of its hartlet: then turn it upon its back, and cut the belly in a strait line down to the bottom in the jointing of the gammons, from three inches below the place where it was stuck to kill it; but do not cut it downwards so far; but that the whole body of the hog may hold any liquor that you put into it, then stretch out the ribs, opening the belly as wide as you can, and strew into it what salt and pepper, you think fit, then having a large iron frame or gridiron with two or three ribs, let it upon an iron stand about three foot and a half high, and upon that lay the hog, spread open with the belly sides downwards with a good charcoal fire under it, broil that side till it is enough at the same side, flouring the back often.
>
> This should be done in some out-house or yard with a tent over it.
>
> When the belly side is done enough and turn'd upwards so as to be steady upon the gridiron or barbecue, pour into the belly of the hog three or four quarts of water and half that quantity of wine. (351)

Ralph Ellison's sharp eye for the way in which the idea of white mastery arises from its reliance on some useful if troubling black element warns against viewing *Dictionarium Domesticum*, or for that matter *The Barbacue Feast*, through the prism of a postcolonial field that can seem preprogrammed to equate "hybridity" with antiracist rebellion. *Invisible Man* helps us see that, far from counteracting empire, the appearance of such "black" pages within these cookbooks only sharpened their ability to envision the British kitchen. They helped situate it at the center of things, imagining it as a "white" space that could admit and assimilate all the foods of the world on its own terms.

At the same time, the discovery that *Invisible Man* resonates with the cultural patterns of eighteenth-century British life just as it does those of the American Republic enriches our view of the latter. Now we can draw parallels, for example, between life in Queen Anne's Britain and life in that U.S. era, known as the Gilded Age, which began with Reconstruction's abandonment. Dominant white culture in this transitional period expressed and enacted its desire to reconcile the warring parties of the U.S. Civil War through its incessant recourse to a new field of black and Indian caricatures. Novels, newspaper advertisements, merchandise, popular songs, and even new photographic technology in this postbellum period let slip a steady stream of racist stereotypes into the national culture. Some stereotypes, from stoic Indians to Joel Chandler Harris's infantilized servant Uncle Remus, could seem benign. Others, however, were downright monstrous. Every fear that the white Christian majority in the United States found it possible to conceive could seem crystallized in these diabolical epitomes of torture, cannibalism, and rape. Whether monstrous or saintly, however, these black and Native stereotypes seem to have provided a nonwhite field that could in turn impress upon white northerners and southerners the fact and importance of their common European ancestry.

The eighteenth-century English craze for all things savage and American that we have explored in this chapter offers a crucial and illuminating precursor to this much-discussed period in U.S. history. News of "savage" barbecue offered 1690s and 1700s London what Uncle Remus and Thomas Dixon Jr.'s rapist Gus in *The Clansman* could offer to postbellum white U.S. culture: a means of reconciliation, of finding succor and peace in the shared contemplation and gift of racial supremacy. In *The Barbacue Feast* as in Gilded Age America, then, the image of a racial Other, circulated ad infinitum in a culture tired of war, could somehow assuage, could somehow comfort the tired and the bitter, buying their peace by doling out white supremacy. Fears of mob rule that we unlocked from the allegories of *The Widdow Ranter* as such seem outmoded, outmaneuvered now. Like the southern conservatives who denounced the racial chaos of election barbecues in the Jacksonian 1820s—we consider them in chapter 4—Behn's portrayal of a white barbecuing mob more savage than savagery itself seems at once insightful and misplaced, prescient and anachronistic, no sooner identifying a genuinely new cultural mode borne of empire than misinterpreting it as a sign of impendent class mayhem. For, as *The Barbacue Feast*'s report suggests, the consummation of Aphra Behn's premonition turned out to be a disarmingly orderly affair, as classbound as any royal pageant. On Peckham Rye in 1707 there stood some of the first-ever recipients of what W. E. B. DuBois once called the "psychological wage" of whiteness: men for whom the barbecue offered the image of an egalitarianism no longer in reach.[72]

Or I guess it is a uniform hieroglyphic,
And it means, Sprouting alike in broad zones and narrow zones,
Growing among black folks as among white,
Kanuck, Tuckahoe, Congressman, Cuff, I give them the same,
  I receive them the same.
—Walt Whitman, "Song of Myself" (1855)

3 Pit Barbecue Present and Past

Of course, even if they wanted it, the organizers of the Black Family Reunion Celebration would never get permission for such a feast. The Washington Mall is far too acclaimed and austere a space to play host to the skirmishes and smoke, the booze and bawdy antics that greeted Ward on that midsummer's day in Peckham Rye. Neoclassical monuments and memorials even now dominate this terrain, granting entry to more spontaneous and free cultures only under certain terms and conditions. A decade or two of good intentions are not enough to break their stranglehold. Kind words cannot quite dispel the suspicion that much of what the Black Family Reunion celebrates does not fully belong to this terrain, and even if permitted entry to its galleries and museums cannot quite challenge its circumscribed vision of U.S. culture. Hip-hop has provided Washington with its soundtrack for some years now. But in this hallowed terrain, in this mythic heart of a city otherwise invisible and poor, it even now sounds strange—irrepressible and strange. Portion after portion of pit barbecue, served up at the edge of the lawn, suffers a similar fate. President after president has courted association with such food, and some even seem to have liked it. Still, however, the impression remains that it is an interloper, a strange black element. Still the smells of spice and smoke, pork butt and grease can conjure up another America—a more American, less Eurocentric, America. Polystyrene cartons still seem to suit it better than china. Disposable, just waiting to be tossed away, these cartons seem almost to conspire with the auspicious memorials, enforcing their verdict that the barbecue in your hands deserves neither cutlery nor respect. Nightfall will come—and this food will disappear. Neither barbecue nor hip-hop will leave a mark on this hallowed, reverent space.

In this chapter I delve further into modern U.S. culture. In particular, I raise my eyes from the colonial archive that I have been exploring so far, asking how the savage barbecue tradition that it invents relates to the kind of pit barbecue that, served up just a few days a year on the Washington Mall, remains a far more familiar feature of life across the U.S. South. We consider two distinct barbecue traditions over the course of this inquiry. On one side looms "savage" barbecue, its mythology imperial, invented, and alive with race. Opposite it stands pit barbecue, a food that has long proven unusually able to bridge even unusually deep racial divides. Ultimately, this chapter offers no definitive account about the specific foodways that gave rise to the second of these two traditions. I leave that history to another. Here, instead, I consider how this southern phenomenon has drawn upon and developed barbecue's old and preexisting savage implications. For, while these two traditions are in certain ways distinct, they do not exist—and nor have they ever existed—in splendid isolation from each other. And pit barbecue culture, as these pages will make clear, playfully draws upon the savage implications of its name, persistently luxuriating in its own barbaric status.

Pit barbecue is conspicuous by its absence from many formulations of the national cuisine of the United States. None of the museums along the Washington Mall seem able to accommodate it. Donna Gabaccia's *We Are What We Eat: Ethnic Food and the Making of Americans* (1998), to take one account of U.S. cuisine, comments on it only cursorily (39–40). Even Sidney Mintz, a man who has done much to establish food and the Caribbean as credible fields of academic study, passes quickly over this food. Indeed, in a doomed odyssey for "regional" American cuisine,

Mintz's failure to consider pit barbecue traditions can seem downright odd. No other cuisine, after all, involves the "active producing of food and producing of opinions about food" that Mintz wants to find quite like pit barbecue. And—as John Shelton Reed's "second-most-quoted sentence" puts it—"Southern barbecue is the closest thing we have in the U.S. to Europe's wines or cheese; drive a hundred miles and the barbecue changes."[1] Mintz seems blind to such diversity, disqualifying pit barbecue for consideration as one of those important foods "around which and through which people communicate daily to each other who they are, . . . validating group membership."[2]

At first glance, the fact that Mintz's quest for U.S. cuisine finds room to mention clam chowders and Boston baked beans might seem to suggest a regional bias on his part. However, much of Mintz's reluctance to consider pit barbecue in fact stems from his horror at U.S. culture in general, being connected to his tendency to contrast its acute commercialization and sheer unhealthiness with the more organic and traditional ways of life that he, like many before him, associates with Mediterranean Europe. If he squints, Mintz can just about see the clam chowder as the U.S. answer to the bouillabaisse of Marseilles or the paella of Valencia; all three seem likewise to esteem "secret" sauces and family recipes, likewise inseparable from the traditional trades of their region, and likewise at home on the menus of the beachside venues favored by locals. And yet, while pit barbecue also answers to a great deal in this description, attracting traditions of connoisseurship and local pride akin to those of the Mediterranean, nonetheless it remains outcast, beyond the culinary pale, because it remains steeped in a fatal American mix of coarseness and commerce—a mix from which Mintz seems to seek disassociation. Even today, some custodians of U.S. cuisine continue to ignore pit barbecue for similar reasons. The great time and effort demanded by this food seem to them betrayed by its unforgivable appearance among ketchup and soda, plastic cutlery and tabletops, and other paraphernalia alien to their idea of culinary excellence.

What these culinary custodians seem to miss is the extent to which pit barbecue culture courts such elitist disdain. Rarely, in their horrified responses, do they concede that pit barbecue might *want* such arbiters of good taste and judgment to hold their distance. Never is it conceded that pit barbecue, whether materializing from hatches or even from the dreaded portal of a *Drive-Thru* window, is delighting in its barbaric associations—is wallowing in grease, reveling in plastic, and generally holding the conventions of Western civilization in a steadfast and almost punklike contempt. The cultural tradition behind pit barbecue culture's hostility toward effete civilization is time and again overlooked. So is the possibility that the dismissal of cutlery in most pit barbecue joints nowadays places them into a cultural lineage that leads right back to, among other places, *The Barbacue Feast* and its repudiation of "Napkin[s]" on Peckham Rye.

Liquid and prone to incessant reinvention, pit barbecue culture is not likely to compromise on its hostility toward civilized polite cuisine. Always it covets the wildness of relief and the relief of wildness, clinging to elements it considers beyond the pale of Europe or civilized life. As Reed puts it, this is a food that even some in the South are ashamed of, a food that insects can judge better than the bourgeois:

> You can still find good barbecue in Atlanta, but most of the joints are hidden away—off the beaten track, in obscure and sometimes unsavory neighborhoods. . . . It's almost as if downtown Atlanta is ashamed of barbecue—finds it too country, too low-rent. . . . The only barbecue Mecca with over a 100,000 population—the only one over 50,000—is Memphis. The South's other cities may have barbecue, sometimes good barbecue, but it's not a religion. . . . Expansion is not good for barbecue joints. That's a rule almost as reliable as [food journalist] Vince Staten's maxim that a place without flies is no good. (You should ask what the flies know that you don't.)[3]

Given such poses, I should perhaps go easy on those who dismiss pit barbecue's culinary credentials or ignore it altogether. In such situations, after all, pit barbecue culture seems to be doing all it can to reinvigorate barbecue's savage associations. The last thing it wants is mainstream acceptance. Stainless steel cutlery and sparkling wine glasses, for many a barbecue fanatic, would spell trouble for the food to come; tablecloths are kryptonite. Perhaps the real mistake of those who disdain pit barbecue lies not in looking down their noses at the food, but in being altogether too quick to oblige it, to present it as it wants to be seen. For, just as most punk artists knew and cared a lot more about music than they liked to let on, so pit barbecue culture sets more store in protocol that it likes to admit, surreptitiously retaining some culinary mores from the civilization it appears to disown even as it spins new ones entirely from this happy and mutual disavowal. Thus, we will now see the passion and resolve with which pit barbecue culture cultivates its rebel status reveal that, though some of its practitioners might wish it were not so, this food qualifies under Mintz's or indeed any current understanding of the dread word *cuisine*.

Slow and Fast Food

Throughout Mintz's *Tasting Food, Tasting Freedom*, the United States exists in antithetical relationship to Mediterranean Europe, its foods seeming more homogenous and industrial, more "invented," than those of France, Spain, or Italy. Cuisine comes to seem a preserve of the Old World; and Mintz grimly predicts that, even there, McDonald's, Pizza Hut, and other agents of Americanization will soon do it in. Pit barbecue tradition, however, upsets this outlook. Under Mintz's logic, after all, pit barbecue tradition's embrace of the logos and products of U.S. corporate capitalism all but announces its capitulation to a brave new world in which cuisine no more belongs than do, say, typewriters or walking. The ideal pit barbecue joint that Lolis Eric Elie imagines in *Smokestack Lightning* (1996), the kind of place connoisseurs dream of, would not strike Mintz as a likely stronghold of culinary prowess:

> First, the place must be small and out of the way; the silverware must be made of plastic, the china of cardboard, and the fine wine of barley and hops. The clientele must be pure and bucolic and have been coming to the place for years, and the proprietor must be old and innocently amused that outsiders find his food so exceptional. Second, such places no longer exist, because if they did, the world would have heard about them long ago and be clamoring to get inside. Such, we are told, is the nature of the world demand for good barbecue. (3)

To many observers, it is almost absurd to think about this idealized location in gastronomic terms. Stepping into what he considers its closest approximation in reality, a Memphis joint called Hawkins, Elie straightaway becomes witness to a host of culinary crimes. Hot dogs and burgers—foods that inspire in Mintz the withering remark, "I don't think anyone wants to call that a cuisine"—await a grill that stands idle before the barbecue pit. Hamburger buns are not likely to have been baked on the premises or locally, and to gourmets would travesty the good name of bread. Ingredients assembled in Hawkins's signature dish of pork shoulder sandwich bypass the use of local produce esteemed by Mintz. Even though its fixing of coleslaw is a hallmark of Memphis barbecue, it is hard to see how cabbages, carrots, or mayonnaise evoke the history or economy of this city more than any other in America.

Masterminding Hawkins's many culinary crimes is its "sole employee," J. C. Hardaway, an unforgettable figure who has the run of the kitchen, who keeps his "hot sauce . . . in an old Palmolive dish detergent bottle" and his "mild sauce . . . in an old salad dressing bottle," and whose unassuming demeanor in general could not seem less like the feted chefs who bark orders and assemble their masterpieces in the pristine kitchens of Michelin restaurants worldwide. "Hardaway," Elie writes,

> has worked here more than half a century. . . . He is a reddish brown man, the color of burnt sienna, . . . [and he] alternates strangely from carefully enunciating his words through his sharp Tennessee twang to mumbling and chewing the edges of them. Whatever word his sentences end on is dragged out just a little. . . . There is a slow deliberation about J. C. . . . except at two points, when he quickens from his characteristic andante to a lively allegretto. First, cleaver in hand, he chops the meat. Short strokes. Cleaver up; cleaver down. This done, he smoothly scoops up the meat and places it on the bottom of one partially toasted bun. The bun serves to measure the portion. When it is sufficiently covered, the meat is taken back off and put on the grill. . . . J. C.'s hot sauce is hot, but there is flavor beneath the pepper and the overall experience brings a smile to the tongue. . . . It is the sort of sandwich that makes you begin debating, halfway through it, whether you should order a second immediately so that it will be ready the moment you finish the first. (3)

In this intriguing portrait, barbecue seems to have captured Hardaway, laying claim to his life. Quietly he saunters around the kitchen, his footsteps from grill to pit and back again balletic and honed to perfection by time. But that ambiguous phrase "sole employee" and the fact that Elie fails to identify Hawkins's owner encourage the suspicion that Hardaway is less than powerful, and that he is in fact controlled, employed, by the barbecue itself, until his expertise in the kitchen comes to seem symptomatic more of its control over him than vice versa. Barbecue, in Elie's account, certainly seems to have seized control of Hardaway, refashioning him in its image. Colonial and Orientalist imaginations have long reinforced the normativity and even the invisibility of whiteness by implying that dark skin is cooked into existence; Elie here subverts this racist tradition to memorable effect, subtly invoking it to suggest that Hardaway's "reddish brown" skin has been, if not "burnt," then gently sealed by its lifelong exposure to smoke. Time and speech undergo similar metamorphoses. As he dances around the kitchen, Hardaway keeps step with the barbecue in the oven, slowing down and speeding up in accordance with its demands. Even his words seem affected in this way, growing somehow calorific as they stretch to fit the languid rhythms of the strangely omniscient pit.

These odd figurations can be read as a comment on pit barbecue culture's ethos of culinary rebellion and disavowal. Ultimately, by suggesting that Hardaway is starting to merge into the food he cooks, Elie implies that he has gone beyond modesty and passed into meekness, entirely reifying his expertise into tradition and perhaps even, at some level, coming to believe barbecue to be junk. At the minimum, it would seem, the outside world has long withheld its cultural and monetary rewards from Hardaway; and Hardaway is starting to think that it must be right. For here is a man who has devoted the better part of his three score and ten to the preservation of culinary tradition. His mind never wanders, his hand never slips in service to this high office. He wields the cleaver with the calm virtuosity of a sushi chef. But whereas such chefs, like the other creative workers of Japanese, French, and Italian cuisine, by and large enjoy high cultural esteem, Hardaway plows his furrow unnoticed. Recognition, like wealth, eludes him.

Hardaway's extraordinary decision to keep his sauces in an "old salad dressing" bottle and in another washed clean of detergent speaks volumes about this cultural marginalization. Financial pressures could, admittedly, explain Hardaway's recourse to secondhand plastic. So, too, could his need to squeeze his sauces out with reasonable accuracy—a need that prevents him from recycling beer or any other more handsome, glass bottles. Saying this, however, cannot rid us of our suspicion that Hardaway is too modest in his decision to present his homemade sauces in soapy and oily bottles barely fit for the purpose. Nor can it explain why he compounds this stark underselling of his culinary prowess by giving his sauces such banal and indistinctive names. Above and beyond all practical considerations, the mismatch between the unprepossessing appearance and delicious contents of these bottles remains hard to fathom. For we can doubtless assume that, even though they are modestly presented, these sauces are secret and the result of Hardaway's lifelong tribute to and improvisation on the recipes of past generations. Although the names he gives them could not be more boring, Hardaway, we can assume, was unsurprised to see Elie respond to their complex flavors with such warm appreciation.

Hardaway's decision to camouflage his delicious sauces in such unappetizing bottles and behind such unimaginative names takes on additional significance when we consider that it occurs in a southern region where, not too long ago, even those whites who adored black culture tended to disparage any claim made on its behalf. At least before World War Two, white elites in Memphis did what they could to inconvenience and insult black cultural practice in the city, banning the likes of Richard Wright from its public library and ridiculing the vernacular tradition that nonetheless flourished on Beale Street. Even those white commentators who praised the blues frequently spoke of its "rough, primitive charm," their celebration of its "barbaric sort of melody" distancing it from Europe's classical tradition.[4]

Hardaway's apparent attempts to disguise his culinary aptitude only begin to make sense once we remember that he started working at Hawkins during the twilight of this Jim Crow era, may still feel caught in its shadow, and has likely inherited not only recipes but habits from a previous generation for whom the merest appearance of uppitiness could prove ruinous. Memories of just how hard white racism once fell on the smallest sign of black cultural ambition, its mocking description of those who could read as "doctors" or "professors," suggest that the culinary tradition that Hardaway has inherited owes much to its originators' need to avoid being singled out as "chefs."[5] Some kind of tongue-in-cheek tribute is thus being paid by Hardaway's secondhand bottles. He is keeping alive memories of the cultural resistance to segregation, maintaining a tradition in which barbecue cooks no sooner accepted their low status, bowing and scraping and submitting to Jim Crow's bipartition of culture and society, than they smuggled new flavors onto the tongue, thrilling it as blues musicians thrilled eardrums, and again confirming that Memphis's genius lay in cultures that city's founders once condemned.

Interwar Joints

Though it seems extreme, and the result of a particular situation of stark racial intimidation, the extravagant modesty of Hardaway's secondhand bottles remains representative of pit barbecue joints in general. Unlike Hawkins, most such barbecue joints popped up outside urban areas as car ownership rose during the interwar years. Across the South, as John A. Jakle and Keith A. Sculle show in *Fast Food: Roadside Restaurants in the Automobile Age* (1999), they appealed not only to locals glad to have someone else spend long hours tending the barbecue pit but also to "automobile travelers seeking the 'real' America of regional traditions and customs" (171). Typically, interwar pit chains like Dallas's Pig Stands Company as well as one-off ventures took a twofold approach to attracting this passing trade, emphasizing their connection to grassroots barbecue traditions even as they harnessed nascent fast-food technology to position themselves as the South's answer to White Castle, Snappy Service, McDonald's, and the other hamburger chains then beginning to do well in the West and Midwest (114–39).

Now that the term *McDonaldization* has become shorthand for the homogenizing effects of global capital, this fusion of fast-food technology with grassroots traditionalism appears incongruous, a marriage, if not of oil and water, then certainly of woodsmoke and plastic forks. To some extent, however, this incongruity is the work of hindsight. Fast-food chains scored many notable successes during the 1920s and '30s, but few at that time predicted that they would mutate into the mammoth multinationals of today. Even after the United States eventually entered World War Two, almost all such businesses remained local affairs. Not least because their owners and customers often lived in the same state, sometimes even in the same county, the idea that most small chains could participate in grassroots tradition was not inherently absurd.[6] Not only trendsetters like East Texas's Pig Stands Company but numerous barbecue businesses in Georgia, the Carolinas, and elsewhere accordingly met little knee-jerk resistance to their attempts to harness the innovations of the emerging fast-food sector. Strategic roadside locations, eye-catching signage, and the sheer novelty of disposable cutlery and dinnerware all proved a help rather than hindrance to their efforts to sell this famously slow food fast. The continuing preference for plastic forks in barbecue joints across the South

4. Marion Post Wolcott, "Sign on Highway from Fort Beauregard to Alexandria, in Pineville, Louisiana," 1940. Courtesy of Library of Congress, Prints and Photographs Division, reproduction number LC-USF34-056537-D.

is one legacy of their success. Another is the global ubiquity of BBQ or "Bar B Q," a classic roadside sign of unknown origin that, under no copyright and recognizable at a flash, even now helps small business owners compete with golden arches among other multinational logos.

Farm Security Administration photographs taken during the New Deal period shed light on the different kinds of pit barbecue joints that opened their doors along southern highways and crossroads between the World Wars. But they also show that, whether part of a new and ambitious chain or too modest even to afford a professional signwriter, these joints shared a similar assessment of barbecue's place in the local economy: that it was a convenient more than a culinary food. Even at its earthiest—even in the hand-painted roadside sign that Marion Post Wolcott photographed during her FSA-sponsored tour of Louisiana in 1940 (fig. 4)—we can see that interwar pit culture is presenting barbecue as a rival to "other" fast foods, sacrificing, or at least playing down, its claims to culinary particularity for the sake of a foothold in the new convenience-driven economy.

5. John Vachon, "Barbecue Stand at Harlingen, Texas," 1943. Courtesy of Library of Congress, Prints and Photographs Division, reproduction number LC-USW3-030829-D.

And yet, although few objected to it in theory, this marriage of slow and fast food met considerable difficulties in practice. The conveyor-belt principles by which McDonald's and other chains assembled their hamburgers, passing them from work station to work station like so many Ford Model Ts, proved stubbornly difficult to apply to the unexpectedly intricate kitchen work done by Hardaway's interwar predecessors. Soon at least some employers realized that, when it came to being called "chefs," these predecessors had been protesting too much. No technological innovation, no new Fordist mode of fast-food production could successfully emulate their handiwork or break it down into tasks simple and discrete enough for teams of unskilled operatives. Only Jim Crow discrimination and its systematic exploitation of even the most skilful black worker made it possible for most pit barbecue joints to operate, permitting them to rely on

6. Arthur Rothstein, "Barbecue Drive-In Restaurant, Fort Worth, Texas," 1942. Courtesy of Library of Congress, Prints and Photographs Division, reproduction number LC-USF34-024569-D.

underpaid and overworked master chefs whom they kept backstage even as they presented an entrepreneurial and self-sufficient face to the world.

Like Hardaway's secondhand bottles, then, pit barbecue culture between the World Wars in general wrapped itself in plastic, embracing the look and feel of the emergent hamburger chains in order to grow a kind of anticulinary, barbaric, junk food skin. Standardization by and large found a warm welcome in these joints. Little distinguished their hamburger buns from each other; drink menus rarely ventured far beyond Coca-Cola, Dr. Pepper, and other major brands of soda and beer. Many locals gave a warm reception to the gimmickry of the Pig Stands chain (fig. 5), greeting the appearance of its outsized pig molds on the borderlands of East Texas neither as a sign of impending McDonaldization nor as some kind of surreal B-movie alien invasion, but as a welcome opportunity to eat a familiar meal in familiar surroundings and at a familiar price.

Crucially, however, as soon as this fast-food regime cut through the skin and began to penetrate the heart of this culinary culture—as soon as the standardization apparent in Pig Stands' use of Identi-kit molds began to affect the barbecue itself—custom fell away. More established joints like the Fort Worth venue photographed by Arthur Rothstein (fig. 6) might have developed a fast-food template that seemed to invite nationwide replication, but the food itself remained stubbornly resistant to such homogenization, its innumerable versions nailed firmly to the specific patches of land considered native to them. Customers elsewhere in the South no more wanted the Texan marriage of barbecue and tomato sauce than the barbecue aficionados of East Texas hankered after the vinegar-based sauces of eastern North Carolina or the dry spice rubs of Memphis. Even as the scene remained nakedly and barbarically procapitalist in appearance, a longstanding precapitalist preference for local variety reasserted itself. As the Arkansas academic Stephen Smith has put it: "There are probably more barbecue joints than Baptist churches in the South, but the exact number in existence is unknown. . . . One newspaper editor in Arkansas suggested, 'it's safe to say that no incorporated municipality lacks at least one barbecue man.'" He conceded, however, "No precise number can be known. There's no Arkansas Rib and Loin Association with an executive secretary to lobby for exemptions from state health regulations and for tariffs on imported barbecues."[7]

As Smith's good joke suggests, barbecue's ability to generate all manner of interstate and even intercounty rivalries, though proving its culinary credentials, at the same time could thwart individual entrepreneurs. The fact that some joints do not even appear in the business census speaks volumes about the difference between pit barbecue, a tradition that Vince Staten labels an "un-fast food," and its burger chain competitors.[8] All manner of testing culinary demands lurked unsuspected in the minds of such venues' allegedly "uncultivated" customers. A sign painted on ramshackle corrugated steel, as captured by Russell Lee in Corpus Christi (fig. 7), seemingly struck them as preferable to the almost plush surrounds Rothstein caught on camera in Fort Worth.

If anything, this pattern has grown stronger with time. Pit joints today continue to cultivate a wild and democratic image, rejecting ostentation and challenging the rigid demarcation of courses and combos. Their attitude to culinary rules and regulation finds a superb and self-conscious symbol in their tendency to hand customers wedges of paper napkins thick enough to suggest that spillages are encouraged. And yet, such mountains of napkins also reveal that this pit barbecue culture has not unchained itself from European cuisine so much as it continues to develop its own unique style out of its acceptance of some of the latter's culinary rules and

7. Russell Lee, "Barbecue Stand Made of Galvanized Steel, Corpus Christi, Texas," 1939. Courtesy of Library of Congress, Prints and Photographs Division, reproduction number LC-USF33-012032-M2.

its rejection of others. Standing in defiance of the pressed linen napkins that silver-service waiters drape over customers' laps, these wedges of napkins, and the fact that many barbecue customers these days would be a little perturbed not to receive them, in other words reveal that pit joints remain in hostile dialogue with the world of official cuisine, subverting and inverting its formalities rather than abandoning them altogether. They reveal that, from this hostile dialogue, pit joints are developing taboos of their own—that customers who enquire into the availability of vegetarian options, who use cutlery throughout the meal, or who dab daintily at the corners of their mouths in such places will soon feel as foolish as the diner at a Michelin restaurant who asks the sommelier "pour une Budweiser" or orders his "flaming yam" well done. New faux pas, and among them, perhaps, the use of a phrase like *faux pas*, flourish in this world as they do in any realm where, in Mintz's words, "ingredients, methods, and recipes" matter much and are used daily "to produce both their everyday and festive foods." To take pit barbecue joints at face value, to accept that where they begin culinary standards end, is to see this culture not as it is but as it wants to be seen: subaltern, rebellious, wild, barbaric.

Bogus Woodpiles

How can we make sense of this confusion, this schizophrenia to be found at the heart of southern pit barbecue culture? If Hardaway's secondhand bottles indeed pay homage to old strategies of black cultural survival, how can we account for white proprietors who seem to share his anticulinary impulses, likewise hiding their slow food behind a fast-food facade? Further, how do such anticulinary gestures relate to the invention and popularization of U.S. barbecue sketched out in the previous chapter of this book? Could that most English text, Ned Ward's *The Barbacue Feast*, be of any help to our search to find a historical explanation for barbecue culture's continuing habit of, effectively, epitomizing cuisine while shunning it?

Preliminary answers to these questions can be gleaned from the last of our photographs of pit barbecue joints (fig. 8). Captured on camera by Marion Post Wolcott in 1940, Big Chief Barbecue, a Georgia outlet positioned between Columbus and the hungry soldiers stationed at Fort Benning, fits easily enough into the paradigm so far elaborated here. Indeed, in the face that Big Chief Barbecue presents to the street, particular products and generic brands seem to enjoy greater harmony than they do in Pig Stands' Identi-kit pigs or the hand-painted Bar B Q sign that caught Wolcott's eye in Louisiana. Local and national logos here intermingle, literally occupying the same level atop the rickety wooden roof that is itself an apt enough indicator of the humble and makeshift character of the place. Admittedly, even here, some flaws in this unlikely marriage are starting to show. You cannot help but wonder whether Big Chief Barbecue's rickety roof is up to the task in hand—its wooden pillars hardly look substantial enough for the forest of signs they support—and its Atlantic Ale and Beer and Dr. Pepper hoardings are noticeably larger than those emblazoning the name of the joint itself. And yet, much as these tensions cast doubt on its marriage of slow and specific barbecue with fast and national food, Big Chief Barbecue clearly remains, in the world of Wolcott's photograph, consummate, pitching its signature dish perfectly and intentionally as a grassroots product nevertheless at home among the paraphernalia of the fast-food age.

Big Chief Barbecue's facade is also intriguing given our focus on racial matters. Pit barbecue culture is often said to be raceless, and Terry Mancour's online history is right to point out that, during the Jim Crow

8. Marion Post Wolcott, "Barbecue Stand near Fort Benning, Columbus, Georgia," 1940. Courtesy of Library of Congress, Prints and Photographs Division, reproduction number LC-USF34-056482-D.

period, many such joints were among the few places where black and white southerners could eat together. Big Chief Barbecue's facade, however, urges us to think twice before treating this fact as proof that pit barbecue joints were bastions of antiracist sentiment or stood in perfect opposition to the segregated lunch counters of the kind that the Greensboro Four famously targeted in North Carolina. Encircled, the smiling and silver-haired waiter who bookends Big Chief Barbecue's biggest sign, holding forth beers that we can imagine gleaming, golden and sirenic, against the Georgia sun, reminds us that what this joint is selling are the kinds of sensual pleasures that Jim Crow culture unfailingly associated with the African presence in its midst. If customers at such eateries could forget about Jim Crow segregation for a while, then Big Chief Barbecue's facade suggests that this had less to do with any commitment to progressive politics than with the fact that owners and customers alike saw these joints as free and de facto non-white spaces in which certain uncivilized appetites could find release.

Questions pivotal to this study now arise. Is there not a striking resemblance between this racial dynamic and that we discovered at the heart of

Ned Ward's *The Barbacue Feast*? Considering the vast differences between the London of 1707 and the Georgia of 1939, does it not seem remarkable that the supposedly civilized members of both societies are growing likewise tired of their civilized life, seeking respite from its dry protocols in the form of this somehow savage, somehow necessary food? Is it not intriguing that the preoccupations that led Ned Ward to compare his *Three Pigs of Peckham* to the bodies of a "Negro wench" and Indian "squaw" should find so close an echo in the triumvirate that Big Chief Barbecue's facade constructs between a smiling black waiter, a doomed pig, and the indigenous authority of its capitalized name? Do these parallels not suggest that, even in its modern usages, *barbecue* retains a barbaric association from the Age of Conquest? Is the notion of this anticulinary food, primitive and instinctive, intrinsic to modernity itself?

Like Elie's snapshots of Memphis pit barbecue joints, Bob Garner's *North Carolina Barbecue: Flavored by Time* (1996) begins by emphasizing the pride barbecue connoisseurs take in their particular way of preparing the food—a pride that soon gives way to contempt when its attention falls on other U.S. traditions. Quintessential to cuisines worldwide, these kinds of intense regional rivalries can draw attention away from the customs and practices that unite all U.S. barbecue traditions. They can downplay the fact that, judging by Garner's account, the pit barbecue joints of North Carolina have been no less reliant on the sweat and toil of the Hardaways of this world than establishments elsewhere in the South. Echoing *Smokestack Lightning*'s melancholic feeling that Hawkins "probably last blazed many years ago" (4), Garner laments the decline of "real" North Carolina pit barbecue:

> Nearly all the real open-pit barbecue houses have someone who's been with the business for twenty or thirty years; who's willing to stay up all night or come to work in the wee hours to tend the pits; who performs a hot, dirty, back-breaking job few others are willing to do—and who will be very difficult to replace once they retire. And in addition to all that, hardwood is becoming more expensive and harder to find, especially hickory wood. . . . The temptations to change to gas or electricity are understandable. . . .
>
> While the number of barbecue places in the piedmont that have given up pit cooking is growing, every barbecue restaurateur with any kind of aspiration to a regional reputation still has a sizable woodpile outside

the restaurant where it's readily visible. (One or two sneaky souls have switched to electric cookers but keep their woodpile as camouflage!) (29–32)

Garner's discovery that some pit barbecue joints are keeping woodpiles on display even though they have long stopped burning such fuel usefully encapsulates our argument so far, clarifying Mintz's reasons for overlooking pit barbecue's culinary status as well as my reasons for challenging this omission. There is a tacky quality to these bogus woodpiles, a kitsch embrace of the commercializing and homogenizing forces that *Tasting Food, Tasting Freedom* deems toxic to its understanding of cuisine. Their presence by the doorway all but condemns the food inside, lending weight to Mintz's insistence that the "bowdlerization of food" remains "less frequent in Europe" than in the United States. Mintz's argument, however, begins to unravel as he goes on to observe that, while "one can eat *bouillabaisse* in a Paris restaurant that resembles *bouillabaisse* in Marseilles, the retail food stores of Paris do not yet offer . . . a *bouillabaisse* 'exactly like the one you ate in Nice'" (115). Now we remember that Mintz is critiquing U.S. cooking culture via a string of unfavorable comparisons with Europe, and that this polarizing approach forces him to understate the impact of commercialization in France and Italy. In other words, Mintz paints himself into a corner here, his argument finding itself at a loss to explain the fact that, when it comes to bowdlerizing their food for tourists, the French have needed few lessons from the United States. The fact that French supermarkets have actually now sold readymade bouillabaisse for some years while North Carolina state laws continue to prevent companies from selling barbecue straight from the fridge immediately alerts us that Mintz's argument is eliding some important complicating factors.[9] Immediately it alerts us that corner-cutting establishments in Marseilles today—the kinds of seafront brasseries that stir defrosted North Sea prawns into packets of granulated fish stock, adding dried rather than fresh bouquet garni—would be quick to grasp the commercial logic that has led some proprietors to plant these bogus woodpiles outside their doors. And this analogy between bowdlerized bouillabaisses and bogus woodpiles alerts us that the latter amount to something less than proof that pit barbecue tradition has now fallen into terminal decline. For the cheap and disappointing bouillabaisses that flood the tourist traps of Provence and the Côte d'Azur may be unwelcome, but they also confirm the dish's continuing prestige, revealing that it remains worthy of pastiche. And the bogus woodpiles that scandalize Bob Garner, if seen in similar light, tend to prove that the traditional methods and meanings of pit barbecue preparation remain alive and well in southern cultures, confirming that this is still a dish prestigious enough to attract the flattering if unwanted attentions of forgers.

Popularized by a host of new local chains, these bogus woodpiles thus add up to powerful if surprising evidence that pit barbecue must be considered a cuisine on a par with the more noted gastronomic traditions of the world. Even in fraudulence they demonstrate the high status of our subject food, referring us back to the existence of "authentic" pit barbecue and reinforcing its mystique. In the course of doing so, however, these woodpiles remind us that they are children of the U.S. South, roadside follies that could not exist in the same way or call forth the same meanings anywhere else in the world. In particular, as the next few pages will show, the South's specific version of frontier mythology saturates these follies, embroiling them in images of rugged fortitude and heroism, of agrarian self-sufficiency, which in turn lift the food up, out of the historical mire of slavery, and into a prelapsarian order somehow scrubbed clean of white guilt.

Signifying the ax, forest clearing, and other arts frontiersmen imbibed from Native peoples, these woodpiles reject slavery, catapulting pit barbecue into a mythic and pristine wilderness run thick with "hickories feathered in mist," in Cormac McCarthy's phrase.[10] They reveal that the historical connotations of pit barbecue—what Allen Pridgen has called its ability to evoke "a past of Jeffersonian small farmers who lived out their lives in close-knit families and communities where self-sufficiency, independence and social intimacy and trust were prized"—are neither spontaneous nor natural, being instead essayed, willed into existence by a dominant southern culture that remains, on the whole, as uneasy about slavery as it is proud of its agrarian past.[11] That is to say, these woodpiles, like other images that modern pit barbecue culture places in circulation, can appear too lowbrow or commercial to merit serious critical consideration; but such consideration soon pays dividends, revealing that these images, rather consistently, trumpet the role that frontier history has played in the career of this American food even as they silence, or at minimum sideline, the contributions that black southerners both slave and free have made to its development. By evoking an era in which customers could relax and reenact the rugged vulgarities that frontier life thrust upon their ancestors, these woodpiles, like the stacks of paper napkins that appear to encourage spillages, thus distance pit barbecue tradition from the history of life on the plantation. Divorcing the food from such "civilized" territories, sending it spinning from the Europhilic etiquette that we now associate, perhaps a little too quickly, with the life of slaveholders, and projecting it onto the altogether more democratic forests of the west—these woodpiles spirit attention away from the kitchen, away from the underpaid and over-worked descendants of slaves so often to be found therein.

Only by recognizing such cultural repositioning can we hope to ar-rive at a full and impartial history of our chosen food. No such history is possible unless we grasp that the frontier mythology that surrounds pit barbecue can and does function as a kind of mask—a smokescreen, even—that orients attention away from other, less comfortable, factors in its development. Given that the spatial and economic organization of pit barbecue joints has long undervalued black labor and craft, it is par-ticularly important that we look beyond this grassroots mythology to ac-count for those elements of this reinvented tradition that reveal its new African and African American influences. For while much in this history remains unquantifiable, it is certainly true that black southerners were a good deal more than mere intermediaries or students of this food—were a good deal more than its smiling waiters, appointed only to ferry it from its Native source out to the tables of white America. Both before and after Emancipation, on the plantation and beyond its disciplinary orbit, such known and unknown figures were instead the innovators, rejuvenators, and reinventors of the food. Contrary to what Big Chief Barbecue's facade among other figurations would suggest, these figures did not belong to barbecue—barbecue belonged to them.

Barbacoa Americanus

Even to his contemporaries Thomas Jefferson could seem something of an enigma, a tangle of contradictory tastes and talents. Though it has esca-lated of late, the excoriation of Jefferson for his hypocrisies in fact began during his own lifetime. The difference is that, while almost every critic of the third president today skewers this hypocrisy in racial terms, citing the ordeal of Sally Hemmings and their offspring to expose the limits of his democratic vision, contemporaries who shared Alexander Hamilton's description of Jefferson as a "contemptible hypocrite" as often grounded their verdict in class, latching onto the jarring disjunction between his extravagant tastes and his status as the architect in chief of the United States' agrarian ethic.[12] For them, Jefferson's underlying tendency to exempt himself from the rigors of his grander democratic visions was chiefly revealed, not by his failure to give up his slaves, but by his continuing thralldom to the trappings of European life. To them, the secular prayers to the simple life that Jefferson offered in his *Notes on the State of Virginia* (1784) could seem less than sincere.

> Those who labor in the earth are the chosen people of God, if ever he had a chosen people, whose breasts he has made his peculiar deposit for substantial and genuine virtue. It is the focus in which he keeps alive that sacred fire, which otherwise might escape from the face of the earth. Corruption of morals in the mass of cultivators is a phænomenon of which no age nor nation has furnished an example. It is the mark set on those, who not looking up to heaven, to their own soil and industry, as does the husbandman, for their subsistance, depend for it on the casualties and caprice of customers. Dependance begets subservience and venality, suffocates the germ of virtue, and prepares fit tools for the designs of ambition. . . . While we have land to labour then, let us never wish to see our citizens occupied at a work-bench, or twirling a distaff. Carpenters, masons, smiths, are wanting in husbandry: but, for the general operations of manufactures, let our work-shops remain in Europe. . . . The loss by the transportation of commodities across the Atlantic will be made up in happiness and permanence of government. . . . It is the manners and spirit of a people which preserve a republic in vigour. A degeneracy in these is a canker which soon eats to the heart of its laws and constitution. (164–66)

In later years Jefferson would don the garb of the commonfolk when campaigning for election and would even, after his defeat of John Adams in 1800, make a point of riding to the Presidential Mansion on horseback. But Jefferson's private correspondence reveals that these agrarian touches were somewhat cosmetic and that, often, he could seem as little acquainted with his "own soil and industry" as the most cocooned European aristocrat. Even his home garden, the part of Monticello that seemed to mean most to him, can emerge from this correspondence as another conflicted space, another locus of illiberal liberalism, on which nameless slaves carry out botanical and agricultural experiments Jefferson seems to have conceived elsewhere, on patrol or in his study. The idea that Jefferson might follow his own advice and lend a hand to their agricultural endeavors was out of the question.

The lingering appeal, even the stranglehold, of European taste and the way in which it discouraged Jefferson from numbering himself among the natural aristocrats of his agrarian vision are nowhere more obvious than in his culinary tastes. Regular shipping orders reveal that, to an even greater extent than contemporaries of similar standing, Jefferson had a weak spot for macaroni, parmesan, and other European foods far beyond the means of the ordinary citizens with whom he sought identification.[13] Describing such pleasures, cataloging the processed fruits of the factories that he wanted to keep out of the United States, Jefferson's correspondence remains all the while silent about the Revolutionary and Republican barbecues that were already a fairly common feature of Virginian life. Jefferson, it would seem, kept his distance from a food that many today seem to see as the ideal accompaniment to his gospel of agrarian democracy.

Given that historians continue to extol Jefferson for having the "most passionately inquiring mind ever to be born in America," his lack of interest in the local phenomenon of the barbecue is intriguing.[14] In 1688, after all, *The Widdow Ranter* already treated the association of pork barbecue and colonial Virginia as common knowledge, and, as we will see, such feasts grew in popularity over the following years, coming to seem, to those who held them, part and parcel of colonial life, even a measure that they were consigning mere survival to the past and were beginning to flourish in the New World. Certainly such barbecues were often said to be inclusive events no less "masterless" than the feast that Ned Ward envisioned for Peckham Rye. It was almost as though their outdoor setting bestowed a public and democratic character upon them. Even those more formal barbecues where toasts were planned, fights rare, and extreme drunkenness more an exception than rule radiated this inclusive and democratic atmosphere. South American revolutionary leader Sebastián Francisco de Miranda's account of a 1783 barbecue held in New Bern, North Carolina, for example, reveals that, upon the birth of the new republic, such feasts were already to be sharply distinguished from the decadent and exclusive banquets of Europe:

> Today the suspension of arms and preliminary treaties with England were celebrated. . . . About one o'clock there was a barbecue . . . with much rum, which they all ate and drank together—from the leading people of the area to the very lowest sort—all shaking hands and drinking from the same utensil. It is impossible to conceive of a more purely democratic assembly without seeing it, no matter how much even the Ancient Greek poets and historians tell us of similar events among the free peoples of Greece.[15]

This revolutionary ceremony would seem a perfect foil to the vision of agrarian freedom and virtue soon to appear in *Notes on the State of Virginia*. Not only did Jefferson cultivate these kinds of comparisons of the United States and Ancient Greece. Years before it grew fashionable to cast doubt upon the ideology of industrial progress, he also saw the need to question the old Greek tendency to see democracy as an urban affair, grasping that "ordinary" Americans instead needed to anchor such freedoms to their land, to the premodern and uncorrupted land from which they drew both sustenance and virtue. One might have thought, then, that barbecues such as that which de Miranda attended in New Bern would have met with Jefferson's approval, the simple need for a whole hog, not to mention the unsophisticated manner of its preparation, tying the event to the farm and, in the process, sheltering democracy from what Jefferson called the "distractions of a town, and waste of life" to be found therein.[16] Here, one might have thought, stood a thoroughly Jeffersonian affair: a simple feast, without "canker" or artifice, innocent of the fussy cutlery and myriad other conceits of Europeanized banquets then and now. But Jefferson's writings remain silent on the subject. Still the idea that he might attend a raucous barbecue of the kind that traveler and diarist Nicholas Cresswell stumbled across in Georgia remains little short of preposterous, as unlikely as the thought of him stopping awhile and lending a hand to the slaves sweating away in his garden:

> *Tuesday, July 26th, 1774.* At Anchor with a contrary wind. About noon a Pilot Boat came along side to invite the Captn. to a Barbecue. I went with him and have been highly diverted. These Barbecues are Hogs, roasted whole. This was under a large Tree. A great number of young people met

together with a Fiddle and Banjo played by Two Negroes, with Plenty of Toddy, which both Men and Women seem to be very fond of. I believe they have danced and drunk till there are few sober people amongst them. I am sorry I was not able to join them.[17]

And so, aloof and loath to experience barbecues firsthand, Jefferson, nonetheless, in *Notes on the State of Virginia* and elsewhere, outlined a vision of agrarian life that could articulate the potent political meanings beginning to surround such feasts. Personal factors help explain why Jefferson appears to have kept his distance from these events—he disliked his own public speaking and abhorred the drunkenness of others—but, at a deeper, more epistemological level, Jefferson's agrarian vision can explain why such barbecues attracted political speakers, and raised thirst in their listeners, in the first place.

Notes on the State of Virginia conveys this through what it does not say as much as through what it does. On its surface Jefferson exhibits a profound yearning to escape the "degeneracy" and "caprice" of modern life. Arguing that the industrializing economy emanating from Europe is placing layers and dependencies between men, he allows that citizens of the new republic might wish to keep a foothold in this system even as he urges that they cling on to a space outside it—a space where they can forever rekindle the "sacred" and democratic "fire" of their free and uncorrupted ancestors. In this respect *Notes on the State of Virginia* resembles *The Barbacue Feast*, Jefferson's suggestion that U.S. citizens avoid civilization's excesses but continue to enjoy its benefits echoing the way in which, in that very English text, every member of Ward's Barbacue Society can relax and become somehow "masterless" without quite forgetting where he stands in the world thus left behind. Both men, it would seem, are here keen to turn their backs on London without abandoning it altogether. Both seem to want to follow the Surrey hoggard—to tarry awhile in the wilderness without losing sight of the enclosures and factories of civilized life. Civilization and wilderness alone thus seem incomplete, insufficient, to Ward and Jefferson alike. Some combination of the two, some overlap or regular shuttling from one to the other, is necessary if the common people are to remain vigorous and worthy of freedom.

Between the lines of *Notes*, however, it becomes evident that this belief that even the most civilized men must keep in touch with nature is altogether more fraught for Jefferson than for Ward. Working at opposite ends of the eighteenth century, and vastly different in personality and reputation, Ward and Jefferson reflected the rational values of their age. Both rejected Calvinist guilt as well as the old Hobbesian belief that humans in their natural state are base and crude, animalistic, and unable to think of much past the "satisfaction of present desires," in Roy Porter's phrase.[18] Both show signs that they had come to believe, instinctively in Ward's case and intellectually in Jefferson's, that the civilizing process that had long insulated men and striven to carry them far from the wildness of the world now needed to reinvigorate them and reacquaint them with instincts long forbidden. And yet, whereas the idea of a savage barbecue slips easily and without friction into Ward's early version of this seminal enlightenment belief, Jefferson's silence on barbecue suggests he finds its barbarity, its stark racial alterity, hard to stomach. Ward's relaxed attitude toward the affinities he uncovers between African or American savages and *The Barbacue Feast*'s band of thirsty Englishmen likewise contrasts sharply with *Notes on the State of Virginia*, forming an intriguing counterpoint to Jefferson's belief that "America" must cleanse itself of slaves as well as machines if it is to realize its "hopeful proofs of genius" (65).

Here, then, Jefferson's rationalistic intelligence as well as the peculiarities of his personal situation have enabled him, years before the South was even called the South, to glimpse as though in silhouette the future politics of that region. Already, in *Notes*, we begin to understand why men who took no profit from slavery would soon fight to save it. Outrage already seems a potential answer to any modern citizen who will not excuse the slaveholder his crimes. A greater blindness, a greater hypocrisy already seems discernible in the behavior of those dependent urban customers whose "subservience and venality" would suggest a failure to connect the clothes they wear and the sugar and tobacco that they enjoy with the peculiar institution that they condemn as the work of others (165). Some of these attitudes, it must be said, have weathered well. To the extent that he sees slavery as a phenomenon of capitalist progress in general rather than of any peculiar talent for brutality on the part of the U.S. South, Jefferson presages the work of C. L. R. James and Paul Gilroy among other postcolonial theorists, anticipating the latter's assertion that African slaves counted among the first to confront the "elaborate" and aggressive "geographical and geopolitical designs" of industrial modernity.[19] The real oddity of *Notes*—indeed, its callousness to our eyes—lies instead in the way in which the feelings of guilt that Jefferson cannot displace by this route, the guilt that he cannot transfer onto industrial modernity, seem to reflect back on his slaves and endow them, for the sake of their master's sanity, with a less-than-human ability to perform monotonous industrial work. Africans, for Jefferson, are not just "inferior to the whites" (143); they are less because they can tolerate more, needing "less sleep" and lacking the "imagination" that finds plantation labor so dull (139–40). The ability of Africans, "after hard labour through the day," to "sit up till midnight" tends to suggest that the real victims of slavery, to Jefferson's mind, are civilized whites (139). Jefferson's insistence that African bodies are strong and "tolerant of heat" tends to implicate them in the introduction of the "canker" of industrial progress into a southern garden otherwise sylvan and free. Moreover, while it seems fairly clear that examples of intercultural mixture of any kind could horrify Jefferson, *Notes on the State of Virginia*'s flat denials of African intelligence contrast so sharply with its melancholic consideration of the tragic Indian as to suggest that Jefferson has reserved his greatest horror for that particular intercultural traffic that flows from quarter to mansion, and from which he, as the likely father of slaves, needs to extricate himself personally.

Notes on the State of Virginia's agrarian vision thus outlines a key national myth, a myth that echoes in many of the ways of seeing barbecue that circulate in modern U.S. culture. Even today a set of displacements and reorientations suggestive of Jefferson legitimizes the idea that such barbecues had little to do with the plantation or its slaves and belonged instead to the wilderness and agrarian west. In their reluctance to mention black Americans as well as their glorification of white settlers as guardians of indigenous knowledge, the frontier barbecues that occur in Rebecca Harding Davis's *Dallas Galbraith* (1868, 157) and in Owen Wister's *The Virginian: a Horseman of the Plains* (1902, 107) clearly belong to this tradition. So, too, did actual extravaganzas like a 1923 Oklahoma barbecue, held to inaugurate John C. Walton's brief but remarkable term as state governor, at which meat of all kinds was smoked in "trenches" said to be a mile long, the progressive crowd gathering to enact a ceremony they could associate with "frontier politics at its exciting best."[20] Even those commentaries that draw attention to the black cooks often found at the heart of such events by and large imply that their culinary exertions had nothing to do with Africa and were merely replicating some template or recipe inherent to the land. Even though Charles Lanman applauds "the unbroken vigilance of expert negro cooks" at an antebellum barbecue, his *Haw-ho-noo: or, Records of a tourist* (1850) refuses to consider that this expertise could be bringing African elements to the white and proslavery table. Barbecue must remain, in Lanman's words, "'a pleasant invention' of the Old Dominion," derived from French even as it remains untroubled by civilization (94–97). Now best practiced by those unaffected by the mixed blessings of white intelligence, it must remain associable as a domain of the common European folk.

Polite and free of prejudice, Bob Garner's *North Carolina Barbecue: Flavored by Time* demonstrates how modern views of barbecue culture maintain elements of this tradition, filleting Jefferson's agrarian ideal while discarding the racism that once accompanied it. Whenever Garner turns his mind to the local history of his favorite food, images of the frontier and its original inhabitants soon surface. Luckily for Garner, key colonial writings support this maneuver. For example, even though it amounts to little more than just another colonial work that seeks to associate "barbecue" with local Amerindians but cannot marshal any evidence for doing so, John Brickell's *Natural History of North Carolina* (1737) and its depiction of how the Algonquian dry and smoke fish and meat "upon Hurdles, keeping a constant Fire under them" (367) is nevertheless often treated in that state as the OED treats Hickeringill's *Jamaica Viewed*—that is to say, anthropologically, and as proof positive that there is a kind of transcontinental, Pan-American native provenance for this word as we know and use it today. The fact that something similar is afoot in other colonial and Revolutionary works about southeastern North America—the fact that, as we saw in chapter 1, Robert Beverley's *History and Present State of Virginia* (1705) and James Adair's *History of the American Indians* (1775) both attribute "barbecue" to Natives without evidencing this attribution—makes it easy for Garner to proceed with his marriage of barbecue and frontier history:

> Wispy blue smoke floating above a coppery brown split pig, hissing and crackling over winking coals, drifts back across many generations of small farmers, sharecroppers, merchants, and traders, finally reaching the native inhabitants of northern eastern North Carolina and tidewater Virginia,

who almost certainly passed along the art of barbecuing to the settlers. It quickly spread throughout the region, but in the aristocracies of those "mountains of conceit," Virginia and South Carolina, barbecuing was often relegated to slaves, its secrets somewhat beneath the notice of polite society. (xii)

In the last two sections of this chapter I hope to show that such modern refigurations of Jefferson's vision of southern history are problematic, not because they commit any glaring historical errors, but because they perpetuate some of the essentializing strategies undertaken and to some extent initiated by *Notes on the State of Virginia*. Something close to Jefferson's need to talk in certainties seizes Garner during these Proustian visions.[21] The words *Indian, slave,* and *white* acquire a permanent, even natural status as Garner accepts a racial worldview that Jefferson, more than many of his contemporaries, had to force painfully, shamingly, and perhaps in repudiation of his own dark children, into life. And so it is that barbecue—this food inseparable from race—this food that people are said everywhere to eat before civilization came along—acquires similar permanence, its essence becoming likewise natural and indigenous without variation and regardless of all subsequent change. So it is that Garner patrols the history of his home state as Jefferson once did his garden, working to prevent the "constant reproduction of weeds" and to concentrate attention on a single, classifiable plant.[22] *Barbacoa Americus.* Slaves only water, only bring back to life, this indigenous food. The Hardaways of this world, intermediaries all, only follow a recipe inherent in the land itself. Frontier knowledge, rather than the countless horrors of slavery, for Garner and others explain pit barbecue as it stands in the Piedmont and other places today.

Barbacoa Africanus

It is difficult to reconcile the secondary and marginal position into which *North Carolina Barbecue: Flavored by Time* casts slave cooks with the primary importance that this food time and again assumes in African American cultural celebration.[23] The images brought together on the roof of Big Chief Barbecue and the association of the food with the frontier and the Native American that ensues from this configuration make it surprising to

turn to the closing pages of Alice Walker's *The Color Purple* (1982), for example, and to find that, when Celie's family ask their West African relatives
Tashi and Adam what they like to eat back home, they "sort of blush and
say *barbecue*" (54). Garner's insinuation that the black barbecuers of North
Carolina and Virginia were little more than the passive inheritors of indigenous tradition certainly stands at some variance to Walker's identification
of such African qualities in the food. Ntozake Shange's excited discovery
that "same oil barrels that we use to barbecue" become steel drums in the
Caribbean can encourage this suspicion that Garner has provided us with
an incomplete historical account of our subject.[24] So can the dynamic and
unifying capacities that pit barbecue acquires in the course of the very different cultural works of David Hammons, Albert Murray, Bobby Seale,
Ntozake Shange, Jean Toomer, and Margaret Walker, among others. The
euphoric opening lines of Ray Charles's "Mess Around" (1953)—"Well you
can talk about the pit / barbecue / the band was jumping / the people
too"—suggest that Garner's rather Jeffersonian narrative seriously under-
estimates the extent to which slaves and their descendants revitalized this
invented tradition and made it their own. Not least in memorializing the
fact that urban black slang once imbued *barbecue* with sexual suggestion,
Louis Armstrong's saunter through "Struttin' with Some Barbecue" (1927)
suggests that, just as banjos and barbecues once went hand in hand in the
antebellum South, so pit barbecue remains able to slip into African American rhythms, nourishing black spirits as well as bodies.

No one did more to celebrate pit barbecue or to embed it within the
African legacies of black southern culture than Zora Neale Hurston. In
their net effect, Hurston's frequent efforts to depict or define barbecue
lend unity to an oeuvre that has been scattered across numerous genres.
Barbecue can draw these scattered writings together just as it can reunite
The Color Purple's transatlantic and far-flung family: references to it connect Hurston's underrated study of political megalomania, *Moses, Man of
the Mountain* (1939), and her enigmatic autobiography, *Dust Tracks on a
Road* (1942), to a single bloodline, a single genealogical relation that can in
turn link both not only to her more treasured works, from *Jonah's Gourd
Vine* (1934) to *Their Eyes Were Watching God* (1937), but also to the many
articles that even now gather dust in the quieter corners of her oeuvre.
Charming northern Jamaica's Maroon leaders into letting her join them

on a traditional hog hunt; smuggling her historical speculations about this "mere" food into the pages of the august *Journal of Negro History*; digressing in her autobiography to envision a utopian barbecue at which "kin-folks" and "skin-folks" can consort together: Hurston wrote and rewrote barbecue scenes throughout her literary career, and each time she did so she effectively dragged the food out of the mythic frontier and plunged it back into the American world that grew out of the horrors and forced migrations and unavoidable cultural interactions of transatlantic slavery. In the process of correcting earlier silences, however—in the process of insisting, in effect, that the likes of Hardaway receive full and overdue recognition for their culinary endeavors—Hurston creates some new silences and new embarrassments of her own. Of her many barbecue visions, those that Hurston developed during the 1930s heyday of her career in particular come uncomfortably close to offering a mere mirror image of the dominant white viewpoint outlined so far in this chapter. In these exuberant diasporic visions, as we will see, Hurston rescues black cooks from their historic denigration, forcing us to recognize that they are neither the intermediaries of barbecue nor its passive heirs, only to cast them as the sole authors of the food. Even in its repudiation the afterglow of Eurocentrism grows apparent as Hurston here and there insists that barbecue had absolutely nothing to do with the frontier and absolutely everything to do with the forced transportation of millions of slaves from West Africa. And yet, as we will also see, something in Hurston's work suggests that she sensed the irony of this reversal. Something seems to make her to think twice about this absolutist position, encouraging her to draw back from it and to complicate it with countervailing visions of the potential barbecues of America's raceless tomorrows.

One of the most astonishing aspects of Hurston's literary career is the fact that she completed *Their Eyes Were Watching God*, her richest novel, in only seven weeks. Upon arriving in Haiti in September 1936, and fresh from a tour of the first black republic's famous beauty spots, Hurston delayed her anthropological fieldwork by only this time in order to write, from beginning to end, her feted novel of Floridian love and labor. Eager to insist that Haiti could be "the heart of Africa for all outward signs," Hurston's letters of this period suggest that the republic itself, and especially the stimulations of its "huge and complicated" culture, helped her finish her masterpiece so quickly.[25] Less romantically, however, *Their Eyes*'s rapid composition also seems inseparable from the fact that, as Alice Gambrell has argued, Hurston practiced a form of "versioning" throughout her career, drawing on fragments of old writings and weaving them into new works, creating new juxtapositions as she did so.[26] Several renowned passages from *Their Eyes* show signs of having undergone such a process. Echoes of earlier writings grow audible even as they are brought into harmony with the particular concerns and imperatives of Hurston's second novel. In particular, a barbecue description in her ethnographic study, *Tell My Horse: Voodoo and Life in Haiti and Jamaica* (1937), echoes in *Their Eyes Were Watching God*'s account of a barbecue held by the Eatonville townspeople to celebrate their acquisition of street lighting:

> The women got together the sweets and the men looked after the meats. The day before the lighting, they dug a big hole in back of the store and filled it full of oak wood and burned it down to a glowing bed of coals. It took them the whole night to barbecue the three hogs. Hambo and Pearson had full charge while the others helped out with turning the meat now and then while Hambo swabbed it all over with the sauce. In between times they told stories, laughed and told more stories and sung songs. They cut all sorts of capers and whiffed the meat as it slowly came to perfection with the seasoning penetrating to the bone. The younger boys had to rig up the saw-horses with boards for the women to use as tables. Then it was after sun-up and everybody not needed went home to rest up for the feast. . . .
>
> Near the time, Joe assembled everybody in the street before the store and made a speech. . . .
>
> "Dis occasion is something for us all to remember tuh our dyin' day. De first street lamp in uh colored town. Lift yo' eyes and gaze on it." . . .
>
> As the word Amen was said, he touched the lighted match to the wick, and Mrs. Bogle's alto burst out in . . .
>
> They, all of them, all of the people took it up and sung it over and over until it was wrung dry, and no further innovations of tone and tempo were conceivable. Then they hushed and ate barbecue. (72–74)

Because it offers Joe Starks such a golden opportunity to speechify and preside, offering Hurston such a golden opportunity to lampoon his pomposity and lay his egotism bare, this "streetlight" hog roast can appear tailor-made for *Their Eyes*. Hurston's journal, however, reveals the huge debt this famous barbecue scene owes to her experiences of life among the Maroon peoples of northern Jamaica.

As Robert Hemenway has shown, Hurston spent the days immediately before her arrival in Haiti living among the communities of Maroons who inhabited (and still inhabit) "the forbidding Saint Catherine Mountains at Accompong." There to research Afro-Caribbean cultures for a new anthropological study that would appear as *Tell My Horse*, Hurston bided her time with the Maroons, drawing on her considerable charm in order to gain new insights into their proud and defiant culture. Eventually the patience of these early months paid off, and Hurston was invited to join the men of the society on what Hemenway calls a "ritualistic hunt for a wild boar."[27] The hunt and its ensuing hog roast clearly gripped Hurston, seizing her imagination as powerfully as the conjure traditions of New Orleans or the Africanist folktales of Haiti. Biographies suggest that she grasped the diasporic significance of the event immediately. She certainly wasted no time, upon her return to the Maroon settlement, in writing down her experiences. After she had worked it up for *Tell My Horse*, Hurston's account of the experience reads as follows:

> [After three days and nights without a sighting, Hurston and her fellow hunters] see the wild boar approach and pass. . . . The men crept closer and Esau chanced a shot. . . . The hog made a half turn and fell. . . .
>
> Then all of the men began to cut dry wood for a big fire. When the fire began to be lively, they . . . put the pig into the fire on his side. . . . Everything was now done in high good humor. No effort was made to save the chitterlings and hasslets, which were referred to as the "fifth quarter." . . . The meat was then seasoned with salt, pepper and spices and put over the fire to cook. It was such a big hog that it took nearly all night to finish cooking. It required two men to turn it over when necessary. While it was being cooked and giving off delicious odors, the men talked and told stories and sang songs. One told the story of Paul Bogle, the Jamaican hero of the war of 1797 who made such a noble fight against the British. . . .
>
> Towards morning we ate our fill of jerked pork. It is more delicious than our barbecue. It is hard to imagine anything better than pork the way Maroons jerk it. . . . We came marching in singing the Karamante' songs.
>
> > Blue yerry, ai
> > Blue yerry
> > Blue yerry, gallo
> > Blue yerry! (36–37)

Tell My Horse and *Their Eyes Were Watching God* are rarely mentioned in the same breath. The fact that the first is an anthropological study of Haiti and Jamaica while the second is a novel of black life in Florida can tend to distance these texts from each other, making them seem unavailable for comparison. By placing their barbecue scenes alongside each other, however, we can begin to restore to them something like the proximity of their creation. In the process we bring to light certain parallels that have long lain hidden from view. We can start to see how barbecue could function in Hurston's oeuvre as a kind of glue, a kind of magic glue that can bind not only her scattered writings together but also the scattered African peoples to whom these writings pay tribute. One anthropological and the other fictional, these barbecue scenes thus sustain a close resemblance that tells us much about how Hurston saw the African diaspora and sought to create it in her work.

As soon as we juxtapose these scenes, their resemblance becomes impossible to miss. In both, for example, men lead the way, being described through broad assertions as a single unit that is then said to "dig" this and "do" that, to "cut dry wood" and to "cut all sorts of capers." Out of Hurston's descriptions of the fire at the center of the feasts similar echoes reverberate: it is "a big fire [of] dry coals" in *Tell My Horse* and a "glowing bed of live coals" in *Their Eyes Were Watching God*. Both prose works then proceed to emphasize the time taken to cook the hog: "all night" in the former, "the whole night" in the latter. In both the meat is then turned by two men, who are identified as Hambo and Pearson in *Their Eyes* but who remain nameless in *Tell My Horse*. A subsequent construction in the former—"while it was being cooked . . . the men talked and told stories and sang songs"—directly echoes a description in the latter—"in between times they told stories, laughed, and told more stories and sung songs." Further echoes strengthen the suspicion that Hurston, writing *Their Eyes* and *Tell My Horse* in quick succession, drew on a single original source: the journal jottings she made in the immediate aftermath of her exhilarating participation in a Maroon hog roast.

Once spotted, the direct similarities between *Their Eyes* and *Tell My Horse*'s barbecue scenes lend new significance to the differences between the two. Much can now be gleaned from those moments where Hurston disrupts the flow of direct echoes, intervening to reinstate the distance between novel and monograph and between black Florida and Maroon Jamaica. Now we can see that, behind Hurston's decision to call Eatonville's favorite alto singer Mrs. Bogle, for example, a rich and complex politics of identity is beginning to develop. Beneath this name alone, so nondescript on its surface, lies a secret network of intertextual connections that at once welcomes Eatonville's barbecue into a wider diasporic culture and chides that culture for its sometime weakness for masculine language. Announced in Paul Bogle's transformation into the female alto of *Their Eyes Were Watching God* is a new womanist politics that wants to celebrate barbecue for expressing diaspora but needs to skewer its homosocial exclusivity when doing so. But the fact that, when writing *Their Eyes* in "the heart of Africa" otherwise known as Haiti, Hurston decided to include some strong women at the Eatonville barbecue and to associate it with the town's entrance into national life also reveals that the fun she has had with the name Bogle, her audacious feminizing of this byword for male black nationalist strength, pivots around her lingering tendency to associate Africa with what is past and the United States with what remains to come. *Tell My Horse*'s reports that the "old African custom of polygamy is rampant" in Haiti and that "all women are inferior to all men by God and law down there" only confirm what is already implicit in this spirited renaming: that the Caribbean retains Africa's bigotries as well as its inspirations, its limits as well as its liberations, and that it is in the United States that women have a chance of finding freedom.[28] The fact that the Maroons are even more keen than Joe Starks to ensure that their hog roast remains an all-male affair signifies that the barbecue they practice is truer in spirit to the African inheritance than the one occurring in consumerist Florida. This conjuring with the name Bogle suggests that, when contemplating and composing the barbecue scenes of *Their Eyes Were Watching God* and *Tell My Horse*, Hurston saw geographical distance as a reliable measure of diasporic authenticity: the further away these events get from Haiti, it would seem, the more removed they become from the "heart" of Africa's cultural spirit.

The barbecue in *Their Eyes Were Watching God*, then, would seem motivated by Hurston's interest in anthropological salvage; it would seem to be striving to record for posterity the African influences of black southern culture before modernization and urbanization do away with them. In this barbecue, held to celebrate a streetlamp bought from a Sears Roebuck catalog, the feast itself seems caught in the process of becoming anachronistic (71). Such traditional community events, it would seem, cannot hold out much longer against the illuminations of U.S. life. Accordingly, and in a manner that is not so removed from *The Barbacue Feast*, *Their Eyes Were Watching God*'s barbecue comes to seem like an elegy for itself: it enacts what it memorializes and memorializes what it enacts. And, even as it commemorates a dying agrarian way of life, it seems a little anxious that its commemoration too might help bring this death one step closer. Only now this sense of preemptive mourning is no longer for the "common treasury" of Old England, nor yet for the "substantial and genuine virtue" of Jefferson's southern yeomanry, but for Africa: for an elusive and mythic ancestral realm whose flaws Hurston can see but whose allure she is powerless to resist.

The invented tradition of American barbecue is thus being radically reinvented here, cast into new terrain. An idea of barbecue originally arising out of European colonial discourse and its genocidal notions of racial barbarism is coming to seem useful to a new black politics that discerns in such barbarism a welcome alternative to the relentless shames and displacements of puritanical white life. At the same time, however, this reinvention remains incomplete. It remains too much beholden to the white narratives that it wants to overthrow. Blood, authenticity, and linearity remain at the center of its vision. Purity remains its point of departure and the object of its fantasies of utopian return. No hybrid exchange, no intercultural complication can be sanctioned or allowed to disturb its development of a linear barbecue history that begins in Africa and extends with all the direct certitude of an arrow into the diasporic heartland of the Americas. Until, rather as the Jeffersonian desire to catapult barbecue into the indigenous wilderness reduces black slaves to intermediaries of barbecue tradition, Hurston similarly silences the Native, similarly shrugging off any claim Amerindia might make upon this resonant and resilient food. Indeed, in her clearest statement on barbecue's origins—the 1927 essay "Cudjo's Own Story of the Last African Slaver"—Hurston places Amerindians into a role every bit as passive and secondary as that into which Bob Garner casts black cooks. In West Africa, Hurston insists, "hogs are prepared by taking brown sage and burning off the hair, then washing the skin thoroughly. The animal is usually roasted whole very much as we barbecue. This was probably the origin of the barbecue in America. The word, however, is derived from a native name in Guiana" (650).

Hurston's proposal here—that the indigenous Guianans managed to give barbecue its name without leaving a mark on its pure and African substance—is not just unpersuasive. Nor does it just amount to another instance in which Hurston could seem, to borrow Paul Gilroy's word, "captivated" by the old and absolutist narratives of race and ancestral belonging.[29] Aired in the *Journal of Negro History*, Hurston's proposal is also deeply ironic. It is counterproductive in effect. For Hurston's acceptance of some of the basic premises of Eurocentrism, from its belief in the possibility of blood purity to its yoking of race and culture, has here led her to develop a rigid genealogy that eventually distracts her from the potential signs of African retention that she places before our eyes.

That is to say, in her scholarly article of 1927, Hurston anticipates the "hogroast" representations that she would produce in the following decade, looking ahead to the way in which *Tell My Horse* and *Their Eyes Were Watching God* accept barbecue's hegemonic status as a primordial food only to repulse this primordial status back across the Atlantic and onto her vision of an Africa more mythic than real. Reports of the invented barbecue traditions of the Maroons of northern Jamaica fuel this project. Positioning Maroon barbecue as a "black" food that has little or nothing to do with the declining Native cultures of the island, Lady Nugent's diaries (1803), R. C. Dallas's *History of the Maroons* (1803), and M. G. Lewis's *Journal of a West Indian Proprietor* (1815–17), among other imperial accounts, all add up to so much grist for Hurston's mill.[30] Directly or indirectly, their ethnographic legacy emboldens Hurston, persuading her to draw a blind eye to the occurrence of interracial contacts and borrowings that might complicate her Africanizing project. The fact that the first black Maroons to escape to the mountains of north Jamaica almost certainly stumbled upon indigenous settlements grows inadmissible as Hurston pursues a pure African genealogy. So does the possibility that these groups exchanged notes on how to survive in the forest, perhaps even hunting in concert and smoking wild pig together in the unclaimed lands of Accompong. So too does the likelihood that the Maroons began to call this smoked food *barbecue* for the simple reason that reports of their isolation from the British presence in the island were greatly exaggerated, and that, from the 1740s if not before, the Maroons often traded with neighboring white individuals and thus had opportunity as well as cause to adopt Europe's repertoire of New World terms.[31] No such untidy complication, no interracial transaction can be sanctioned as Hurston struggles to preserve a single genealogical line, a single arrowlike trajectory, by which to get back to Africa without delay. *Barbacoa Africanus*. Amerindians only name, only haunt, this African root. It is inherent to diaspora. As in the closing pages of *The Color Purple*, it holds the key to blackness itself.

In this Afrocentric configuration, as Haiti turns into Africa's transplanted heart and as Florida and Georgia come to occupy the outermost edge of its diasporic influence, the chief innovation of *Their Eyes Were Watching God*'s Eatonville barbecue—the fact that its characters dig "a big hole" and place their hog into this pit—can no longer denote anything but a concession to modernity. The logic of Hurston's historical vision demands that we see such trenches as a culinary counterpart to macho Paul Bogle's transformation into ethereal Mrs. Bogle—as another symptom of the Americanization of Eatonville's barbecue, another measure of the distance it has traveled from the exotic custom of the Maroons. Under no circumstances can it appear more authentically African than the barbecue that the children of fugitive slaves conduct in the wilds of northern Jamaica.

Here lie the ironies of Hurston's vision. Southern antebellum writings, after all, often call attention to the fact that exactly these kinds of barbecue trenches should be dug by black men. As they do so, one begins to suspect that, in addition to the obvious laboriousness of such digging, some kind of controlled concession to West African cultural knowledge is being made. In its suggestion that not only the digging but also the observing and overseeing of such trenches was best left to "expert negro cooks," Charles Lanman's *Haw-ho-noo* (1850) was far from alone.

In 1944, for example, North Carolina's official state photographer, John Hemmer, produced a series of photographs that confirm that, well into the twentieth century, landowners and privileged white southerners could still regard the creation and overseeing of barbecue trenches not only as labor but also as craft, and a craft to be left to African American inferiors (see figs. 9 to 12).

These photographs are of a barbecue that the North Carolina politician Thomas J. Pearsall held in 1944 for his friends and associates at Braswell plantation, near Rocky Mount. Ten years later Pearsall would serve as chairman of the North Carolina Committee on Education, a panel tasked with working out how best to desegregate the state schools, and his suggestion of having black classes and white classes within single institutions would be noted at a national level.[32] But while Hemmer took these

9. John Hemmer, "Thomas J. Pearsall's Annual Barbecue at Braswell Plantation, North Carolina: Unidentified Black Cook Oversees the Barbecuing Pigs," 1944. Courtesy of the North Carolina State Archives.

10. John Hemmer, "Thomas J. Pearsall's Annual Barbecue: White Guests Enjoy Barbecue, Bread, and Soda," 1944. Courtesy of the North Carolina State Archives.

11. John Hemmer, "Thomas J. Pearsall's Annual Barbecue: Black Cook Bastes Barbecuing Pigs," 1944. Courtesy of the North Carolina State Archives.

photographs at an earlier phase in Pearsall's career—a phase when the state representative preferred to call himself "farmer"—they too suggest a paternalist view of race relations. Like 1950s speeches in which Pearsall would "stress . . . a history of blacks and whites working together in good faith for the good of all" while trying to "encourage . . . support of . . . voluntary segregation," the plantation pit barbecue captured by Hemmer reveals a social system that could sanction, and even celebrate, moments of racial intimacy on the understanding that the division between black and white would remain ironclad.[33] Moreover, these photographs confirm that this careful social system gave rise to a complicated situation in which the need to yoke civilization and white southerners together could allow enviable and invigorating if "wild" forms of cultural practice to fall into the hands of their black neighbors. Indeed, what Hemmer's photographs capture is not just the Jim Crow exploitation of black labor but, in addition, a kind of standing back, a kind of impressed withdrawal of white authorities from the vital heart of barbecue creation.

12. John Hemmer, "Thomas J. Pearsall's Annual Barbecue: Unidentified Black Elder Spoons Basting Sauce over Barbecuing Pig," 1944. Courtesy of the North Carolina State Archives.

In their combined effect, these images present a world split into two spheres, one black and one white, separate and unequal. Yet Hemmer—a New Yorker who would settle in North Carolina, remaining there even after he succumbed to blindness in 1970[34]—also seems alive to, and interested in, the ways in which these worlds echo one another. In figures 9 and 10, we can see Hemmer views the long trench in which the pit barbecue is smoked and the long table on which it is eaten from a similar vantage point. Each shot taking the long rectangle as its focus, Hemmer draws attention to the geometric resemblance between the table and trench. This resemblance sharpens our awareness of the contrast between the two, associating it with their interdependence on each other. It reveals that the leisure of the table results from the labors of the trench. It suggests that some southerners are at ease because other southerners toil. And it indicates that white segregationists needed to find ways of justifying this outrageous situation—needed to fashion a culture that could assure them that theirs was the civilized estate, and the fruits of inequality their natural due. After all, this table can convey white mastery in a dozen ways far subtler than its exclusion of black faces. In contrast to the customers of pit joints who disdain cutlery and revel in spillages, those standing around this plantation table seem determined to enjoy the "savage" barbecue without allowing it to untidy the protocols of civilized life. Napkins sit idle on the tablecloth as guests demonstrate their ability to eat this messy meal without ruining their white shirts or ties. Women stand together at the table, their customary role in Jim Crow culture as apogees of maternal innocence and virtue apparent in their reluctance to dispense with their plastic knives and forks. Not that the men opposite them are exactly wallowing in grease. Instead, their ties still unloosened, they turn to the loaves of bread that run up the center of the table, studiously lifting forkfuls of meat into the white slices. Indeed, as they thus surround the barbecue, these slices of bread could be said to function as the table overall functions: as a kind of white blanket, a white envelope that contains the vital black element, carrying it far from the swinish, savage trench.

But the full sequence of Hemmer's photographs also suggests that this Jim Crow worldview cannot quite believe its own myths about race and civilization. If only because he took more shots of the former than the latter, it is clear that Hemmer took far greater interest in the "black" preparation of the feast than in its "white" consumption. In these more numerous images, like that of the incidental white figures caught on film, Hemmer's attention centers on the processes involved in the production of the pit barbecue. In figure 9, in a barn or outhouse elsewhere on the plantation, he joins the white overseer in focusing on the shovel, poised above the trench, with which the black cook distributes the smoldering coals as evenly as possible. For figure 11 Hemmer zooms in farther, centering his camera on the bowl of basting sauce, perhaps taken from one of the steaming cauldrons, which this unidentified cook is now ladling over the pork. In figure 12, moreover, his camera follows the barefoot boy and the girl in her fine dress and hat, centering on the bearded elder who spoons more basting sauce from a jug onto another pig carcass. Indeed, if we consider Hemmer's photographic gaze alongside that of the people he captures on film, it becomes apparent that almost everyone—and even the civilized diners standing around the white table—are staring at the same thing: the barbecue itself. For all the propriety of the feast, it would seem, the wild element at its heart retains an allure, a fascination with which the more genteel products of Jim Crow civilization cannot compete.

These photographs, then, confirm that the dominant culture of 1940s eastern North Carolina often delegated the work of pit barbecue culture to black cooks. But Hemmer's gaze, and the way it mirrors the gaze of those it captures, also implies that there was more to this delegation than raw Jim Crow economics. They suggest that, while middle-class southerners no doubt bequeathed the preparation of pit barbecue to black cooks because such work was dirty and onerous and uncivilized, at another level they did this because the food struck them, if not as wholly African, then certainly as less than European in origin. Inflected by contemporary racist ideology, these white North Carolinians yielded ground to leave a space in which forms of African cultural knowledge could flourish. Rather as North Carolina's slaves, centuries earlier, had applied West African irrigation and planting techniques to "establish . . . rice as a plantation crop," so it at least seems possible that, here, free black cooks are involved in the "diffusion of" another "significant African knowledge system."[35] Even as Jim Crow's strategic stultification of black expression reached its zenith—even as the parents and grandparents of Hardaway's generation were forced to do what they could to disguise all signs of their intelligence from unknown white eyes—landowning authorities could nonetheless still concede ground to a field in which culinary procedures suggestive of West Africa—culinary procedures evocative of the outdoor drying of cassava to form the *gari* of Benin and *egba* of Nigeria, for example—could resurface and acquire a new and more carnivorous incarnation on American ground.

The irony is that Hurston's essentialist decision to cast Haiti as the African heartland of the Americas has ushered her to a kind of epistemological impasse from which she cannot then countenance this possibility. Her commitment to Africanist Haiti prevents her from recognizing that the barbecue tradition before her eyes—the pit barbecue tradition of the southeastern United States, the barbecue she grew up with—could conceivably be *as* Yoruban or even *more* Iboan than the smoking practices still practiced by the Maroons of northern Jamaica. Hurston's failure to dismantle Eurocentrism's epistemological scaffolding, her acceptance of its linear account of historical knowledge, and her continuing belief in blood have forced her into a paradigm in which the pit dug at the beginning of *Their Eyes Were Watching God*'s Eatonville barbecue instead amounts to a sign of the town's Americanization. Embryonic Afrocentrism has blinded Hurston to the potential Africanness of the pit barbecue, forcing it to pale in comparison with the guaranteed and unsurpassable negritude of primitive Haiti.

The Barbecue Rhizome

Quite apart from the culinary cynic of *Tasting Food, Tasting Freedom*'s conclusion, there is another Sidney Mintz—a Sidney Mintz who has done more than anyone to show that the sociocultural area of food studies and the geographical area of the colonial Caribbean amount to serious academic fields too long neglected by Western scholarship. Indeed, this chapter—and its contention that pit barbecue arose from a complex transatlantic traffic, amounting to a hybrid form that has flirted with its simplifying "savage" association—owes much to Mintz's *Caribbean Transformations* (1974) and other studies in which Mintz sets out his belief that the American territories of transatlantic slavery boast "as much ethnic . . . heterogeneity as can be found in any region of comparable size in the entire world."[36] In particular, Mintz's theorization, with Richard Price, of the experiences of those slaves who found ways of dealing with each other to create "integrated cultural subsystems," coping with New World experience and forging cultures against the odds, would seem evinced in the possibility that they had a hand in pit barbecue's formation.[37] Moreover, Mintz's reconfiguration of the cultural map of slavery in the Americas, his insistence that we approach this terrain as a founding site of industrial modernity, and his interest in its interdependency with the urbanized North are all clearly apposite to this study, helping to explain how invented barbecue tradition underwent such incessant reinvention and could slip, overnight, into the routine rhythms of metropolitan life. His recognition that Caribbean peoples were the first to endure the disciplinary routines and racial punishments characteristic of industrial modernity—a position that bears comparison to Paul Gilroy's recent suggestion that Nazism and fascism "brought" the full impact of modernity "back home"—similarly holds great value to this book, revealing the need to retain a realistic appraisal of cultural hybridity and to avoid overestimating its powers of political or racial subversion.[38] As Mintz puts it, the

> modernization of the Caribbean took place in the constant presence of multicultural Others. People who came from other places and who are not *in* their own culture can become modern, in part because institutional recourse to a standard common tradition is not immediately available. Soon after the Conquest, Caribbean people began coming from somewhere else. Most of them had to come with imperfect institutions, and in the company of others culturally unlike themselves. Most came without kinfolk. . . . The processes set in motion by the creation of New World plantations have never stopped. But in their earliest overseas phases, they were concentrated within a definable area, of which the relatively tiny Caribbean colonies were a part. It was what these reborn enterprises achieved in mobilizing resources, adapting to stolen labour, producing capitalism's first real commodities, feeding the first proletarians, and changing the outlooks of so many people on both sides of the Atlantic, that embodied a dawning modernity.[39]

Not until the advent of poststructuralist theory in the 1970s did scholars begin to undertake a full exploration of the kinds of "reborn enterprises" that Mintz's pioneering research identifies in the experiences of those living in and around the Caribbean plantation. Indeed, there is a sense that Mintz, in this characteristic discussion, is apprehending that Caribbean history cannot easily fit the epistemological models to which Western historians have long grown accustomed, and that he is casting around, groping in the dark, for a new vocabulary that could enable him to find a way through that history without artificially imposing order on it or otherwise organizing it into various neat and tidy units. Already, in this pioneering work, Mintz seems to grasp what I have suggested in relation to *Notes on the State of Virginia* and *Their Eyes Were Watching God*: that an epistemological approach that can only talk in terms of the linear, a historical vision still enchanted by racial purity, is a mode of enquiry that cannot help but simplify the protean cultural life of America's slaveholding territories. Already, in other words, it is as though Mintz is looking ahead to the more fluid historiographic models at which leading poststructuralist theorists would arrive over the course of the 1970s and '80s. Certainly Mintz's scathing indictments of the continuing allure of racial purity, like his insistence on the need to emphasize "process" and "adaptation" when appraising Caribbean history, suggest that he would share poststructuralists Gilles Deleuze and Félix Guattari's impatience with traditional models of identity, sympathizing with their sense of being "tired of trees" and with their demand that we "stop believing in trees, roots, and radicles. They've made us suffer too much."[40] Mintz, it is easy to imagine, would feel much sympathy for Deleuze and Guattari's noted attempt to get away from such "rootlike" or "arborescent" historical thinking, agreeing with their *A Thousand Plateaus* (1980) and its proposal that the "rhizome" represent an "antigenealogy" by which we might conduct a more diffuse and less constrictive kind of cultural history (23). Rhizomes, Deleuze, and Guattari suggest, are

> very different from the tree or root, which plots a point, fixes an order. . . . A rhizome may be broken, shattered at a given spot, but it will start up again on one of its old lines, or on new lines. You can never get rid of ants because they form an animal rhizome that can rebound time and again after most of it has been destroyed. Every rhizome contains lines of segmentarity according to which it is stratified, territorialized, organized, signified, attributed, etc., as well as lines of deterritorialization down which it constantly flees. (7–10)

A number of writers have revisited *A Thousand Plateaus*, seeing in its praise of the rhizome a formula through which to reinvigorate postcolonialism's exhortation of the democratic possibilities of intercultural hybridity. Paul Gilroy, among others, argues that the "rhizomorphic principle" introduced by Deleuze and Guattari can help us to see how an open and fluid understanding of the "idea of diaspora offers a ready alternative to the stern discipline of . . . rooted belonging."[41] Such redeployments of the rhizomorphic principle have proven useful to postcolonialist studies: it has allowed us to recognize how different African phenomena or ideas can surface in different forms in different circumstances, and it has enabled us to avoid that more traditional and "rootlike" language that would want to equate such difference with the reduction or diminution of some putative African essence. At times, however, these postcolonial redeployments seem to intimate that, as a new mode of cultural inquiry, this rhizomorphic principle is potent enough to escape the "lines of differentiation," allowing us to forget the corrective disciplinary counterweight with which, in

A Thousand Plateaus' original vision, it is always connected. Again, when contemplating postcolonial theory's adoption of this poststructuralist concept, one comes to feel that the value of cultural hybridity has been overstated, its critical appraisal accelerating far beyond its actual ability to undo actual racism. The dismal resilience of racial logic again comes to seem somewhat inexplicable, its longevity again confounding the brilliant account postcolonialism gives of hybrid culture.

It is not hard to identify the rhizomatic qualities of barbecue tradition. Like ants, like the wild pigs with which it is associated, barbecue constantly invents and reinvents itself throughout the Americas. Here and there, throughout this massive field, this resilient food breaks ground. Wherever people take flight from civilization or seek fleeting shelter from it, it comes to surface. Wherever people covet the thrill of the barbaric or yearn for outdoor freedoms, this food, rhizomatic and protean, undergoes another repositioning, another reinvention, embedding itself into diverse human cultures otherwise opposed. No sooner does barbecue resurface, however, than new "lines of differentiation" are drawn. Always its violation of racial borders stands in the most delicate balance and the finest of tension with the rooted fantasies that it seems to prompt. Barbecue, hatched in conquest, spreads throughout America. In its snaking course across and between racial boundaries it challenges the racial edifice. But it is a child of this edifice—it is a product of European racial discourse. Rhizomatic, it cannot escape the racial world it subverts.

Let us conclude this chapter by turning to another reference to barbecue that appears in Hurston's oeuvre. *Dust Tracks on a Road* (1942) is a confused and confusing book. In the words of Hurston's first biographer, Robert Hemenway, it is an "autobiography at war with itself."[42] This autobiography repeatedly obfuscates the past; as she looks back at the remarkable life that led her from rural Florida to the erudite world of Barnard College and the Harlem Renaissance, Hurston seems at a loss to offer insight or explanation. Yet while this confusion is almost always seen as a matter for great regret—Alice Walker calls it "the most unfortunate thing" Hurston "ever wrote," for example—perhaps we have been too quick to rule out the possibility that the confusions of this exasperating autobiography—the war it wages with itself—could be productive.[43] Certainly it is hard to see how we might regret the appearance of such beautiful, resonant declarations as the following:

I have no race prejudice of any kind. My kinfolks and my "skin-folks" are dearly loved. My own circumference of everyday life is there. . . . In my eyesight, you lose nothing by not looking just like me. I will remember you all in my good thoughts, and I ask you kindly to do the same for me. Not only just me. You, who play the zig-zag lightning of power over the world, with the grumbling thunder in your wake, think kindly of those who walk in the dust. And you who walk in humble places, think kindly too, of others. There has been no proof in the world so far that you would be less arrogant if you held the lever of power in your hands. Let us all be kissing friends. Consider that with tolerance and patience, we godly demons may breed a noble world in a few hundred generations or so. Maybe all of us who do not have the good fortune to meet or meet again, in this world, will meet at a barbeque.[44]

Redolent of *Their Eyes Were Watching God*'s famous opening page, this passage is puzzling, borderline nonsense. It fluctuates between meaningfulness and meaninglessness. It is a warning and a temptation. Pressures make themselves felt; Hurston seems strangely to resist the postracial utopia toward which her logic impels her. Split desires are astir: Hurston wants to envision a America beyond race, but she also wants to keep hold of the heroic and nourishing narrative of African American survival; and she is palpably afraid that these wishes will prove incompatible. Hence the schizophrenia of the passage, its shifting modes of address, its shifting *you* and *we*; hence the strange manner in which race is no sooner declared unimportant ("you lose nothing by not looking just like me") than it becomes all-important ("you who walk in humble places"). And hence, too, our difficulty in deciding whether or not "barbeque" as it is being envisioned here is rootlike or rhizomatic. The contradictions that Hurston puts on display here make the passage impossible to gauge: one moment it feels redolent of the Africanizing conclusion of Walker's *The Color Purple*, the next it suggests Deleuze and Guattari's *A Thousand Plateaus*.

Stepping beyond the vexed question of her racial or political inclinations, however, Hurston's work regains importance once we recognize its ability to lay bare contemporary ideological or epistemological assumptions, and to reveal, in ways she sometimes noticed and ways she sometimes did not see, that these assumptions were powerless to cope with the sheer variety of human experience. Indeed, Hurston was far from alone among contemporary scholars and cultural practitioners in producing work that sacrificed the troublesome plurality of U.S. history to preserve the integrity of existing criteria and systems of scientific or rationalist categorization. What was different about her work, perhaps, was that, in their stark contradictions and sudden surges of speculation, you can sometimes still see the scars such sacrifices left behind.

Left to its own devices, unlit by the spotlights of the story and before the first fitting session with the designers, the world is neither orderly nor chaotic, neither clean nor dirty. It is human design that conjures up disorder *together* with the vision of order, dirt together with the project of purity.

—Zygmunt Bauman, *Wasted Lives*

4 Barbecue between the Lines

Edward W. Said's *Orientalism* (1978) has held great importance for *Savage Barbecue* as it has for numerous inquiries into race, identity, and the cultural bases of empires old and new. Almost thirty years after its publication, *Orientalism*'s frank talk of the United States as an "Imperium" following in the footsteps of Britain and France now seems less controversial than it once did, while Said's identification of the fundamentalist Muslim as the emergent nemesis of Western cultures has come to appear prescient. No less influential, at least in postcolonialist and likeminded circles, has been Said's understanding of Orientalism as that at once bureaucratic and academic discourse by which Europe has historically fixed the "Orient" in place, nurturing its own pristine image by projecting its barbarisms eastward. *Orientalism*, of course, was not the first to call attention to this dialectic process. Years before Frantz Fanon had pioneered this approach, drawing on Marxist and Hegelian tradition to insist that, in the colonial system, "the settler's town" and the "town of niggers and dirty arabs" depend on each other and determine each other's identity.[1] What always distinguished *Orientalism*, however, was its insistence that writing and culture lie at the heart of this dialectical process. Ernest Renan, Gustave Flaubert, and others receive a starring role in *Orientalism*, Said's masterpiece effectively approaching Western letters as a hegemonic if rich and complex discourse powerful enough to call empire into existence:

> In short, as a form of growing knowledge Orientalism resorted mainly to citations of predecessor scholars in the field for its nutriment. . . . In the system of knowledge about the Orient, the Orient is less a place than a *topos*, a set of references, a congeries of characteristics, that seems to have its origin in a quotation, or a fragment of a text, or a citation from someone's work on the Orient, or some bit of previous imagining, or an amalgam of all these. (175–77)

Effectively, over the course of this book, I have tried to draw attention to the range of rhetorical strategies that, appearing in diverse writings about America, bear comparison to those Said uncovers from Europe's invention of the Orient. Embarking on this project has led me to realize that even now our discourse remains surprisingly reluctant to recognize in full the close resemblance between Europe's Orientalization of Asia and its Americanization of America. But it has also made clear that this reluctance begins life in Said's own thinking and stems in part from the fastidious care he takes to heed particularities of time and place and to avoid oversimplifying global culture's chaotic and finally uncountable transactions. For such care and attention, while undeniably admirable in almost all respects, in this particular instance can lure Said toward the old sirens of U.S. exceptionalism, his works here and there falling a little under the spell of democratic progress among other nationalistic mantras and compromising his ability to uncover in full the imperial origins of the United States. In *Culture and Imperialism*'s outstanding vision of the grim procession of Eurocentric power, something unspoken seems to ordain that the United States should inhabit the last word and occupy the final chapter. Promises of democracy and freedom do their old clandestine work, at some level excusing the United States its imperial expansion and insulating it a little from outright attack. America's magic persists, allowing the United States to cling to its familiar status as a less naked imperial power whose imperial credentials we must work that much harder to reveal.

Even as *Orientalism* heeds cultural specificity almost to the point of closing off its wider imperial applications, it remains easy to see how the American frontier might be regarded in Orientalist terms as another liminal territory that is "less a place than a *topos*, a set of references, a congeries of characteristics." To critics of U.S. hegemony if not always to Said himself, it is clear that, in the history of America's colonial settlement as in Orientalism, numerous cultural commentators and political authorities have found it necessary to write racial subjects into existence and to formulate notions of racial classification. As in Orientalism it is clear that in this history of settlement there was never a time when leading attitudes about Amerindians and slaves did not derive in the first instance from the loaded "quotation[s]" of art and writing rather than from direct encounter or objective report. Nor was there a time when writing did not offer a huge and overwhelming archive that could invent the inferiority of Amerindian slaves very much as Orientalist writing could invent the inferiority of Fanon's "niggers and dirty arabs." Moreover, just as *Orientalism* repeatedly implies that such received Orientalized images helped colonials to dictate terms and issue instructions to the colonized, so America's likewise invented and likewise inferior racial images were no sooner concocted than they acquired a kind of overnight and insuperable authority, straightaway setting the agenda for actual black and Amerindian behavior. In the historical process of Americanization as in Orientalization, no sooner did colonial adventurers imagine Indians, no sooner did slaveholders and their guests imagine slaves, than these subjective and purposeful scribblings acquired a kind of stranglehold over their living and breathing referents, growing powerful enough to extract patterns of behavior from them and to mete out punishments in accordance to some preexisting and unassailable design.

> There was, at the outset, no difficulty in accounting for the genesis of the savage. Almost universally it was agreed that the Indians were of the race of men, descendants, in order, of Adam, Noah, and those Asiatic Tartars who had come to America by a land-bridge from northern Asia. This opinion, orthodox in the seventeenth century, allowed Puritans to account simply for the savage, heathenish state of the Indian. Was he not perhaps the farthest of all God's human creatures from God himself? Descended from wanderers, had he not lost his sense of civilization and law and order? . . . And wasn't he, as a direct result of this loss, in the power of Satan?[2]

By recognizing that not only Puritan New England but all North American colonies were highly literary societies that accessed and formed their ideas about Indians through written works, Roy Harvey Pearce's *Savagism and Civilization* (1953) unearths a number of processes of cultural domination akin to those Said associates with the Orientalization of Asia. Certainly any lingering feeling that writing is little more than a mere echo of history is dispatched as summarily by *Savagism and Civilization* as it is by *Orientalism*. One American in subject and the other Asian, these studies issue a joint challenge to the idea that writing is a passive or reactive activity that men and women turn to only after the dust of action has settled and a certain calm objectivity has been restored. Together they remind us that this way of thinking, while perhaps fair enough for the study of Walt Whitman's "When Lilacs Last in the Dooryard Bloom'd" (1865) or other elegies, omits those very different episodes in which history has drawn its fundamental shape from literature and other kinds of writing. It overlooks, cannot quite countenance, the many moments when written myths and philosophies have preceded history, providing explorer after explorer with a fundamental lens through which to view the subaltern territory and make it intelligible.

Encouraged by *Savagism and Civilization* and *Orientalism*, this recognition that writing not only records history but just as often *engenders* it is necessary if we are to reach a full understanding of the role that barbecue, as a trope more than as a food, played in the emergence of independent U.S. nationhood. As this final chapter shows, barbecue, as a literary and cultural trope, has in a small way determined the shape of some of the most significant turns in colonial and early Republican life. Outrageous allegations of indigenous violence, the fun and frolics of democratic sovereignty, a new Jacksonian politics squarely centered on the earthy wisdom of the common man: all took shape from what they understood to reside in this savage barbecue trope. Even the architects of racist violence often seemed to organize their violence through this kind of engagement, explaining not only the "butchery" of the lynching but also its peculiarly festive qualities, its cohesive and familial connotations, via their audacious elaboration of the barbecue parallel. Elsewhere in U.S. literature high and low, new notions about race and renewal, about civilization and the savage instinct adrift within its soul, can be seen to develop via the contemplation of this replete and volatile food. And from this contemplation, what some have called Jacksonian savagism and others the U.S. myth of regeneration through violence took shape.[3] Something about this food, at least from the 1820s onward, confirmed white Americans in the feeling that they were unique; something clarified that they differed from the English or Germans or other "indoor" peoples because they, alone in the West, had come to know savagery firsthand.

But it bears repetition that the seeds of this process were sown in writing, and in English and European writing at that. It bears repetition that barbecue, if it began anywhere at all, began life in the writings and art of early modern Europe. Out of this culture's need to find new and less incriminating outlets for the physical and psychological appetites that were being ostracized from civilized life arose a desire to recalibrate the functions of barbarism, to mold it into a more pleasurable field of cultural adventure that civilization could then enjoy without ever colonizing in full. Opportunities to project this remodeled and more pleasurable barbarism onto the American territories subsequently opened a clear route into which European art could displace all things forbidden safe in the knowledge that these things would only wash back after they had come to wear the new and disassociated skin of American savagery. Safely deposited on the other side of the Atlantic, colonial barbecue might have looked, smelled, and tasted American; but only insofar as America itself remained of European genesis.

We have already explored the political and philosophical twists and turns that pivot around barbecue in the work of Aphra Behn, Edmund Hickeringill, Ned Ward, and other transatlantic writers identified with England. Now, to conclude this book, we will turn to the food as it appears in the writings of Cotton Mather and William Byrd, among other transatlantic writers identified with America. Quickly, as we do so, it will grow clear that much common ground exists between these "American" writers and their "English" counterparts, the work of both exhibiting the kinds of epistemological dilemmas and instant nostalgias encapsulated in *The Barbacue Feast*. Like Ned Ward, Mather and Byrd work hard to treat barbecue as a natural and savage phenomenon in which civilization has played no meaningful part. Their writings, too, conform to a basic pattern—a pattern we now know well. Like their English counterparts they, effectively, loiter on the edge of civilization. When no one is looking, they cast barbecue into the wilderness. Eventually, having waited a while, they take our hand and lead us into those "barren" realms. In time discovering the fold of virgin land into which their barbecue has landed, they stand back, awestruck, inviting us to share their astonishment to discover this proof positive of a barbarism not yet touched.

Both *Orientalism* and *Savagism and Civilization* help expose this clandestine and surreptitious throwing and fetching that has for so long gone on behind our backs. They draw attention to what Zygmunt Bauman would later characterize as the cultural conjuration of disorder, reminding us of the existence of all manner of established literary and cultural assumptions that have posited barbarism and civilization as separate states and that have endowed the two with a set of distinctive qualities whose appearance can then help the observer classify them as such. They help us see that, in this Eurocentric archive that has come down from classical writings, drawing new nourishment from the ethnographic and philosophical discourses of the Enlightenment, barbarism has been situated as humankind's default condition and thus as the condition to which humankind may revert should civilization overreach itself or too eagerly obstruct its visceral and libidinal outlets.

And they help us see that, to the vision of barbecue emerging from this epistemological field, different writers offer different responses. Some follow Ned Ward and treat the food as a welcome opportunity to escape the stolid thoroughfares of civilized life—to wallow awhile in the bliss of primordial nothingness. Others stress the violence of barbecue, associating it with the kinds of cannibalistic or sadistic crimes envisioned in Hickeringill's *Jamaica Viewed*. But all of these accounts, *Orientalism* and *Savagism and Civilization* help us see, amount to differences of emphasis rather than differences of kind. All interpretive options remain open in all cases. Seemingly benign visions of such feasts can get nasty at the drop of a hat. Good times can only be had by all if all agree to relax the cannibal taboo to a dangerous extent. Bad deeds forever now carry horrific echoes with the field of cultural pleasure. Aphra Behn's white cannibals reawaken as approving and disapproving commentators alike grasp in the Jacksonian barbecue an exercise in white savage incorporation. Here, then, the slow fires of Indian smoke cookery could again burn a little brighter, could again balk on the fat that could fall from human flesh. Here again imperial words beget imperial deeds: conjuring disorder from the obliteration of an all-too-human world.

Bad News, as Expected

The frontier long ago left the North Carolina coastline, migrating over the Blue Ridge mountain country and into the western territories beyond it. Straight lines were long ago etched into this land, dividing it into plantations and then dividing it again into row upon row of indigo stem, tobacco shrub, and sugarcane stalk. Railroads and other augurs of industrial modernity long ago completed this process of demarcation; but the angular and geometric sensibility that they brought to completion was long before heralded in the colonnades and porticos of the wealthier Big Houses. Traveling down one such straight line, however—watching the Carolinas roll by from an Amtrak seat—it is not hard to find, still scattered throughout the state, the patches of wildness that persist. Palmetto woodland still interrupts the ordered and productive farmland intermittently, painting the train windows cabbage green. Swampland still seems impenetrable, immune to colonization. Clearings, as remote from the plantation system of old as from the industrial-agricultural system of today, still seem to offer spaces beyond civilization's orbit. Here may come weekending bikers, teenagers on illicit missions, worshippers seeking clean water and air, anyone wanting time away from the TV and supermarkets of humming, wasteful America. Here, too, resonant memories lurk: the footsteps that runaway slaves once left in the mud, the eyes thought to peer from within the web of tree branches, haunt this space and hold it in a state of perpetual wildness.

> In Pontiac's career, . . . Parkman found a subject which would take him
> to the vital center of American history. . . . His Pontiac is concretely and
> particularly and immediately the savage, conceived in a period when the ac-
> tuality of the Indian was everywhere known to symbolize and to image the
> idea of savagism. Knowing what Pontiac meant, Parkman could show what
> he was. For knowing what history was, Parkman could show what it was.[4]

Such wildness, however, was from the start and remains even now constructed. Not only the sojourners of the postindustrial United States but even the first European explorers in fact looked upon this "virgin" land much as frontier historian Francis Parkman, according to *Savagism and Civilization*, once looked upon the face of Ottawa leader Pontiac. Early pioneers likewise greeted the sight of North Carolina's coast and interior in the manner of men who knew what they looking for and who were duty bound to find it. Accompanying their every western foray, their every Indian campaign or mission, were numerous received images—and the image of racial barbarism in particular—through which they could make sense of this New World and name it as "wild." Perhaps they had never set eyes on Theodor de Bry's sensational engravings of Tupinambán cannibalism, nor read *Jamaica Viewed*'s savage doggerel, nor attended a dinner as exotic as that reported in *The Barbacue Feast*. But they certainly shared a culture in common with those who had—a culture that knew how to invent wildness in order to deal with it.

On this original frontier, mysteries occurred daily. Baffling indigenous behavior, strange symptoms of unknown diseases, extremes of temperature and climate, exotic flora and fauna, and the urgent need to work out how to farm the American land: all guaranteed that the first European settlers of North Carolina, like those of other New World colonies, would work hard to manage the mysteries of everyday life and to manage the fact that some of these beguilements would always defeat explanation. The Bible and classical literature provided settlers with a navigational aid by which they could find a path through the mysteries of American life. New Testament parables and Old Testament judgments, Greek and Roman myth, and tales and warnings disseminated by word of mouth all assumed new importance as they offered settlers a kind of cultural compensation for their lack of American experience and for their failure to absorb indigenous knowledge in full. Although we tend to associate the biblical allegorizing of American experience with the Puritan oligarchs of New England, in fact all settlers in all colonies—and even those Puritans condemned as irreligious—negotiated the puzzles and confusions of American life via this kind of resort to scripture as well as to more general European traditions of story and myth. Erudite and devout Puritan leaders might have liked to condemn North Carolina as a dissolute and ungovernable colony, a mere frontier outpost to which the dregs of Europe had fallen, but even among such "dregs" many found guidance in biblical stories that were not even the preserve of the literate, let alone New England.

Travel writer and land speculator John Lawson and Swiss Palatine leader Christoph de Graffenried, traveling down the Neuse River in 1711, certainly seem to have looked shoreward in anticipation of indigenous eyes and in the foreknowledge that those eyes could "image the idea of savagism."

Myths proliferate in colonial accounts of their journey, as we will see in a moment: but this wayward attitude toward the truth in itself indicates that, as their slaves oar them farther from the coastal settlements, both men are accessing myths about savagery and the barbaric and are using these myths to filter the new world laid out before them. When de Graffenried writes that he and his companion traveled down that river wary of savage tribes, their suspicion in part precedes its explanation. For them, what Richard Hofstadter might have called the "paranoid style" of colonial exploration is calling the wilderness into existence, helping them imagine its dangers and the demons hidden within it. De Graffenried's report of Lawson's bucolic vision of the source of the river as a bounteous terrain rife with "good wild grapes" clearly derives, for example, not from the eyewitness accounts of colonial predecessors, nor from translated Native testimony, but in the first instance from a longstanding European tradition of comparing America to the Garden of Eden.[5] Hazards or obstacles standing between the men and this lush and fertile destination as clearly result, not just from genuine Native menace, but also from a Calvinistic narrative of pilgrimage in which both the religious baron and his more entrepreneurial companion need and crave such menace in order to justify their pursuit of Eden itself. Danger of attack, a cynic might say, hardly inconveniences either man: it steeps their mission in bravery, it masks their baser economic goals, and it even draws attention away from their reliance on the slaves who row them from dawn to dusk out of civilization's reach. Thus the suspicion remains that de Graffenried and Lawson know their lines: that their anxieties are somehow premeditated, rehearsed.

> I . . . resolved to take that trip, and we took provisions for 15 days; I, however, asked Mr Lawson whether there were any danger on account of the Indians, especially on account of those which we did not know. He answered that there was no danger in that direction, as he had already taken that trip once, that surely there were no savages living on that branch of the River that they used to be very far from it. But, in order to feel all the safer, we took with us two Indian neighbors, which we knew well, and to whom I had done much good, with two negroes to row. One of the Savages knew English, and we thought that, as we had those two Indians with us, we had nothing to fear from the others. So we went peacefully on our way; . . . the whole day we went up the river,—by night we pitched our tents near the water, and early in the morning we proceeded further.[6]

In the days before their fateful journey, de Graffenried and Lawson had become embroiled in that North Carolinian quarrel that we somewhat aggrandize by the name the Cary Rebellion. Doubtless their sojourn into the wilderness was not entirely unconnected to their earlier decision to side with their colony's ruling council against Thomas Cary, thus helping to thwart this "open and declared rebel" as he jockeyed for greater influence (912). Having two months earlier put his name to a letter urging the Virginian Colonel Spotswood to take action to foil such unrest, calling North Carolina "the most distracted country in the Queen's Dominions," de Graffenried certainly had good reason to absent himself from the developing political situation.[7] Not that either he or his companion saw their journey into the west as a soft option. Written after his earlier and altogether more professional exploration of the Carolinian interior, Lawson's own *The History of Carolina: containing the exact description and natural history of that country* (1718, posthumous) repeatedly mixes its supposedly objective reports of local indigenous customs with more fearful allusions to the savage tribes that remain outside his anthropological compass. Returning to the wilderness with his companion de Graffenried, Lawson, it seems clear, would have possessed a vivid sense, not only of its dangerousness, but of the precise character that those dangers could take. Vainly endeavoring to reassure himself, de Graffenried seemingly saw the wilderness as Lawson did: in the light of *The History of Carolina*, through the screen of its lurid descriptions of unknown savages and of the unimaginable but imaginable forms of cannibalistic torture that they might inflict. De Graffenried's revealing decision to start capitalizing his references to Savages halfway through his account suggests he has yet to shake off *The History of Carolina*'s grislier reports:

> the *Sinnagers* . . . are fear'd by all the savage Nations I ever was among, the Westward *Indians* dreading their approach. They . . . keep Spies and Out-Guards for their better Security. . . . Captives . . . they intend to burn, few Prisoners of War escaping that Punishment. The Fire of Pitch-Pine being got ready, and a Feast appointed, . . . the Sufferer has his Body stuck thick with Light-Wood-Splinters, which are lighted like so many Candles. (47)

Like its constant references to the "fat barbecu'd Venison" and "Turkeys" of the friendly Santee (18), *The History of Carolina*'s detailed description of the all but cannibalistic forms of torture perpetrated by the unfriendly and untamed Seneca fails to offer any reliable or firsthand evidence by way of support. Much as this raises suspicions, however, leading us to doubt its subtitle's claim to provide "exact description[s]" of native life, such doubts must not persuade us to mistake *The History of Carolina* for a dishonest or insincere account. As mythological as we might find it, *The History of Carolina*, to its original writer and readers, legitimately supplements its pioneer account by drawing evidence from respectable fields of classical knowledge, out of this mélange producing a vision of savagery that is earnest and sincere to the extent that it fulfils the foregoing and no less earnest and sincere need to know that such savagery *exists*. Classical literature, and in particular Pliny's account of the tribes of Scythian man-eaters who dwell on the edge of the world, are proof enough for the cannibal habits of the unknown Seneca.[8] Outlandish though they might seem now, Lawson and de Graffenried's fears of falling prey to such cannibal fires were, in a word, real. No irony nor incredulousness alleviates the force of such visions. But nor could either man allow that these nightmare visions might submit to rational explanation. Neither could allow that their presence in the wilderness alone manifested a military provocation sufficient to spark Native action. And neither man could grasp that Lawson's likely involvement in a gang that had "captured Tuscarora women and children and sold them into slavery" amounted to sufficient provocation for the dangers that lay upriver.[9]

In the turbulent six weeks that followed their departure, no European knew for sure the fate of these two men. Kidnapping or slaughter seemed possible, but most left behind in the white towns and other settlements surely knew that they were little more than speculation, ways of filling the void of understanding into which the men had vanished. Only a statement that their former associate Christopher Gale presented to the North Carolina ruling council could offer any way out of this void, providing some welcome explanation for a mystery more malignant than most:

> Charleston, S.C.
> November 2, 1711
>
> My Dear:—. . .
> I will not trouble you with repetitions, but refer you to the after-written memorial which I laid before the government, and shall only acquaint you how far I had been concerned in the bloody tragedy, if kind Providence had not prevented.

About ten days before the fatal day, I was at the baron's, and had agreed with him and Mr. Lawson on a progress to the Indian towns; but before we were prepared to go, a message came from home, to inform me that my wife and brother lay dangerously sick; which I may call a happy sickness to me, for on the news I immediately repaired home, and thereby avoided the fate which I shall hereafter inform you.

The baron, with Mr. Lawson and their attendants, proceeding on their journey, were, on the 22nd of September (as you will see by the memorial) both barbarously murdered; the mat, on which the baron used to lie on such like voyages, being since found all daubed with blood, so as we suppose him to have been quickly dispatched. But the fate of Mr. Lawson (if our Indian information be true) was much more tragical, for we are informed that they stuck him full of fine small splinters of torchwood, like hogs' bristles, and so set them gradually on fire. This, I doubt not, had been my fate if Providence had not prevented; but I hope God Almighty has designed me for an instrument in the revenging such innocent Christian blood.

Gale's letter proceeds to tell the council what they already know: that the ambushing of Lawson and de Graffenried on the Neuse River amounted to the opening shot in a terrifying onslaught that had then culminated with the Tuscarora's massacre of the men, women, and children of New Bern. Gale reassures the council that he will "not trouble you with a particular relation of all their butcheries," confining himself instead to the report of isolated atrocities "by which you may suppose the rest." In the account that follows, however, it is hard to imagine what details Gale spared his readers:

Women were laid on their house-floors and great stakes run up through their bodies. Others big with child, the infants were ripped out and hung upon trees. In short, their manner of butchery has been so various and unaccountable, that it would be beyond credit to relate them. This blow was so hotly followed by the hellish crew, that we could not bury our dead; so that they were left for prey to the dogs, and wolves, and vultures, whilst our care was to strengthen our garrison to secure the living.[10]

In his *Roots of American Racism: Essays on the Colonial Experience* (1995), Alden Vaughn outlines a common view in colonial America, arguing that, in this period, "frequent and ferocious hostilities, regardless of who was at fault, [transformed] . . . the Indian in English eyes from potential friend to inveterate enemy."[11] With its embellishments and silences, Gale's letter confirms aspects of this common historical outlook even as it challenges others. No sooner does Gale's missive confirm the existence of this process of Indian demonization than it reminds us that such demonization took place in the European imagination first and foremost, and that it did so *before* and *during* as well as *after* military hostilities. That is to say, in Vaughn's view, military action seems to predate cultural *reaction*; literature and other forms of writing appear to exist in a secondary relationship to war. Like many other colonial dispatches, however, Gale's letter turns to literary myth in the very heat of war, drawing on foregoing myths from the start to discover what that war might mean and how that war might look.

Gale's letter is more than a letter. It is also a call to arms—an American Jeremiad, which masterfully biblicizes frontier experience to unite Christian men against savagery in all its guises.[12] Indeed, it is striking that, just as, only four years earlier, barbecue had somehow united Ned Ward's London society, bringing them together in the shared contemplation of the savage feast, so, in Gale's letter, the internal differences that had recently been tearing that colony apart melt away. Operating in a more political and violent mode, Gale's letter nonetheless shares with *The Barbacue Feast* a desire to pin savagery down and open it up to a general observation via which white men can then come to recognize the whiteness that unites them. Extraordinary care is taken by Gale as he moves through his report. In contrast to Lawson's sincere *History of Carolina*, this letter, throughout, seems keen to avoid lying; but not so keen that North Carolina's councilmen will fail to grasp the urgency of the situation. Indeed, Gale's rhetorical mode here relies heavily on what Huck Finn would later call "stretchers." He leans against the facts. He embroiders and exaggerates, speculates and dismisses. And he acknowledges the existence of other explanations only to pursue a particular savage explanation to the point where these other explanations shrivel up and die. Out of this delicate textual performance, race is fixed in place. Ongoing enslavement among the other ordeals that convinced the Tuscarora of the need for desperate measures, persuading them to ambush Lawson and de Graffenried and then to try to raze New Bern to the ground, become inadmissible as Gale rejects explanation and endeavors to fix the atrocity in place as a "massacre" that only savagery could contemplate or commit. Aflame with racial fury, determined to conflate biology and morality, Gale is here doing what he can to ensure that the "nefarious villainy" committed against his erstwhile companions as well as at New Bern are greeted as crimes of race.

> I very much fear that upon strict inquiry, it would be found that the whole nation of the Tuscaroras (though some of them may not yet be actors) was knowing and consenting to what was done; and that the success of those already in motion, if not put a stop to, will at last induce the rest to join with them in carrying on these bloody designs. Beside the daily expectation of a considerable number of Senekoes [Seneca], which we are certainly informed are coming to cohabit with the Tuscaroras, our enemies, this winter, and become one nation, which in time may affect our neighboring governments as well as us.[13]

The horror of Gale's account, combined with our knowledge that a massacre on New Bern did indeed take place, can encourage us to think twice before criticizing his surge into macho rhetoric. Here, we can feel, is the terrible logic of war. Here is the inevitable call for blood by the soldier distraught at the fall of his friends. Before we indulge Gale's letter on these terms, however, several problems must be faced. For one thing, as Gale surely hopes has escaped our notice, nobody here knows for sure that either of his companions is really dead. As a matter of fact, de Graffenried will return to haunt Gale. But even Lawson's ordeal can complicate matters. For, although Lawson at least has the decency to die, no European, not even Gale, witnessed the manner of his death. And this clarifies that, for a man who is meant to be stricken with grief, our writer has here been a bit too quick to try to capitalize on the lack of information that surrounds Lawson and de Graffenried's disappearance. In fact, for one who makes so much of his "Indian information," Gale is imagining Lawson's demise in terms that bear a striking resemblance to *The History of Carolina* and its unsupported references to Seneca torture. Gale's premonition of the Tuscarora's future alliance here reflects little more than his own bad faith; this alliance is a ghostly trace, a poor substitute for any admission that his friend's death has actually sent this "survivor" scuttling back into the pages of the dead man's *History of Carolina*.

Even before rigor mortis has set in, then, Lawson's corpse has cued an intertextual dialogue of a kind that literary critic Harold Bloom could understand: the death of the author has led his successor to produce a creative "misinterpretation" of the "parent" work, conjuring from this careful misinterpretation a dead body—a corpse whose desecration can now shock all white men into acting against their savage foe.[14] Hence, in the course of this rather Orientalizing rhetoric, a myth of savage violence is leeching off the atmosphere of the reality it has usurped. Massacre, Indian terror are being mythologized, given concrete form. The depredations that some Tuscarora undoubtedly committed in the heat of battle have ballooned out of proportion, coming to prove, to Europeans, the diabolism of their race.

It would have been funny to see the look on Gale's face when he first learned that the Tuscarora had set de Graffenried free. Perhaps some fleeting terror flickered across his eyes. Perhaps those who brought him the good news were surprised by how little it pleased him. Or perhaps not—perhaps Gale knew what we know today: that de Graffenried's miraculous liberation and return to the devastation at New Bern would barely disturb the mythologization of Tuscaroran cannibalism that his and Lawson's disappearance had helped unleash. Perhaps Gale knew that de Graffenried's insistence that his captors actually kept the "execution" of Lawson "very secret" would barely interrupt the proliferation of a legend of savage torture first aired in the dead man's book. Actual events proved powerless to resist this legend's elevation to the status of truth. Nobody seems to have been prepared to accept De Graffenried's testimony that the Tuscarora had probably just cut Lawson's throat. Few were about to allow de Graffenried's testimony get in the way of a good story.

Already, in Gale's 1711 letter, it is possible to extrapolate *The History of Carolina*'s sunny references to all manner of savage and barbecued foods onto its lurid and uncorroborated accounts of Seneca torture. Exposing that a cannibal impulse lies dormant in the savage even when he is barbecuing "Turkeys" is central to Gale's propagandist revision of Lawson's book. But it is also clear that Gale's tone must remain understated throughout this letter. Just coming out with it—just naming Lawson's murder as a cannibal depravity or otherwise comparing its manner to acts of savage cooking—would ruin his evident need to look as though he is sticking to the facts. No such obligations restricted those who wrote about these actions in journals or in correspondence with friends. As they heard about events in the Carolinas, colonial settlers elsewhere seem to have been quick to grasp that what Gale was describing was, in a word, *barbecue*. Again, it is impossible to gauge the extent to which this ability to fit Gale's and other reports of Tuscaroran atrocity onto the paradigm of barbecue tradition derived from settlers' familiarity with Hickeringill's *Jamaica Viewed* or de Bry's cannibal engravings. But this is certainly a possible explanation for why Cotton Mather—whose library was one of the largest in colonial America and who had extraordinary command of the literature of discovery and conquest—so swiftly grasped that the atrocities in "wick'd and ruin'd" Carolina could be viewed through the prism of barbecue, or, as he liked to spell it, "barbikew."[15] Regardless of what recommended the trope to him, however, Mather's letter to the Edinburgh theologian Robert Wodrow seems likewise rehearsed, likewise familiar with the lines it must perform. Relating the latest piece of bad news to emerge from Carolina, Mather certainly knows how to talk about barbecue, presenting it in curious, but by now familiar, fashion as an American neologism that nonetheless needs no explanation:

> The colony of Carolina, to the southward of us, is nearly destroyed by the dreadful judgments of God, for which an uncommon measure of iniquities had ripened it. . . . the barbarities perpetrated by the Indians are too hideous to be restated. There were a sort of inhumanity in the very relation of such things. . . . Major Cochrane . . . was one of the first seized by the Indians, who bound him, and then stript his lady, and abused her with all possible and infandous prostitution before his eyes. Then they struck her flesh with splinters of that oily wood which they burn for candles, and set them on fire. In this condition, and with these lingering torments,—but how horrid!—she was two or three days broiling and wasting to death, in which time they roasted her sucking infant, and compelled her to eat of it; and when these diabolical operations were gone through, they finished all by barbikewing of the gentleman![16]

The important thing to stress here is that the lack of factual verification and indeed the sheer libidinal fury of these secondhand reports have proven no bar to the promulgation of the cannibal barbecue trope. Something behind this trope propels it forward, allowing it to bulldoze contradicting evidence and force its way into the works of writers otherwise calmer and more humane in outlook. Pierre Marambaud sharply distinguishes Virginia planter William Byrd II from Cotton Mather, for example, insisting that the former had little time for the New England patriarch's simplistic habit of pigeonholing Natives as "devils incarnate, heathens who richly deserved complete destruction." In *The History of the Dividing Line* (1728) and other prose, Marambaud insists, Byrd offers "a fairly objective account of Indians and Indian life in colonial Virginia."[17] And it is true that *Dividing Line* takes some care when reciting the facts of Lawson's death, calmly informing us that the Tuscarora "cut his throat from ear to ear" (303). Scrutinizing *Dividing Line* more closely, however, it becomes evident that sober and objective Byrd is in fact as eager to utilize the cannibalistic trope as Lawson in *History of Carolina* and Gale in his fantasies about Lawson's death. No less clear is the fact that the mere mention of barbecue can now call this fantasy into being, furnishing its fundamental shape. Byrd's barbecue references reveal that, for all Marambaud's protestations, *The History of the Dividing Line* repeats the basic structure of *History of Carolina* among other more "aggressive" and "colonial" writings, and fully shares their fluency in what we might call the satanic poetics of American savagery. In Lawson's *History of Carolina* and Byrd's *The History of the Dividing Line*, for example, the Natives closest to white settlement—respectively, the Santee and the Catawba—are held to be gentle, intriguing, and worthy of an objective and anthropological gaze; while those at the edge of the world—those whom Lawson called "Sinnagers," and those whom Byrd will only call "the northern Indians" (258)—remain barbaric and as diabolical as anything or anyone Mather had ever dreamed up. Comparing these "northern Indians" to the Scythian tribes—*The History of the Dividing Line* is littered with echoes of Pliny's *Natural History*—Byrd continues:

> They are very cunning in finding out new ways to torment their unhappy captives, though, like those of hell, their usual method is by fire. Sometimes they barbecue them over live coals, taking them off every now and then to prolong their misery; at other times they will stick sharp pieces of lightwood all over their bodies and, setting them on fire, let them burn down into the flesh to the very bone. And when they take a stout fellow that they believe able to endure a great deal, they will tear all the flesh off his bones with red-hot pincers. While these and suchlike barbarities are practicing, the victors are so far from being touched with tenderness and compassion that they dance and sing round these wretched mortals, showing all the marks of pleasure and jollity. (259–60)

Nor does the barbecue trope come to a stop here. It bulldozes its way well into the twentieth century. Perhaps it even continues to this day.

Genealogical connections certainly exist between *The History of the Dividing Line*'s cannibal barbecue and, say, H. L. Mencken's report of a 1920s fantasy about dancing "with glee around the bonfire of human flesh; and [imagining that] . . . a barbecue was on hand."[18] The lynch mob's occasional tendency to invoke barbecue—a tendency that stands behind Mencken's report of this 1920s fantasy—likewise indicates that this word, our invented tradition, long continued to help some deal with their violent feelings by projecting them onto an externalized notion of racial primitivism.[19] Seeing violence as a breakdown or failure of civilization, believing that all of us harbor primitive instincts deep within, and projecting such primitive instincts onto the regions of the world beyond Europe: all of these assumptions remain embedded in Western culture, and all of them can, even now, cluster around barbecue and call back to life its residual savage associations. The consequences of John Lawson's death—or, rather, the consequences of the historical atrocity into which Christopher Gale successfully transformed it—continue to reverberate, disseminating myths of frontier conquest and primitive violence that still elude complete interrogation.

In 1783, seventy years after the Tuscarora attacked the Swiss settlement at New Bern, the town, rebuilt and thriving, honored the visit of revolutionary leader Francisco de Miranda with that barbecue to which (as we saw in the previous chapter) every local white man, from "the leading" to the "very lowest sort," was invited.[20] John Hemmer's 1940 photographs of the pit barbecue held at the Braswell plantation not so far from New Bern suggest that the overlaps between the "fun" barbecues of civilization's center and the fiendish barbecues of its putative margin developed in a particularly intimate and local fashion in this northeastern patch of North Carolina. But similar stories—similar collisions of the violence and fun of barbecue—have unfolded in similarly intimate settings throughout the region that we now know as the U.S. South. Common lands long seen as suitable grounds for barbecues punctuate the southern landscape of today. One might even say that the concurrent thrills and dangers explored in this book, from Ned Ward's keen eye for the hedonistic pleasures of the American feast to Cotton Mather's horror at its cannibalistic potential, lead in only one direction: toward the Jacksonian era and its popularization, throughout the region of plantation slavery, of the election day barbecue.

Perhaps such an understanding is a little too neat. Perhaps the idea that everything that this book has considered leads inexorably toward the Jacksonian barbecue is a little reliant on hindsight. Perhaps, too, it regrettably shuts down the international character of this tradition, once more scapegoating the South for a racial mythology that has actually encompassed the Anglophone world. Without forgetting such caveats, however, the mythology of barbecue traced in these pages still seems to present a "perfect fit" for the politics of Jackson and his men. After all, it is not difficult to connect the convergence of violence and pleasure that *The Barbacue Feast* and other written works achieve through their contemplation of savagery to the Jacksonian outlook and its wild oscillation between feelings of empathy and feelings of antipathy for the Indian. Just as the Barbecue Society rejuvenated collective English civility through a shared enjoyment of savage culture, so the frontier soldiers of Jacksonian America could, in Michael Paul Rogin's words, slip "unselfconsciously from killing Indians to scalping corpses and participating in Indian victory rituals."[21] All foregoing connotations of barbecue, from the most savage to the most pleasurable, surface in the life and autobiographical writings of Davy Crockett, for example. The friendliest of cannibals, Crockett held his public enthralled as he told of his savage actions in the fields. Crockett presented himself as a "man turned beast, the white man who scalps Indians, the uncultured civilizer."[22] As for all of Jackson's followers—as for all those acolytes who could seem more Jacksonian than Jackson himself—frontier barbecue, as an invented tradition, thus presented Davy Crockett with a perfect food. Here, it could seem, was a food endowed with all the qualities, from savagery to democracy, and from independence to power, with which he courted association. No one expected such men to sing the praises of soup. No one wanted Crockett and his ilk to march off to the Alamo with a bellyful of cheese croquettes. Only barbecue could present a feast equal to these new American warriors. Only barbecue could appease their hunger for savagery as well as meat.[23]

The American Chief

Death always knew how to find Andrew Jackson. In an age when mourning was stitched firmly into the fabric of everyday life, Jackson still stood out as being unusually unfortunate, his allotted time on earth unusually stockpiled with death. Born fatherless, Jackson lost his two brothers as well as his mother to illness before he turned sixteen. Misfortune followed him into adulthood. Back in Tennessee, slaves on the Hermitage sometimes died so often as to seem unseasoned, like new cargo unloaded from Senegal or Dahomey, while Jackson's adoptive Creek son Lincoyer—a fellow orphan, whom U.S. troops in 1813 found "pressed to the bosom of . . . [the] lifeless mother" they had killed—succumbed to tuberculosis in 1827.[24] In December 1828, Rachel Jackson's last decline at the end of her husband's successful presidential campaign brought more public grief. Sorrow ate at Jackson's face, scoring lines of anguish onto his forehead and even down as far as his chin, where they fell into and rose out of the pockmarks that were a permanent reminder that he alone survived the sicknesses that befell his family.

Other terrors wrote themselves on Jackson's face. Supporting or attacking his presidential hopes, newspapers agreed that, however frozen in grief, it remained that of a man of war—a man some might call "General" and others "killer," but whom all knew as an agent and prosecutor as much as a victim of death. Actually, like several of his successors, Jackson saw less actual armed combat than his public image suggested. Nonetheless, this presidential candidate's reputation for violence remained intact. To his opponents, emphasizing Jackson's readiness to duel, scalp, and execute could make him seem a liability, too hotheaded for the responsibilities of high office. But to his supporters it confirmed his status as the candidate of change—the democratic choice, who did not look down upon enfranchised Americans but shared their fears and prejudices, and understood that national security could not be achieved without a good measure of muscle and might. *John Quincy Adams can write,* they sloganeered, *but Andrew Jackson can fight,* and the anti-intellectual couplet implied other things, too—that Adams was a man of thought, Jackson of deed; that Adams was an Anglophile, Jackson an Anglophobe; and that, while classicist Adams was intent on building a new U.S. aristocracy, Jackson alone knew what it meant to face down the Natives, discipline slaves, work the land, and generally make himself a free white man of independent means.

On the early steps of the long journey that eventually led him to the White House, it was this second Jackson—the Jackson who was not the servant but the master of death—who prevailed. The Tennessean oligarchs who promoted Jackson's presidential hopes quickly realized that their candidate's appeal resided in his tough frontier upbringing and heroic military actions, and that it was best to say as little as possible about the eminent legal positions he had held or his antipopulist belief that "the rights secured to the citizens . . . are worth nothing" without judicial assent.[25] Jackson's Nashville boosters maintained an equally careful silence about the fact that their general was anything but a reluctant hero, thrust suddenly into the theater of war. As Michael Paul Rogin puts it, Jackson needed war, not simply for political reasons, but to expunge the emasculating knowledge that, in his youth on the Tennessean frontier, he "had done nothing heroic to establish his own right to the land" and had even "fled" the scene of "an Indian ambush."[26] Jackson had to wait until his forty-sixth birthday for the chance to bloody his hands, finally leading U.S. troops against the Creek people in the War of 1812. His letters and addresses, dispatched from Tennessee during lulls in the hostilities, in turn seem prerehearsed, already familiar, as well-versed in existing Indian myth as Lawson's *The History of Carolina*. Delivered the moment battle ended, Jackson's address to his victorious soldiers at Fort Williams in March 1814 is again that of a man who already knows his lines—a man who has long known what savagery means, and who is now gratified to find some available source onto whom he can graft such a priori truths.

> [After the] battles of Talishatchey, Talladega, Emuckfau and Enop-
> tichopc . . . our borders must no longer be disturbed by the war-hoop of
> the ruthless savage, or the cries of the suffering victims. That torch which
> they lighted up on our frontier has blazed and must blaze again in the
> heart of their nation. They shall see by its blaze, the gleamings of that
> sword which their cruelties and tracheries has compelled us to unsheath.
>
> But how has this war been waged . . . ? Have we emulated them as an
> example by the disorder of our movements, and savageness of their war-
> fare, no, fellow soldiers; great as was the grievance that called us from our
> homes, we never ought to permit . . . the dominion of unruly passions.[27]

On its surface, this patriotic address stages the military confrontation with savagery as an almost spiritual experience whereby Jackson and those he leads have discovered what it means to be Christian, white, and free. Some knowledge exists in the wherewithal, even in the savagery, of the savage, arising in him just as he arises in the wilderness. Now the acquisition of racial mastery demands that the U.S. soldier find a way of confronting this wherewithal and mastering it without surrendering the civilized supremacy embodied in his white skin. If only because he already knows how to turn this recent military experience into useful propaganda, however, this encounter with "savageness" in the field is clearly less surprising than Jackson would have us believe. No epistemological crisis, no shattering exposure to barbarisms unsuspected, has in fact occurred. Jackson, instead, has placed his latest military engagement into a longstanding tradition of exaggerating Native violence in order to justify its massive military response.

Implied here is an idea the U.S. soldier had secured "our borders" only after having undergone a complex and twofold identification whereby, in the heat of battle, he made contact with the savagery inside him before, in the calm of armistice, finding a way to force it back down his throat. In his victorious rationalization of U.S. violence, Jackson certainly seems to know something of the "dominion of unruly passions" that he declares taboo. He is, one might say, dismissing the possibility of white savagery for the good reason that he has seen it in action. For the Jackson who assures his troops that they have not "emulated . . . savageness" might have forgotten playing with a tomahawk and spear as a boy, but he could certainly remember writing to Thomas Pinckney, just one month before delivering this address, that "I have on all occasions preserved the sculps of my killed."[28] This abrupt switch from a profound identification with to an equally powerful alienation from the Native supplies what Rogin's *Fathers and Children* calls the "consistent pattern" of Jackson's military talks:

> He first described the atrocities of the "inhuman butchers" against
> women and children. His images, as he put it in describing the Duck
> River massacre, made the Indians' victims "our own." They roused his
> men to "pant with vengeance." They aroused primitive identification with
> Indian violence. Jackson then insisted that his troops must not fight like
> "barbarians." . . . Discipline distinguished white volunteers from Indian
> warriors. Such control permitted primitive identification with savages to
> eventuate not in chaotic violence but in victorious authority. (148–49)

Writing about racism today often tends to treat it as a deviant or pathological condition. Novelists, journalists, and academics often depict racism as a warping of the world: as an ideology that sets itself the impossible task of making people fit spurious biological criteria of its own design. In this view, the well-known sadism of racists—their apparent tendency to burst suddenly and without warning into acts of cruel and libidinal violence—comes to seem symptomatic of a kind of mental fatigue, becoming, to this growing consensus, a venting of the pressures accumulated from their endless and eventually unbearable distortion of humanity. Forty years since Frantz Fanon's *The Wretched of the Earth* drew attention to a French government agent in Algeria who "stuffed his ears with cottonwool in order to make the screams [in his head] seem less piercing," Fanon's groundbreaking conclusion that racism does psychological damage to the racist now borders on the status of received wisdom (213).

Just because Jackson's conduct contradicts his rhetorical insistence that Americans were free from savagery does not mean that his statement fits this diagnosis. Unlike many planters and overseers of his time, Jackson seems never to have sought to assure himself of the superiority of his own body by physically and sexually abusing his slaves. His was a more settled, more stable, racial style. Frontier culture in the early republic, after all, naturalized and normalized white supremacy, largely assumed that democracy was the birthright of Europe's children, and only sometimes felt it necessary to invoke science to vindicate such racial claims. A paternalist slaveholder and U.S. soldier, Jackson duly developed a complex racial outlook quite alien to today's understanding of racist thought. Jackson lacked the fear of biological mixture and pollution that, epitomized in Nazism, is now generally considered an inevitable hallmark of racism. Apparently free to consort with American Indians and even to mimic their behavior, Jackson felt secure enough in his racial superiority that he could use such contacts to revolutionize whiteness—to rid it of English callousness and European artifice by exposing it to the "blaze" of a regenerating but "primitive" native spirit. Indeed, in Jackson's very different racial outlook, turning self-consciously "savage" violence against indigenous peoples paradoxically becomes a way of optimizing whiteness, offering an opportunity to kill your teachers while displaying your mastery of the lessons they taught.

And so Jackson, as *Fathers and Children* puts it, cannibalistically "incorporated in combat the Indians' magic—their heroism, their violence, their land" (149). Like the black droplets that produce the dazzling white paint in Ralph Ellison's *Invisible Man*, every scalp that Jackson took and every "savage" act that he performed merely made his yellow rheumatic skin glow white. Jackson, as I say, was the master, not the servant, of death. He was the man, sought by death, who sought in the Indian a sign of the country's future path. Against the bookish and the elite, the John Quincy Adamses of this world, he alone seemed to know that U.S. civilization had no choice but to turn savagery back against the savage. Such a terrifying man, his face petrified and pockmarked by the death he kept cheating, Jackson was thus an unprecedented electoral proposition. His candidacy would turn the turbulent elections of 1824 and 1828 into national referendums on violence, and his victory would rest on convincing the electorate that their country faced a nightmare, and that only he could save it. Somehow growing out of the wilderness, somehow emanating from the field of American savagery, the invented tradition of the election day barbecue was a superb platform from which to launch such a manly and ominous campaign.

Different Ideas of Fun

Barbecue! For one day at least, leave toil behind and eat your fill of hog meat and beef! Get yourself good and drunk without spending a dime! Sing, reel, and dance to the fiddle! Revel with friends! Laugh with the politician who donated the meat! Assure him that you would not be so rude as to vote for the other man! Stay steady for the stump speeches ahead! Do not get so drunk as to disgrace the republic! Give in to some temptations! Resist others! Steer clear of those James Kirke Paulding called "roysterers, tosspots and Barbecue villains," who in merriment or crime ply you with rotgut![29] Remember who you are! Remember why you are here! Remember that, however humble your beginnings, here you stand, enfranchised, a man of status in this new world!

> [With] the coming of the Jacksonian epoch, there was . . . an increase in hilarity and boisterousness in the celebrations. . . . all business and labor came to a stop, and everybody celebrated. . . . The crowds, composed of men, women, and children, yea all "the little niggers in town," yelled and shrieked and screamed like mad. These crowds, however, were assembled with a purpose that was serious, almost holy. They . . . greeted the Declaration and the oration with enthusiastic applause. Instead of a dinner for the select few, barbecues were prepared for everybody. At one barbecue, "long tables groaned beneath the fat of the land." . . . Of food there was

enough and to spare. But instead of drinking the toasts in Madeira and imported liquors, as the early assemblies had done, these "motley crews" drank domestic wines and liquors, even lemonade.[30]

The specifically southern tradition of the election day barbecue, as described by Fletcher M. Green, first came to prominence during Andrew Jackson's presidential campaign of the early 1820s. Although sometimes ignored, Jackson's association with this invented barbecue tradition was there from the beginning of his political career. While it is impossible to say when Jackson's pursuit of the White House really began—1820s U.S. society liked its candidates reluctant, preferring that they left open electioneering to their political allies—the likeliest point is summer 1822 and the "enormous barbecue . . . at McNairy's Spring on the purlieus of" Nashville, where no one "breathed an allusion to the topic in every mind—the Presidential election" of 1824.[31] From this point forward, the General's campaigners used barbecue to stoke what his contemporaries would call "Jackson Fever," promoting the grassroots credentials of their man by associating him with the most grassroots of American foods.[32] As one historian has put it, the "Jacksonians were using parades, barbecues, and Hickory Clubs to stir up the masses."[33] Jackson biographer Robert Remini concurs:

> Much of this ballyhoo was conceived and organized by the new breed of politicians who appeared following the War of 1812. They encouraged the public to feats (hitherto unknown) of organized mayhem. Parades, barbecues, dinners, street rallies, tree plantings (hickory trees for Democrats) and patriotic displays of every variety occurred throughout the Union— and most of them for Jackson.[34]

By the 1810s and '20s, then, the invented tradition whose colonial and English origins I have traced over the course of *Savage Barbecue* began to fall into the hands of the anti-Indian and anti-English politicians then rallying behind Andrew Jackson. Many of the original hallmarks of this invented tradition, from its association with pork to its disdain for cutlery, not to mention its peculiar combination of identification with and hostility toward indigenous or slave culture, were if anything reinforced even as this movement positioned itself as a new phenomenon born of frontier experience. Given all that we have already considered, this new political position thus requires careful consideration. What was it about this barbecue's invented tradition that so strongly appealed to the architects of Jacksonian democracy? In this important and transitional period of national democracy, as politicians began to refine their appeal to the white male electorate, what was signified by the mountains of meat that lay, ignored by history, at their ceremonial heart?

Evocative as it is, Green's forty-year-old portrait of the feast is flawed. His prose drips with the same Revolutionary nostalgia that, Green claims, led even the most uproarious Jacksonian mob to still itself for democratic participation. Green's eyes mist over as he fondly contrasts these ribald and "'motley crews'" with the sedate civility of those who drank Revolutionary "toasts in Madeira and imported liquors." He blinds himself to the fact that, as Charles Sydnor reminds us, during the War of Independence the republic's forefathers "barbecued" their fair share of election "oxen," serving them alongside "kegs of rum" that soon got all present "roaring drunk."[35] The veil Green draws across such preceding Revolutionary extravaganzas of beef, ballots, and booze perhaps indicates that he is trusting too much in those outraged citizens of the Jacksonian period for whom the drunken barbecue marked a new and unsavory departure in U.S. life. In their public statements, such naysayers certainly liked to drape their prudery in nostalgia, depicting these feasts as dissolute binges, linked to Jackson, which sounded the death knell of any remaining Republican dignity. To them, indeed, the binary opposition appeared immaculate: democratic debate in the early Republic had been upstanding and dispassionate; Jacksonian barbecues were legless and, as will soon become clear, savage.

Daniel Dupre's article on political barbecues in Madison County, Alabama, unearths striking examples of such naysayers. Exploring local press opposition, Dupre quotes one correspondent who, under the pen name *An Old Resident*, waxes especially nostalgic about the democracy of yore, insisting that candidates in the early Republic never "'rode to and fro through the county. . . . They never paid for barbecues and ordered bottles of whiskey to be set out. . . . They were never seen first with their arm on one man's shoulder and then on another, going aside having little chats and then coming back to drink a glass of whiskey together.'"[36] A second correspondent, calling her- or himself Barbecuensis, agreed, condemning the treating of the present by "sarcastically" invoking "the 'martyr blood' of the American Revolution, spilled to secure 'that most sublime of all human rights . . . the right of self-barter.'"[37] Using alliteration, anaphora and other techniques indicating an education in rhetoric, Barbecuensis elsewhere takes on what a third correspondent called the new "'*barbecue gentry.*'"[38] These bogus aristocrats, Barbecuensis alleged, were violently uprooting U.S. democratic tradition from its rightful site—the minds of the voters—and forcing it down into their bellies.

> The question now, is not, what is his mental capacity? But, what are the dimensions of his stomach? Not, does he read and think? But, does he eat and digest? Not, if he will enact wholesome laws and promote and preserve the peace, happiness and prosperity of the State, but if he will drink raw whiskey, eat rawer shote [shoat, a young hog], dance bare foot on a puncheon floor, . . . and pull at a gander's neck.[39]

Revolutionary culture made naked class snobbery seem, if not taboo, then a little unpatriotic. But it also set before the country's oligarchs a mass of ordinary white folk who had fought for democratic independence and now considered it their due. Opportunities for snobbery thus multiplied as the need to make it euphemistic grew pressing. Barbecuensis displays great fluency in the aliases and alibis that subsequently came to cloak class antipathy. Seemingly despising democracy in action despite supporting it in principle, her or his letters cleverly turn the fear of social leveling into a question of polite convention, even of morality. Manners become the main thing for Barbecuensis: he or she is cognizant of the need to couch objections carefully—to present them as a matter, no longer of snatching the vote back out of the hands of the great unwashed, but of upholding propriety, stopping drunkenness, curbing excess. The paradox then vanishes altogether, spirited away by the alchemy of race, as Barbecuensis describes how, at these events, "'slavery forgot its chain, and the tawny sons of Africa danced, sung, and halooed in sympathetic freedom.'"[40] As Dupre observes, such naysayers felt that

> the men who swilled whiskey and gorged themselves in the hot noon-day sun and who listened to the rantings of the candidates on the stump with the same measure of seriousness as they danced to the fiddle had lost their reason in fits of passion. They abandoned their self-control to revel in licentiousness and, as a result, they marched to the polls on election day no better than slaves.[41]

Certain questions become pressing at this point. For one thing, why on earth would Jackson seek to associate himself with such racial topsy-turvyism? In a political culture more or less defined by the policing of the racial boundary, why on earth would he set foot in a ritual that encouraged "'slavery'" to forget "'its chain'"? Barbecuensis's version of events clearly found little to no reflection among those who actually went along to such festivities. To them, clearly, such events were neither a spanner in the works of U.S. politics nor nothing more than a way of letting off steam. On the contrary: it must have seemed to them an enactment, a culmination of democracy. The proliferation and recurrence of election day barbecues alone suggest that Stanley Elkins and Eric McKitrick are right to suggest that such events attracted "increasing numbers of young men in the poorer counties" into political participation.[42]

Certainly the racial mythology outlined throughout *Savage Barbecue* makes Barbecuensis's fears appear misplaced. On such election days, after all, slaves would have gained little beyond a chance to take a break from work—if they were lucky. No doubt they trod carefully through the day, and found themselves the victims of even more drunken jibes, not to mention violent attacks, than was ordinary. Power surely met no extraordinary challenge, nor found itself dissipated even for one fantastic day. Instead it must have displayed itself, paraded its brutishness, and remained at all times exactly where it was meant to be, in the hands of the empowered. Barbecuensis's fears were groundless. Nostalgia for the Revolution might have led him or her to disdain the whiskey-drinking men "who listened to the rantings of the candidates on the stump," and even to paint them as being "no better than slaves." But these men, of course, would have seen things very differently. Democratic participation, for them, was surely a welcome sign not of slavery but its opposite. Likely it struck them as part of what W. E. B. DuBois later called the "psychological wage" of whiteness.[43] If whiskey got you so bad that you could no longer follow what was being said, maybe, in the morning, your hangover came with a sense of renewed gratitude that you were born the right side of the color divide. And if you were compos mentis enough to take it all in, maybe you felt connected with the very birth of the republic, kith and kin to the forefathers whose legacy some said you were disgracing.

Onlookers and participants' radically divergent responses to the barbecue rehearsed an equally radical split in attitudes toward primitivism and its uses in the national culture. Mentioned earlier, the attack on those at the barbecue who "drink raw whiskey, eat rawer shote, dance bare foot on a puncheon floor, . . . and pull at a gander's neck" confirms Barbecuensis's gift for striking at the heart of the matter. Though fanciful, its exaggeration ferrets out the barbecue's subconscious status as a savage ceremonial. To Barbecuensis this subconscious savagery was the mark and proof of the barbecue's guilt, demonstrating that its participants were abandoning European civilization for a primitive zone in which they shed clothing, danced shoeless, and sought to outbid one another in pulling geese's necks while on horseback. Although Jacksonian barbecues customarily required several hours of preparation, Barbecuensis refers to the consumption of raw pig, which seems to imply his or her perception of the ceremony as not only violent but savagely so. By ignoring that this food is cooked far longer than anything else in the American repertoire, Barbecuensis essentially strips barbecue of culture, forcing it into the "raw" and "natural" corner of Lévi-Strauss's culinary triangle, labeling it fit only for primitive consumers.[44]

Once again, those attending the barbecue would have seen such matters differently. The machismo of the event was surely overwhelming. It is hard to imagine that gander pullers could easily express their misgivings or squeamishness at torturing innocent birds. No comparable gender pressures, however, compelled men to dance barefoot. Genuine pleasure was to be had in the thudding of naked toes on puncheon, "the flat surface of a split log, smoothed with an ax,"[45] that some associated with slave quarters and others with the backcountry "primitive log-cabin[s]" that produced such men as Daniel Boone.[46] Perhaps revelers furthermore preferred not to drink "Madeira and imported liquors," feeling thankful to wash barbecue down with "raw" home brew. And perhaps these mountains of meat in turn connoted a power over violence in a way no other food could. Perhaps prospective politicians kept planning this particular event because, even as it offered opportunities to display public generosity, it declared to all in town that they were *men*—warriors, even. Slowly rotting in the summer sun, the piles of pig would have announced a kind of power, a mastery over rather than servitude to death. War veterans, after a drink or two, could comment on the meat, contemplating its resemblance to the roasted and dismembered Native corpses they had seen. As the white American electorate eyed the west covetously, consciously and unconsciously contemplating the violence that its conquest would involve, the rise of the political barbecue was anything but accidental. Jackson, destined to become the first "backwoods President," could not have wished for a more fitting stage.[47]

The Savage Inauguration

March 4, 1829. No one doubted the magnitude of the day. For Jackson's men, it came four years late. Sour-faced John Quincy Adams, they were convinced, stole the election of 1824, receiving the nod under dubious circumstances and enjoying the most sumptuous of all presidential inauguration despite not winning the vote. Jackson himself shared their dismay, at least in private, writing soon afterward that "Adams was inaugurated amidst a vast assemblage of citizens having been escorted to the Capitol with a pomp and ceremony of guns & drums not very consistent, in my humble opinion, with the character of the occasion." Anger often fuels Jackson's writing, building through his long and coiling sentences, and this letter works up a typical head of steam. "Twenty four years ago when Mr. Jefferson was inducted into office no such machinery was called in to give solemnity to the occasion.—he rode his own horse and hitched himself to the enclosure."[48] In the words of an Ohioan election ticket, a victory in 1828 would allow Jackson and his men finally to "sweep the Augean stable." It would avenge Adams's shoddy backroom politicking. It would give the presidency back to the people. And it would reverse the country's worrying drift away from the Republican simplicity that Jefferson, for all his books and slaves, somehow still embodied.

If Jackson's desire to keep democracy vital recalls the political barbecue's emphasis on promoting contact between voters and their officials, then his opponents' diatribes echo Barbecuensis's letters even more strikingly. Again collapsing white oafishness into savagery, the shudders of disgust that the "war-whoop[s]" of "King Mob" sent down Joseph Story's spine reveal that the patrician judge was as fluent in the new alibis and aliases of class fear as Barbecuensis, and could easily outdo the latter's horror at the boozing, barbecuing, barefoot-dancing mob. Yet in this democratizing era, as the franchise mushroomed and manners were said to have declined, many more than just Story and Barbecuensis grew skilled in the art of scapegoating Jackson, and much sport was had in blaming the haggard Tennessean for "ushering in the spirit of leveling and riotous partisanship," thereby placing the Constitution in "the hands of roughnecks and radicals."[49] Though it was by no means exclusive to the New England intelligentsia, Daniel Webster encapsulated this feeling that Washington, in the run up to the inauguration, was a city laid to siege, swamped by vagabonds and rednecks agog at their man's impending ascent: "Today, we have had the Inauguration. A monstrous crowd of people is in the City. I have never seen anything like it before. Persons have come 500 miles to see Genl Jackson; & they really seem to think that the Country is rescued from some dreadful danger."[50]

Shades of this attitude color *President's Levee*, the drawing of the inauguration that Robert Cruikshank produced from the other side of the Atlantic in 1841 (fig. 13). In his alternative title—"or, all Creation going to the White House"—Cruikshank shows that he is aware of the U.S. citizenry's new nickname for the president's Executive Mansion. Superficially, however, his picture seems blind to the racial implications of this new name, ignoring the equivalence of color that it generates between the president's skin and the walls of his office. Indeed, Cruikshank seems determined to disregard Jackson's savage reputation and to see him in terms of class upheaval. Cruikshank's White House is a thing of wonder, so white and perfect he seems to have forgotten that his fellow Britons tried to burn it down. Dazzling and clean, it looks less and less American, and more and more like one of those immaculately white "sugar subtleties" that monarchs in medieval Europe, keen to impress visitors with the riches at their command, had paraded between courses at state dinners. Buzzing around this "subtlety" are the mass that Cruikshank labels "all Creation": the backwoodsmen, hunters, and rednecks from Kentucky, Ohio, and Tennessee. Some stand in the windows and others on the porticos, looking out at the masses surrounding the White House; some swarm up and down its curving staircase. Others stand in the foregound of the picture, talking and smoking. In the middle ground others get roughed up by horses—get flung out of carriages, get separated from their hats. And toward the picture's rightmost edge, others still get whipped up into a Jacksonian frenzy, raising their arms in the air and seemingly behaving in a manner liable to make Joseph Story, not to mention Barbecuensis, shudder.

13. Robert Cruikshank, "President's Levee, or All Creation Going to the White House, Washington," 1841. Courtesy of the Library of Congress, Prints and Photographs Division, reproduction number LC-USZ62-1805.

By making their faces featureless and their outlines very alike, Cruikshank suggests that this is something more than a wild and lawless multitude. It is also leveled. What it is about to do to the White House has long ago been done to it. An idealistic but premature expansion of the democratic franchise has flattened this Jacksonian throng, forcing the loftiest among its rank to succumb to instincts universal to it. At the same time, however, this is also an explicitly white crowd. By shading some of the skin in this picture but leaving most of it unmarked, Cruikshank is delegating the business of racial identification to the bleached canvas on which he draws. Rather than making a decisive artistic intervention of his own, he is harnessing the unremarked-upon whiteness of his material, allowing it to do his work for him. Unalloyed class fear here allows itself to go about its day, untroubled by a transatlantic mirror from which the racial complexity of the United States has been magically, materially deflected.

Eyewitnesses to the inauguration viewed the event quite differently. Four years before the Nullification Crisis that would see him withdraw his

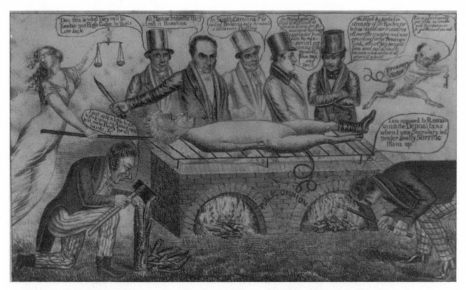

14. Jack "Zek" Downing, "The Political Barbecue," 1834. Courtesy of the Library of Congress, Prints and Photographs Division, reproduction number LC-USZ62-9647.

support of the president, the new Governor of South Carolina James H. Hamilton wrote Martin Van Buren:

> It was a glorious day yesterday for the *sovereign* who . . . called here to the account of some 15 or 20,000 who hailed the Chief. . . . The ceremony went off well, and the principal personage acquitted himself with a grace and "composed dignity" which I never saw surpassed. The address itself is excellent chaste patriotic sententious and dignified it says all that is necessary to say on such an occasion . . . As far as I have heard . . . it has given universal satisfaction. . . .
>
> After the ceremony the old Chief retired to the Palace where we had a regular saturnalia. The mob broke in, in thousands—Spirits black yellow and grey, poured in in one uninterrupted flow of mud and filth, among the throngs many fit subjects for the penitentiary and not the fewest among these . . . for Liberia. It would have done Mr. Wilberforce's heart good to see a stout black wench eating in this free country a jelley with a gold spoon at the President's House.[51]

This is a curious, clever letter. There is something excessive about the praise it lavishes on Jackson, and there is something too fierce about its denunciation of the mob. By referring to Jackson's dignity not once but twice, and by generally making free with the superlatives, Hamilton here betrays his surprise that the new president neither stumbled up the Capitol's steps nor succumbed to an old and embarrassing childhood habit, and started dribbling halfway through his "excellent" and unexpectedly "chaste" inaugural address. If combined with his horror at the savagery of this inauguration, indeed, Hamilton's excessive personal praise for Jackson could suggest that this letter was meant to be read as a kind of sounding out, pushing certain buttons to let Van Buren know that its author will remain loyal only if certain conditions are in future met. At the very least, the fact that, less than four years after this, Hamilton will stand in open contempt of the president suggests that we would be unwise to take his letter's exaltation of the chief at face value. Nor should we ignore the association that this repeated and somewhat Indian moniker sets up with the "stout black wench" who augurs the potential racial topsy-turvyism of the future as she waves a gold spoon about amid the splendors of the East Room.

This is to read Hamilton's letter as it wants to be read: as a poised statement to the incoming administration, which dutifully offers support even as it intimates that this support is limited and subject to a range of conditions. There are other ways of reading this letter, however. In particular, the cultural paths and crossroads that this book has led us down encourage us to pay more attention to Hamilton's symbolic associations, and less to his political machinations. After all, if read in the light of this book and against the grain of Hamilton's own ideological assumptions, the single black woman's infiltration of the East Room comes to seem neither scandalous nor subversive, and instead presents a human counterpart to the drops of black paint that, in *Invisible Man*, optimize Washington's spectral whiteness. In this view, Hamilton's need to isolate and humiliate this single black woman fails in its efforts to find a surreptitious way of denunciating Jackson. Instead of exposing Old Hickory's racial irresponsibility, instead of revealing the reckless dangers of Jacksonian savagism, this unnamed woman, reduced to a symbol, sits like so much barbecued meat in the belly of the White House. And, in turn, Hamilton's worries turn out to seem as groundless as those of Barbecuensis: the system, here, it now becomes clear, has not capitulated to this woman, nor has it been fatally polluted by her, but rather it has grown magically stronger as a result of its contact with what it considers to be her barbaric presence. Barbarism, the very breath of it warming the skin of the white mansion, revitalizes and intensifies the office of U.S. civilization. Walls strengthen all around the black woman, swallowing her and enacting a more genuine cannibal threat.

The feeling with Jackson always seems to be that he could not control the force he unleashed into American life. Jacksonian philosophy, the consensus seems to suggest, soon outgrew Jackson the man. He himself could not grasp and nor could he recover awareness enough to see that his name had become a byword for a kind of democratic evangelicalism whose radical postures far outstripped his own beliefs. So it was with his connection to barbecue. White Americans grasped that there was in Jackson's harnessing of the campaign barbecue a declaration that his was the "savage" ticket, the "cannibal" ticket that could be set against the urbane refinements of John Quincy Adams. They could see that Jackson, here, was courting association with a primitive feast that, even in its politest incarnations, belonged to the same paradigm by which men like John Lawson once, supposedly, were tortured to death.

Zek Downing's *The Political Barbecue* (1834, fig. 14) visualizes this way of thinking about Jackson. The barbaric tradition whose invention we have traced in these pages becomes reanimated here as Downing depicts a brick barbecue fueled by kindling, with Jackson suspended above the flames on a gridiron. An apparatus that bears no closer connection to indigenous practice than Edward Hickeringill's Carib barbecues, but which somehow still maintains an unassailable barbaric aura, here grows powerful enough to animalize the seventh president, turning his extremities swinish, savage. Coils of smoke rise and turn him brown. All around him the great and the good gather, unmoved by their leader's predicament. Opponents of Jackson's bank program stand behind the barbecue. Among them Daniel Webster wields a knife, announcing, "In Massachusetts they call it Roasting." Webster Preston, adding a touch of intriguing local detail, comments, "In South Carolina t'is called Barbecue only he wants a little more Basteing." Impish Van Buren, flying away from the scene, meanwhile announces, "T'is my business to get folks in trouble and their business to get themselves out."

Forced to converse with each other, these old political allies and adversaries as such congeal into a macho, homosocial circle. They gather together, debate the barbecue method together like the Carpenters and Galenists of Ned Ward's *The Barbacue Feast*. Together, like that London crew, they gather to watch a pig that is not a pig, a man that is not a man. Together they indulge the barbarism that they project outward, laughing and joking in the face of death. And they seem oblivious to the dehumanization of the indigenous and African subject that these jokes and this laughter would cause. They seem almost to believe their assertion that these tawdry visions of cannibalism do not spring from their own culture. They seem almost convinced—as we are convinced—that violence involves a journey away from civilized life, a journey back into the arms of some primitive memory. A regression that latches onto and humiliates the black and Native subjects in American life seems to call into existence this cannibal feast. You could almost believe it was true. You could almost forget that here were the true barbarians, the white savages who wash their hands of the violence they have sent out into the world.

NOTES

Introduction

1. Ferguson, "Smithsonian's Mitsitam Café."
2. Web site of the National Museum of the American Indian. Accessed 30 Nov. 2006 at http://www.nmai.si.edu/subpage.cfm?subpage=dc&second=visitor&third=in side#museumcafe.
3. For a good discussion of how, in the immediate wake of the Great Migration, "food came to represent the resilience of the African American people in the South," see Poe, "Origins of Soul Food," 97.
4. Zibart, "Caribbean Islands," 333.
5. S. Johnson, *Dictionary of the English Language*, n.p.
6. Hobsbawm, "Mass-Producing Traditions," 268.
7. Pleck, "Making of the Domestic Occasion," 774.
8. O'Leary, *To Die For*, 100.
9. Dudley, "Taking the Slow Road to Perfect Barbecue," 5.
10. Web site of the National Museum of the American Indian.
11. Fiddes, *Meat*, 2.
12. "In the Shadow of Two Gunmen," part 2, *West Wing* 2:2.
13. Reed, "Barbecue Sociology," 79.
14. Quoted in G. Ward, *Jazz*, 78–79.
15. Burns, preface, vii.

Chapter One. From Barbacoa *to* Barbecue

1. Flint, *Imaginative Landscape of Christopher Columbus*, 118.
2. Kurlansky, *Cod*, 22–23.
3. Fernández-Armesto, *Columbus*, 73.
4. Kurlansky, *Basque History of the World*, 352–53.
5. Martire d' Anghiera, *Decades of the newe worlde*, 41.
6. Columbus, *Journal of the First Voyage*, 15–17.
7. Indeed, synthetic capsaicin is used in antimugger sprays. See Davidson, *Penguin Companion to Food*, 204.
8. Columbus, *Journal of the First Voyage*, 89.
9. Ibid., 181. Present scholarly consensus suggests that Babeque refers to the Baha-

man island Great Anagua, while Bohío refers to Hispaniola. See Lemos, "Voyages of Columbus," 699.

10. Flint charts these shifts in Columbus's attitudes well in *Imaginative Landscape*, 123.

11. Lemos, "Voyages of Columbus," 704–12.

12. Bernáldez, "History of the Catholic Sovereigns," 120–22. Washington Irving did much to popularize this anecdote, amending it for American tastes in his *Life and Voyages of Columbus* (*Works of Washington Irving* 3:1–460, 418).

13. Nader, "Andrés Bernáldez," 64–65.

14. Lemos, "Voyages of Columbus," 709.

15. Castillo, *Performing America*, 23.

16. Quoted in Bucher, *Icon and Conquest*, 4.

17. In this intriguing chronicle Caribbean Indians are said to "patiently endure hunger, [so] that after they are returned from fishing they will have the patience to broil their fish over a soft fire on a wooden frame made like a Gridiron, about two foot high, under which they kindle so small a fire, that sometimes it requires a whole day to make ready their fish as they would have it: Some of the *French* affirm, that have eaten some of their dressing, they have lik'd it very well: It is observable generally in all their meat, that they dress all with a very gentle fire" (Rochefort, *History of the Caribby-islands*, 297–98).

18. Hale, *Civilization of Europe*, 504.

19. Calloway, *New Worlds for All*, 11.

20. Rouse, *Tainos*, 5. For Columbus's early attitude to the Caribs, see *Journal of the First Voyage*, 169.

21. Flint, *Imaginative Landscape of Christopher Columbus*, xi.

22. Mazumdar, "Impact of New World Food Crops," 61.

23. Steingarten, "Going Whole Hog," 262.

24. Tylor, *Researches into the Early History*, 262. In *Anahuac*, Tylor describes *barbacoa* as "a native Haitian word" (335).

25. Gray, "Captivating Animals," 522.

26. Elie, *Smokestack Lightning*, 86.

27. Hulme, *Colonial Encounters*, 16–17.

28. Purchas, *Purchas his pilgrims*, 1534.

29. Hakluyt, *Discovery and Conquest of Terra Florida*, 39–41, emphasis added.

30. Shubert, *Death and Money in the Afternoon*, 7.

31. Walcott, "Muse of History," 40–41.

32. Warnes, *Hunger Overcome?*, 42–44.

33. Stedman, *Narrative, of a five years' expedition*, 114–15.

34. Sollors, "Introduction," xx.

35. Petersen, "Taino, Island Carib, and Prehistoric Amerindian Economies," 129.

36. See Hickeringill, *Jamaica Viewed*, 7. *Wild Majesty*, Peter Hulme and Neil Whitehead's definitive anthology of writings on the Caribs, offers no basis for Marvin Harris's assertion, stated in *Cannibals and Kings*, that "barbecue . . . comes from the

Carib word babricot" and from the first referred to their "cannibal feasts" (132). *Wild Majesty* demonstrates that colonial attacks on the Caribs were likelier to emphasize the rawness of their cannibal victims. Fire, when mentioned, tends to encourage colonial commentators to lapse into biblical rhetoric rather than to parrot indigenous words. Far more compelling evidence seems to surround the Carib derivation of the word *tamale*. Interestingly, in Hulme and Whitehead's collection, the word *barbecue* is first used in reference to Carib culture in a 1941 description by Yorkshire anthropologist Douglas Taylor; see *Wild Majesty*, 308.

37. Hillhouse, "Notes on the Indians of British Guiana," 230.

38. Jameson, *Late Marxism*, 104.

39. Hickeringill to Ralph Thoresby, 31 May 1702, in *Letters of Eminent Men*, 2:13.

40. The phrase "odor memory" appears in Orlando Patterson's intriguing discussion of lynching in the Jim Crow South, "Rituals of Blood," 127.

41. Hickeringill, *Mushroom*, 6.

42. Erikson, *Wayward Puritans*, 158.

43. Carlton, *Going to the Wars*, 257.

44. E. Morgan, "Making Use of a New World," 13.

45. Hulton, "John White's Publisher," 17.

46. J. Morgan, "'Some Could Suckle over Their Shoulder,'" 173–75.

47. Schneider, "Reading for Indian Resistance," 169.

48. Hans Stade utters this phrase during his capture by "the wild tribes" of eastern Brazil (*Captivity of Hans Stade*, 59).

49. Vaughn, *Roots of American Racism*, 36.

50. The list of U.S. writers for whom barbecue has seemed the obvious way to prepare cannibal foods is long and growing. Half-human Brer Fox threatens to "bobbycue" Brer Rabbit before resolving to cast him in the briar patch in J. C. Harris, *Uncle Remus*, 53; his threat in fact inspires an extended cartoon sequence in Walt Disney's *Song of the South* (1946). *Moby-Dick*, meanwhile, like the National Museum of the American Indian, seems to see through *barbecue*'s veneer of native authenticity; the fact that the cannibal "barbecues" of Polynesia only give Queequeg "dyspepsia" certainly suggests a wry knowingness on Melville's part. See *Moby-Dick*, 95. It is possible that Robert Louis Stevenson first heard of barbecue during his journey around California in 1879. But it is also possible that he read it before he heard it, in the pages of *Moby-Dick*. Long John Silver's possession of a pegleg could be Stevenson's nod to Ahab, while the conjunction of his barbaric nickname with his slippery racial status—he ends the novel seemingly reunited with "his old negress"—certainly seems thoroughly Melvillean. See *Treasure Island*, 52. Space is limited here, but it would worth reflecting further on William Faulkner's decision to describe Joanna Burden's murder as an "emotional barbecue" in *Light in August*, 217, and to ponder the tangle of associations that leads Cormac McCarthy to associate cavemen and dynamite with the fear of getting "barbycued" in *Orchard Keeper*, 141.

51. Sayre, *Les sauvages américains*, ix.

52. Jantz, "Images of America in the German Renaissance," 98.

53. Ibid., 98–100.

54. Greene, "Petrachism among the Discourses of Imperialism," 154.

Chapter Two. London Broil

1. Dyer, *White*, 75.

2. Mullen, "Optic White," 74.

3. Ellison, "Change the Joke and Slip the Yoke," 53.

4. J. Roberts, "'Hidden right out in the Open,'" 125.

5. As Bauman puts it, it is the "presence of the stranger, of a stranger conspiring to trespass, to break in and invade, that makes the gate tangible." See *Life in Fragments*, 136.

6. Hechter, *Internal Colonialism*, xxix.

7. Deloria, *Playing Indian*, 37.

8. Hickeringill elsewhere refers to "the poor silly *Indians* . . . that are but just one degree (if they be so much) remov'd from a Monkey"; see *The Ceremony-Monger*, in *Works*, 2:377–543 (446).

9. Hill, *Reformation to Industrial Revolution*, 124.

10. J. L. C. McNulty, "Edmund Hickeringill" in *Oxford Dictionary of National Biography*, 27:1–4.

11. Mintz, *Sweetness and Power*, 61.

12. Hill, *Century of Revolution*, 199.

13. Cressy, *Bonfires and Bells*, 175.

14. Ibid., 87.

15. Dillon, "Republican Theatricality," 555.

16. Behn, *Widdow Ranter*, 288. As Edmund S. Morgan has shown, Virginians began to plant orchards in earnest in the mid-seventeenth century; and by the time of Bacon's Rebellion apparently valued fermented cider not for its intoxicating effects but because, unlike a water supply vulnerable to infection, it was generally safe for human consumption. *American Slavery, American Freedom*, 183.

17. Quoted in E. Morgan, *American Slavery, American Freedom*, 259.

18. Hakluyt, *Discovery and Conquest of Terra Florida*, 24, and Bridenbaugh and Bridenbaugh, *No Peace Beyond the Line*, 420.

19. J. W. Harris, *Making of the American South*, 23.

20. Wallace, *Premodern Places*, 241.

21. Mintz, *Sweetness and Power*, 141.

22. Wilson, "Ideal Meals and Their Menus," 110.

23. Pope, *Works*, 3:325.

24. Rogers, *Grub Street*, 24.

25. Ibid., 37.

26. Fairer, *English Poetry of the Eighteenth Century*, 32.

27. See Witt's discussion of the "twinned responses of attraction and repulsion that a mention of soul food often seems to arouse," *Black Hunger*, 86.

28. Rogers, *Grub Street*, 39.

29. E. Ward, "The Humours of a Coffee-House: A Comedy," in *Collection*, 2:349.

30. E. Ward, "A trip to Jamaica," in *Collection*, 2:168.

31. Pope, *The Dunciad*, in *Works*, 3:75–279 (111).

32. Ackroyd, *London*, 692.

33. Robert J. Allen, for example, upbraids Ward's *Secret history of clubs* (1707) for obscuring "the facts concerning both the origins and the nature of the Kit-Cat society." Although Allen sniffily points out that Ward wanted "to amuse a group of readers whose stomachs were strong enough for anything by administering certain perfunctory thrusts at the depravities of low life, rather than to depict genuine London brotherhoods," the fact remains that *The Barbacue Feast* is full of details, specifying ticket prices as well as the date of the event, even as it looks back to a feast plausibly encountered at New Dock. See Allen, *Clubs of Augustan London*, 186.

34. *Midsummer Moon*: In England during Ward's lifetime the summer solstice was "venerated in the church calendar as the Nativity of St John the Baptist"; a month perhaps seemed a respectable interval before holding this raucous and ribald barbecue. See Cressy, *Bonfires and Bells*, 25. *Rotherhitheans*: People from nearby Rotherhithe, another town on the south bank of the Thames. Like Southwark, Bermondsey, Deptford, and Greenwich, Rotherhithe had long been dominated by the sea; a century earlier, Christopher Jones, commanding officer of the *Mayflower*, kept a house in the town. *Kill-Devil-Punch*: The English began calling rum Kill-Devil by the mid-seventeenth century. The derivation arose as "a man who imbibed it promptly became boisterous, reckless and daring" (Bridenbaugh and Bridenbaugh, *No Peace beyond the Line*, 92). *Rum*: Like Columbus's decision to name Caribbean chili after Asian pepper, Ward's description of rum as a kind of "punch" here knits ideas about America and the Orient together. Such interknitting also occurs in contemporary accounts of the Mohocks, who many at the time said were marauding around London after dark. *Train oil* was made from the blubber of a whale.

35. Derived from the waterproofs that they wore at sea, *Tarpaulins*, like its abbreviated form *Tars*, refers to common sailors.

36. Unlike other settlements mentioned by Ward, *Peckham* lies a few miles south of the Thames, and the society's decision to hold its feast on this common land thus befits its hopes of assimilating barbecue into English life. The fact that Surrey and Sussex drovers heading for London's Smithfield Market still liked to pause for refreshment at Peckham's inns further suggests that the town is a fitting venue for the feast.

37. *Hoggard*: The Barbacue Society had good reason to call this *Hoggard* "brother" and otherwise do what it could to keep on the right side of him. Hoggards and drovers "were inclined to have fun stampeding cattle on the way to market; tormented beasts took refuge in shops and houses. (This is probably the origin of the phrase 'a bull in a china shop.')" See Weinreb and Hibbert, *London Encyclopaedia*, 812–13.

38. Then a familiar term for contrariness, the origins of *cross-grain'd* in carpentry arguably help associate the Hoggard further with an agrarian and artisan England, an England very different to the civilized thoroughfares and squares into which he is about to lead his doomed pigs.

39. "Shrove Tuesday, the day before Lent begins in the Christian calendar, "was Pancake day, and is still so called in some parts of England. . . . London apprentices were notorious for their riotous behavior at Shrovetide, which usually took the form of harassment of presumed prostitutes and attacks against the . . . brothels" (Cressy, *Bonfires and Bells*, 18). St. *Bartholomew's* Revels: Scene of the annual Bartholomew Fair, and envisioned in Ben Jonson's play of that name as a kind of microcosm of London in all its dirt and vitality, Smithfield Market was and remains the city's largest meat market. Efforts to civilize Smithfield began as early as the 1630s; their success can be gauged from the "hideous and discordant din" and "squalid" and "dirty figures" that Dickens would emphasize in *Oliver Twist* as late as 1837 (202). No doubt Smithfield's persisting wildness had something to do with its historic status as a place of spectacular and lynchlike execution. Scottish insurgent William Wallace was famously disembow-eled and decapitated at the market in 1305; for the next three centuries, many would suffer a similar fate.

40. This gastronomic alchemy, by which pigs eat but do not break down certain foods, instead allowing them to languish in their bellies to form instant (and disgust-ing) "hogs puddings," carries important echoes. One such is the long English tradition of distributing meat to the poor, which was carried on in early New England (see Cressy, *Bonfires and Bells*, 205). Arguably, however, in the sheer squalor of its magic, Ward's conceit also echoes the particularly noisome anti-Catholic antics of November 1677, in which a London mob paraded "a most costly" effigy of the pope, "his belly filled with live cats who squalled most hideously as soon as they felt the fire" (letter of Charles Hatton qtd. in Cressy, *Bonfires and Bells*, 177).

41. Introduced to English audiences by Samuel Purchas and John Smith, *sagamoor* was a corrupted version of the Penobscot term for leader, being universalized by Ward's lifetime to refer to the chief of any Amerindian people.

42. *The Barbacue Feast*'s description of the apothecary as a Galenist fits with its gentle mocking of his verbal diarrhea and unnecessary complication of a mode of cooking that is, lest we forget, meant to be savage. Since the 1680s improved "scientific understanding of the body" had made Galen's classical Greek ideas seem "empty and barren" (Porter, *Flesh in the Age of Reason*, 54). Ward remains unclear about the age of the pigs throughout *The Barbacue Feast*. Members of the Barbacue Society alternately call these animals *shoats* (young and recently weaned piglets), *pigs* (slightly older speci-mens), and *hogs* (sexually mature specimens over five months in age). See Davidson, "Pig" in *The Penguin Companion to Food*, 727.

43. *Pettitoes*: pig's feet. The word, a compression of *petit* and *toes*, refers in jest to human's feet in Shakespeare, *A Winter's Tale*, 4.4.677.

44. St. *George's* Dragon: England's acquisition of St. George as its patron saint amounts to another invented tradition. "The tale of the saint's battle with and success over the legendary dragon . . . captured the imagination of English people during the Middle Ages and gained official status as a feast of the Church in 1415. . . . Despite the high esteem in which the saint was held, the feast . . . was eliminated from the . . .

calendar during the Reformation as the worship of saints came under attack from Protestant reformers" (McClendon, "Moveable Feast," 4).

45. Swine which the Devil had pickled in Salt Water: Given *The Barbacue Feast*'s incessant personification of Peckham's hapless pigs, it is unsurprising to find Ward alluding to the incident in the Book of Matthew, in which two men "possessed with devils" harangue Jesus only to be dispatched into a "herd of swine" who run "violently down a steep place into the sea, and perish . . . in the waters" (Matt. 8.30–31).

46. To change their Colour: The "Indian manipulation of skin color" almost straightaway preoccupied William Strachey and other early English observers of the New World. Fascinating to some and troubling to others, face painting formed a particularly vexing counterpoint to the talcum, powders, and oils of English aristocratic ladies. See Kupperman "Presentment of Civility," 208–9.

47. Key, "Political Culture and Political Rhetoric of County Feasts and Sermons," 242.

48. Arditi, *Genealogy of Manners*, 174.

49. Winstanley, "True Levellers' Standard Advanced," 77.

50. Winstanley, "An Appeal to the House of Commons," 120.

51. Starkey, *European and Native American Warfare*, 54.

52. E. Morgan, *American Slavery, American Freedom*, 328.

53. Ashton, *Social Life in the Reign of Queen Anne*, 221–22.

54. Gidley, "*Representing Others*: An Introduction," 9.

55. H. Roberts, *Downhearth to Bar Grate*, 6.

56. E. Morgan, *American Slavery, American Freedom*, 404.

57. Feild, *Irons in the Fire*, 41.

58. Day, "From Murrell to Jarrin," 105–6.

59. Hinderaker, "Four 'Indian Kings,'" 518.

60. Ibid., 524.

61. Steele, in Addison et al., *Spectator* 324 (12 March 1712), 3:186–90.

62. Hinderaker, "Four 'Indian Kings,'" 524.

63. Steele, in Addison et al., *Spectator* 324 (12 March 1712), 3:186–90.

64. Budgell, "The Manifesto of Taw Waw Eben Zan Kaladar, Emperor of the Mohocks," in Addison et al., *Spectator* 347 (8 April 1712) 3:295–97 (296).

65. Steele, in Addison et al., *Spectator* 324 (12 March 1712), 3:186–90.

66. Dabydeen, *Hogarth's Blacks*, 34.

67. Ibid., 18.

68. Hill, *Century of Revolution*, 311. An exception to this, though one whose idiosyncrasies rather proves the rule, is Garry Wills, *Cincinnatus*.

69. Cannadine, *Class in Britain*, 35.

70. Similarly, Gordon Wood's desire to celebrate the American Revolution for creating, "almost overnight, the most liberal . . . and the most modern people in the world" tends to explain his reluctance to allow the English Revolutions of the previous century a full or objective reckoning (*Radicalism of the American Revolution*, 7).

71. Ellison, "Change the Joke," 53.

72. DuBois writes: "It must be remembered that the white group of laborers, while they received a low wage, were compensated in part by a sort of public and psychological wage. They were given public deference and titles of courtesy because they were white. They were admitted freely with all classes of white people to public functions, public parks, and the best schools. . . . Their vote selected public officials, and while this had small effect upon the economic situation, it had great effect upon their personal treatment and the deference shown them. . . . Thus every problem of labor advance in the South was skillfully turned by demagogues into a matter of inter-racial jealousy" (*Black Reconstruction in America*, 700–701).

Chapter Three. Pit Barbecue Present and Past

1. Reed, "Barbecue Sociology," 78.

2. Mintz, *Tasting Food, Tasting Freedom*, 97–98.

3. Reed, "Barbecue Sociology," 80–81.

4. Scarborough, *On the Trail of Negro Folk-songs*, 128, 264. Richard Middleton provides a good overview of such white attitudes in "O Brother, Let's Go Down Home."

5. Litwack, *Trouble in Mind*, 317–18.

6. Jakle and Sculle suggest that McDonald's among other chains took its first real steps toward its present status as a "super-corporation" during the 1960s, its gross profit soaring from $37 million in 1960 to $226 million in 1967. See *Fast Food*, 141.

7. S. Smith, "Rhetoric of Barbecue," 62.

8. Staten, "Real Barbecue Revisited," 139.

9. Garner, *North Carolina Barbecue*, 26.

10. McCarthy, *Orchard Keeper*, 177.

11. This is not a verbatim quote but Bob Garner's recording from a conference paper that Allen Pridgen had not yet placed for publication. See Garner, *North Carolina Barbecue*, 17.

12. Hamilton to James A. Bayard, 16 June 1801, in Hamilton, *Papers*, 25:319–24.

13. See, for example, list of baggage shipped by Jefferson from France, 1 Sept. 1789, in Jefferson, *Papers*, 15:375–77.

14. Brogan, *Penguin History of the United States of America*, 179.

15. Translation from Cox, "Spain and the Founding Fathers," 108. The original Spanish version appears in *Diary of Francisco de Miranda*, 1:5–6.

16. Jefferson to James Monroe, 18 Dec. 1786, in Jefferson, *Papers*, 10:611–13.

17. Cresswell, *Journal*, 30.

18. Porter, *Enlightenment*, 58.

19. Gilroy, *Between Camps*, 64.

20. Fite, "Oklahoma's Reconstruction League," 552–53.

21. Foucault, *Order of Things*, 151.

22. Jefferson to J. Reibelt, 12 Aug. 1807, in Jefferson, *Garden Book*, 351.

23. This concluding portion of the chapter revisits and develops further work that I originally published as "Barbecuing the Diaspora" in *Hunger Overcome?* 65–79; a tran-

sitional essay is "Guantánamo, Eatonville, Accompong: Barbecue and the Diaspora in the Writings of Zora Neale Hurston." Some phrases and references already occur in those earlier publications.

24. Shange, *If I Can Cook*, 65.

25. Hurston to Henry Allen Moe, 6 Jan. 1937, in Hurston, *Letters*, 391.

26. Gambrell, *Women Intellectuals, Modernism and Difference*, 14.

27. Hemenway, *Zora Neale Hurston*, 228–29.

28. Hurston, *Tell My Horse*, 58.

29. Gilroy, *Between Camps*, 234.

30. For imperial references to the barbecues attributed to the Maroons of northern Jamaica, see Nugent, *Journal*, 70; Dallas, *History of the Maroons*, 90–91; and Lewis, *Journal of a West Indian Proprietor*, 92.

31. Long, *History of Jamaica*, 1:429.

32. D. Douglas, *Reading, Writing, and Race*, 29.

33. Peebles-Wilkins, "Reactions of Segments of the Black Community," 114.

34. "John Hemmer."

35. Carney, *Black Rice*, 163.

36. Mintz, "Groups, Group Boundaries and the Perception of 'Race,'" 437.

37. Mintz and Price, *Birth of African-American Culture*, 46–47.

38. See Gilroy, *Between Camps*, 54–96.

39. Mintz, "Enduring Substances, Trying Theories," 295–96.

40. Deleuze and Guattari, *Thousand Plateaus*, 17.

41. Gilroy, *Between Camps*, 123–25. Bill Ashcroft offers a troubled analysis of how imperial power can operate rhizomatically, suggesting that the "institutions of metropolitan 'centres' may have the *appearance* of tap roots plunging deep into the colonial earth, but this is only appearance. The *rhizomic* nature of imperialism might be likened more to a laterally spreading parasite. It is rhizomic because it has interlinked centres everywhere, but it *appears* monolithic because underlying all of these centres is a consensus about its vertical structure. . . . Once we understand this we see that certain ways of talking about post-colonial or resistance discourse have fallen into a very deep trap set for them. For if we see imperialism as monolithic, then its resistance becomes polarised. We then fall into all kinds of egregious binarisms" ("Rhizome of Post-Colonial Discourse," 118–19).

42. Hemenway, *Zora Neale Hurston*, 277.

43. Walker, "Zora Neale Hurston," 91.

44. Hurston, *Dust Tracks*, 285–86.

Chapter Four. Barbecue between the Lines

1. Fanon, *Wretched of the Earth*, 30.

2. Pearce, *Savagism and Civilization*, 24–25.

3. For a landmark account of Jacksonian savagism, see Rogin, *Fathers and Children*, 125. For Richard Slotkin's idea of regeneration through violence, see *Fatal Environment*, 374–75.

4. Pearce, *Savagism and Civilization*, 167.

5. Christoph de Graffenried, "De Graffenried's Manuscript," in Clark, *Colonial Records of North Carolina* (hereafter *CRNC*), 1:905–84, see p. 926.

6. Ibid., 926.

7. President and council of North Carolina to Colonel Spotswood, 29 June 1711, in *CRNC*, 1:760.

8. Pliny the Elder describes the "Scythian tribes . . . which eat human flesh" and tells us that "very recently, it was the custom of tribes beyond the Alps to practice human sacrifice, which is only one step removed from cannibalism" in *Elder Pliny on the Human Animal*, 61. In the same volume Beagon observes that "severe cultural anomalies such as cannibalism tended to place their practitioners on the very edge of the world," 123.

9. Cooper and Terrill, *American South*, 63.

10. Gale to North Carolina Council, 2 Nov. 1711, in *CRNC*, 1:825.

11. Vaughn, *Roots of American Racism*, 21–23.

12. In particular, the rhetorical movement that leads Gale from his catalogue of abomination to his demand for military vengeance recalls the Book of Jeremiah. His voice echoes that of this book's righteous and wrathful God, and of especially apocalyptic visions such as the following: "And first I will recompense their iniquity and their sin double; because they have defiled my land, they have filled mine inheritance with the carcases of their detestable and abominable things" (Jer. 16.18). Sacvan Bercovitch, *American Jeremiad* remains the seminal study of Jeremiah's importance to the formation of colonial and Republican American culture.

13. Gale to North Carolina Council, 2 Nov. 1711, in *CRNC*, 1:826.

14. Bloom, "The Anxiety of Influence," 1804.

15. Mather to Daniel Williams, ? June 1715, in *Diary of Cotton Mather* 2:316.

16. Mather to Robert Wodrow, 17 July 1715, in Wodrow, *Correspondence*, 2:149–50.

17. Marambaud, *William Byrd*, 254. As Gordon S. Wood observes in *Radicalism of the American Revolution*, the fact that Byrd could be seen "blithely" eating "the corn pone served to slaves" could seem to confirm this tolerant reputation (42).

18. Mencken, "Sound and Fury," 196–97.

19. The 1916 lynching of Jesse Washington at Waco, Texas, produced a particularly notorious example of this cannibal analogy. Joe Myers, a car mechanic in the town, bought one of the commemorative postcards showing Washington's charred and mangled corpse, and signed on the back of it a message for his father: "This is the barbecue we had last night" (Allen, *Without Sanctuary*, 83). Not unsurprisingly, dominant American culture has long remained silent about such shocking analogies; but African American writers have seized upon them and have used to frame their fictions of dissent. Baleful allusions to such analogies thus occur, for example, in Ralph Ellison's "A Party Down at the Square," in *Flying Home*, 3–11. Other invocations of this barbecue analogy, both by white supremacist aggressors and their racial targets, are not hard to come by.

20. Cox, "Spain and the Founding Fathers," 108.

21. Rogin, *Fathers and Children*, 119.

22. Smith-Rosenberg's excellent article shows that Crockett's dream in the 1837 *Almanac* of "swallowing a nigger whole without choking" is no isolated incident but a key part of his public cultivation of an image of über-Jacksonian savagism ("Davey Crockett as Trickster," 335–39).

23. References to Crockett's down-home prewar barbecues appear in W. Davis, *Three Roads to the Alamo*, 408.

24. Jackson to Rachel Jackson, 29 Dec. 1813, in Jackson, *Correspondence*, 1:416.

25. Jackson to Andrew J. Donelson, 5 July 1822, in ibid., 3:167.

26. Rogin, *Fathers and Children*, 134.

27. Jackson, General Orders 24 March 1814 [?], in Jackson, *Correspondence*, 1:486–87.

28. Jackson to Thomas Pinckney, 17 Feb. 1814, in ibid., 1:465.

29. Quoted in Watkins, "James Kirke Paulding and the South," 222.

30. Green, "Listen to the Eagle Scream," 124–25.

31. James, *Andrew Jackson*, 32.

32. Peter B. Porter to Henry Clay, 26 Oct. 1827, in Clay, *Papers*, 6:1189–90.

33. Thomas, *Pursuit of the White House*, 18.

34. Remini, *Andrew Jackson and the Course of American Freedom*, 131.

35. Sydnor, *Gentlemen Freeholders*, 184.

36. Dupre, "Barbecues and Pledges," 492–93, quoted from Huntsville *Democrat*, 9 May 1833.

37. Dupre, "Barbecues and Pledges," 492, quoted from Huntsville *Southern Advocate*, 10 Aug. 1827.

38. Dupre, "Ambivalent Capitalists on the Cotton Frontier," 233, quoted from Huntsville *Democrat*, 26 June 1829.

39. Dupre, "Barbecues and Pledges," 492–93, quoted from Huntsville *Southern Advocate*, 13 July 1827.

40. Dupre, "Barbecues and Pledges," 490, quoted from ibid., 10 Oct. 1827.

41. Dupre, "Barbecues and Pledges," 498.

42. Elkins and McKitrick, "Meaning for Turner's Frontier," 577.

43. DuBois, *Black Reconstruction in America*, 700.

44. Lévi-Strauss, "Culinary Triangle," 29.

45. Wyeth, *With Sabre and Scalpel*, 60.

46. Hartley, *Life of Daniel Boone*, 270.

47. Ogg, *Reign of Andrew Jackson*, 115.

48. Jackson to Samuel Swartwout, 5 March 1825, in Jackson, *Correspondence*, 3:280–81.

49. McLellan, *Joseph Story and the American Constitution*, 44.

50. Webster to Achsah Pollard Webster, 4 March 1829, in Webster, *Papers*, 2:405.

51. Hamilton to Martin Van Buren, 5 March 1829, in Van Buren, *Papers*.

BIBLIOGRAPHY

Ackroyd, Peter. *London: The Biography.* London: Chatto and Windus, 2000.

Adair, James. *The History of the American Indians: Particularly those Nations adjoining to the Mississippi, East and West Florida, Georgia, South and North Carolina, and Virginia.* New York: Johnson Reprint, 1968.

Addison, Joseph. *Cato, a tragedy.* Dublin: Peter Wilson, 1750. Accessed 1 July 2007 via Eighteenth Century Collections Online, http://www.gale.com/eighteenth century/.

———. "The Manifesto of Taw Waw Eben Zan Kaladar, Emperor of the Mohocks." In *The Spectator, with illustrative notes,* 295–97. London: Geo Cawthorn, 1799.

———. "Of the Mohocks: *The Spectator,* 12 March 1712." In *The Spectator, with illustrative notes,* 167–69.

Addison, Joseph, and Richard Steele, et al. *The Spectator.* 5 vols. Edited by Donald F. Bond. Oxford: Clarendon Press, 1965.

Allen, James, [ed.] *Without Sanctuary: Lynching Photography in America.* Santa Fe, N.M.: Twin Palms, 2000.

Allen, Robert J. *The Clubs of Augustan London.* Cambridge, Mass.: Harvard University Press, 1933.

Arditi, Jorge. *A Genealogy of Manners: Transformations of Social Relations in France and England from the Fourteenth to the Eighteenth Century.* Chicago: University of Chicago Press, 1998.

Ashcroft, Bill. "The Rhizome of Post-Colonial Discourse." In *Literature and the Contemporary: Fictions and Theories of the Present,* edited by Roger Luckhurst and Peter Marks, 111–25. Harlow, U.K.: Longman, 1999.

Ashton, John. *Social Life in the Reign of Queen Anne: Taken from Original Source.* London: Chatto and Windus, 1929.

Bailey, Nathan. *Dictionarium Domesticum, being a new and compleat houshold dictionary. For the use both of city and country* . . . London: C. Hitch and C. Davis, 1736. Accessed 6 July 2007 via Eighteenth Century Collections Online, http://www.gale.com/eighteenthcentury/.

Bauman, Zygmunt. *Life in Fragments: Essays in Postmodern Morality.* Oxford: Blackwell, 1995.

———. *Wasted Lives: Modernity and its Outcasts.* London: Polity, 2004.

Behn, Aphra. *The Widdow Ranter*. In Aphra Behn, *Oroonoko, The Rover, and Other Works*, edited by Janet Todd, 249–328. London: Penguin, 2003.

Bercovitch, Sacvan. *The American Jeremiad*. Madison: University of Wisconsin Press, 1978.

Berkhofer, Robert F. *The White Man's Indian: Images of the American Indian, from Columbus to the Present*. New York: Vintage, 1979.

Bernáldez, Andrés. "History of the Catholic Sovereigns Don Ferdinand and Doña Isabella, Chapters 123–31." In *Select Documents Illustrating the Four Voyages of Columbus: Including those contained in R. H. Major's Select Letters of Christopher Columbus*, translated by Cecil Jane, 114–68. London: Hakluyt Society, 1930.

Beverley, Robert. *The History and Present State of Virginia*. Edited by Louis B. Wright. Charlottesville, Va.: Dominia, 1968.

Bhabha, Homi K. *The Location of Culture*. London: Routledge, 1994.

Bird, S. Elizabeth, ed. *Dressing in Feathers: The Construction of the Indian in American Popular Culture*. Boulder, Colo.: Westview, 1996.

Bloom, Harold. "The Anxiety of Influence." In *The Norton Anthology of Theory and Criticism*, edited by Vincent B. Leitch, 1797–805. New York: Norton, 2001.

Brickell, John. *The natural history of North-Carolina. With an account of the trade, manners, and customs, of the Christian and Indian inhabitants. Strange beasts, birds, fishes, snakes, insects, trees, and plants, &c*. London: Charles Corbett, 1743. Accessed 6 July 2007 via Eighteenth Century Collections Online, http://www.gale.com/eighteenthcentury/.

Bridenbaugh, Carl, and Robert Bridenbaugh. *No Peace Beyond the Line: The English in the Caribbean, 1624–1690*. New York: Oxford University Press, 1972.

Brillat-Savarin, Jean Anthelme. *The Physiology of Taste*, translated by Anne Drayton. London: Penguin, 1994.

Brogan, Hugh. *The Penguin History of the United States of America*. Harmondsworth, U.K.: Penguin, 1990.

Brown, Sterling A. *The Collected Poems of Sterling A. Brown*. Edited by Michael S. Harper. Evanston, Ill.: Triquarterly, 1996.

Bucher, Bernadette. *Icon and Conquest: A Structural Analysis of the Illustrations of de Bry's Great Voyages*, translated by Basia Miller Gulati. Chicago: University of Chicago Press, 1981.

Burns, Ken, "Preface." In G. Ward, *Jazz*, vii–x.

Byrd, William. *History of the Dividing Line betwixt Virginia and North Carolina Run in the Year of Our Lord 1728*. In *The Prose Works of William Byrd of Westover: Narratives of a Colonial Virginian*, edited by Louis B. Wright, 157–338. Cambridge, Mass.: Belknap Press of Harvard University Press, 1966.

Calloway, Colin G. *New Worlds for All: Indians, Europeans and the Remaking of Early America*. Baltimore: Johns Hopkins University Press, 1997.

Cannadine, David. *Class in Britain*. London: Penguin, 2000.

Carlton, Charles. *Going to the Wars: the Experience of the British Civil Wars, 1638–1651*. London: Routledge, 1992.

Carney, Judith A. *Black Rice: The African Origins of Rice Cultivation in the Americas.* Cambridge, Mass.: Harvard University Press, 2001.

Castillo, Susan. *Colonial Encounters in New World Writing, 1500–1786: Performing America.* London: Routledge, 2006.

Castillo, Susan, and Ivy Schweitzer, eds. *A Companion to the Literatures of Colonial America.* Malden, Mass.: Blackwell, 2005.

Clark, Walker, ed. *The Colonial Records of North Carolina.* 10 vols. New York: AMS, 1968.

Clay, Henry. *The Papers of Henry Clay.* 10 vols. Edited by James F. Hopkins and Mary V. M. Hargreaves. Lexington: University of Kentucky Press, 1972.

Colley, Linda. *Britons: Forging the Nation 1707–1837.* New Haven: Yale University Press, 2005.

Columbus, Christopher. *Journal of the First Voyage (Diario del primer viaje),* translated by B. W. Ife. Warminster, U.K.: Aris and Philips, 1990.

Cooper, William J., Jr., and Thomas E. Terrill. *The American South: A History.* New York: McGraw-Hill, 2002.

Cox, R. Merritt. "Spain and the Founding Fathers." *Modern Language Journal* 60, no. 3 (1976): 101–9.

Cresswell, Nicholas. *The Journal of Nicholas Cresswell, 1774–1777.* New York: Dial Press, 1924. Accessed 27 Nov. 2006 via Library of Congress Digital Collections, http://memory.loc.gov/.

Cressy, David. *Bonfires and Bells: National Memory and the Protestant Calendar in Elizabethan and Stuart England.* Stroud, U.K.: Sutton, 2004.

Dabydeen, David. *Hogarth's Blacks: Images of Blacks in Eighteenth Century English Art.* Mundelstrup, Denmark: Dangaroo, 1985.

Dallas, R. C. *The History of the Maroons: From Their Origin to the Establishment of their Chief Tribe at Sierra Leone, Including the Expedition to Cuba for the Purpose of Procuring Spanish Chasseurs and the State of the Island of Jamaica for the Last Ten Years, with a Succinct History of the Island Previous to that Period.* London: Cass, 1968.

Dampier, William. *A New Voyage round the World, describing particularly the Isthmus of America.* London: James Knapton, 1698.

Davidson, Alan. *The Penguin Companion to Food.* London: Penguin, 2002.

Davis, Rebecca Harding. *Dallas Galbraith.* Philadelphia: J. B. Lippincott, 1868. Accessed 9 Jan. 2007 via Making of America Books, http://www.hti.umich .edu/m/moagrp/.

Davis, William C. *Three Roads to the Alamo: The Lives and Fortunes of David Crockett, James Bowie, and William Barret Travis.* New York: Harper Perennial, 1998.

Day, Ivan. "From Murrell to Jarrin: Illustrations in British Cookery Books, 1621– 1820." In *The English Cookery Book: Historical Essays,* edited by Eileen White, 98–150. Totnes, U.K.: Prospect, 2004.

Defoe, Daniel. *Moll Flanders.* London: Penguin, 1989.

———. *Robinson Crusoe.* London: Penguin, 1985.

Deleuze, Gilles, and Félix Guattari. *A Thousand Plateaus: Capitalism and Schizophrenia*, translated by Brian Massumi. London: Continuum, 2004.

Deloria, Philip J. *Playing Indian*. New Haven: Yale University Press, 1998.

Dickens, Charles. *Oliver Twist*. Hammondsworth, U.K.: Penguin, 1985.

Diehl, Daniel, and Mark Donnelly. *Eat Thy Neighbour: A History of Cannibalism*. Stroud, U.K.: Sutton, 2006.

Dillon, Elizabeth Maddock. "Republican Theatricality and Transatlantic Empire." In Castillo and Schweitzer, *Companion to the Literatures of Colonial America*, 551–66.

Douglas, Davison M. *Reading, Writing, and Race: The Desegregation of the Charlotte Schools*. Chapel Hill: University of North Carolina Press, 1995.

Douglas, Mary. *Purity and Danger: An Analysis of Concepts of Pollution and Taboos*. London: Routledge, 2006.

DuBois, W. E. B. *Black Reconstruction in America: An Essay Toward a History of the Part Which Black Folk Played in the Attempt to Reconstruct Democracy in America, 1860–1880*. London: Cass, 1966.

Dudley, David. "Taking the Low Slow Road to Perfect Barbecue." *Baltimore*, July 2000.

Dupre, Daniel. "Ambivalent Capitalists on the Cotton Frontier: Settlement and Development in the Tennessee Valley of Alabama." *Journal of Southern History* 56, no. 2 (1990): 215–40.

———. "Barbecues and Pledges: Electioneering and the Rise of Democratic Politics in Antebellum Alabama." *Journal of Southern History* 60, no. 3 (1994): 479–512.

Dyer, Richard. *White*. London: Routledge, 1997.

Elias, Norbert. *The Civilizing Process: The History of Manners and State Formation and Civilization*, translated by Edward Jephcott. Oxford: Blackwell, 1994.

Elie, Lolis Eric, ed. *Cornbread Nation 2: The United States of Barbecue*. Chapel Hill: University of North Carolina Press, 2004.

———. *Smokestack Lightning: Adventures in the Heart of Barbecue Country*. New York: Farrar, Straus and Giroux, 1996.

Elkins, Stanley, and Eric McKitrick. "A Meaning for Turner's Frontier: Part II: The Southwest Frontier and New England." *Political Science Quarterly* 69, no. 4 (1954): 565–602.

Ellison, Ralph. "Change the Joke and Slip the Yoke." In *Shadow and Act*, 45–60. London: Secker and Warburg, 1967.

———. *Flying Home and Other Stories*. London: Penguin, 1998.

———. *Invisible Man*. Harmondsworth, U.K.: Penguin, 1965.

Erikson, Kai T. *Wayward Puritans: A Study in the Sociology of Deviance*. New York: John Wiley, 1966.

Fairer, David. *English Poetry of the Eighteenth Century, 1700–1789*. London: Longman, 2003.

Fanon, Frantz. *The Wretched of the Earth*. London: Penguin, 1990.

Faulkner, William. *Light in August.* London: Vintage, 2000.

Federmann, Nikolas. *Belle et agréable narration du premier voyage de Nicolas Federmann le jeune, d'Ulm, aux indes de la mer océane, et de tout ce qui lui est arrivé dans ce pays Jusqu'a son retour en Espagne.* Paris: A. Bertrand, 1837. Accessed 1 July 2007 via Google Book Search, http://books.google.co.uk/.

Feild, Rachael. *Irons in the Fire: A History of Cooking Equipment.* Ramsbury, U.K.: Crowood, 1984.

Ferguson, Eve M. "The Smithsonian's Mitsitam Café." In *Global Rhythm: The Destination for World Music.* Accessed 30 Nov. 2006 at http://www.globalrhythm .net/Food/TheSmithsoniansMitsitamCaf.cfm.

Fernández-Armesto, Felipe. *Columbus.* Oxford: Oxford University Press, 1991.

———. *Food: A History.* London: Pan, 2001.

Fiddes, Nick. *Meat: A Natural Symbol.* London: Routledge, 1991.

Fite, Gilbert C. "Oklahoma's Reconstruction League: An Experiment in Farmer-Labor Politics." *Journal of Southern History* 13, no. 4 (1947): 535–55.

Flint, Valerie I. J. *The Imaginative Landscape of Christopher Columbus.* Princeton, N.J.: Princeton University Press, 1992.

Foucault, Michel. *The Order of Things: An Archaeology of the Human Sciences.* London: Routledge, 2004.

Gabaccia, Donna. *We Are What We Eat: Ethnic Food and the Making of Americans.* Cambridge, Mass.: Harvard University Press, 1998.

Gale, Christopher. "A Letter from Christopher Gale." In *The Colonial Records of North Carolina,* vol. 1, *1662 to 1712,* 825–26. New York: AMS, 1968.

Gambrell, Alice. *Women Intellectuals, Modernism, and Difference: Transatlantic Culture, 1919–1945.* Cambridge: Cambridge University Press, 1997.

Garner, Bob. *North Carolina Barbecue: Flavored by Time.* Winston-Salem, N.C.: John F. Blair, 1996.

Gidley, Mick, and Ben Gidley. "The Native-American South." In *A Companion to the Literature and Culture of the American South,* edited by Richard Gray and Owen Robinson, 166–85. Malden, Mass.: Blackwell, 2004.

———. "*Representing Others*: An Introduction." In *Representing Others: White Views of Indigenous People,* 1–13. Exeter: University of Exeter Press, 1992.

Giles, Paul. *Atlantic Republic: The American Tradition in English Literature.* Oxford: Oxford University Press, 2006.

———. "The Culture of Colonial America: Theology and Aesthetics." In Castillo and Schweitzer, *Companion to the Literatures of Colonial America,* 78–93.

Gilroy, Paul. *Between Camps: Nations, Cultures and the Allure of Race.* London: Penguin, 2004.

Glaisyer, Natasha. *The Culture of Commerce in England, 1660–1720.* London: Royal Historical Society, 2006.

Godden, Richard. *Fictions of Labor: William Faulkner and the South's Long Revolution.* Cambridge: Cambridge University Press, 1997.

Gray, Kathryn Napier. "Captivating Animals: Science and Spectacle in Early American Natural Histories." In Castillo and Schweitzer, *Companion to the Literatures of Colonial America*, 517–32.

Green, Fletcher M. "Listen to the Eagle Scream: One Hundred Years of the Fourth of July in North Carolina, 1776–1876." In *Democracy in the Old South, and Other Essays*, edited by J. Isaac Copeland, 111–56. Nashville, Tenn.: Vanderbilt University Press, 1969.

Greene, Roland. "Petrachism among the Discourses of Imperialism." In *America in European Consciousness, 1493–1750*, edited by Karen Ordahl Kupperman, 130–65. Chapel Hill: University of North Carolina Press, 1995.

Hakluyt, Richard. *The Discovery and Conquest of Terra Florida by Don Ferdinando de Soto, and Six Hundred Spaniards his Followers. Written by a Gentlemen of Elvas, Employed in All the Action, and Translated out of Portuguese, by Richard Hakluyt.* London: Hakluyt Society, 1851.

Hale, John. *The Civilization of Europe in the Renaissance.* London: Harper Perennial, 2005.

Hamilton, Alexander. *The Papers of Alexander Hamilton.* 27 vols. Edited by Harold C. Syrett and Jacob E. Cooke. New York: Columbia University Press, 1961–87.

Harris, Joel Chandler. *Uncle Remus: His Songs and His Sayings.* Edited by Robert Hemenway. Harmondsworth, U.K.: Penguin, 1986.

Harris, Marvin. *Cannibals and Kings.* London: Vintage, 1991.

Harris, J. William. *The Making of the American South: A Short History, 1500–1877.* Malden, Mass.: Blackwell, 2006.

Hartley, Cecil B. *Life of Daniel Boone, the great western hunter and pioneer, comprising an account of his early history, his daring and remarkable career as the first settler of Kentucky . . . By Cecil B. Hartley. To which is added his autobiography complete as dictated by himself.* Philadelphia: J. E. Potter, 1865.

Hazlitt, William. "On Londoners and Country People." In William Hazlitt, *The Plain Speaker: Opinions on Books, Men, and Things*, 86–105. London: George Bell, 1894.

Hechter, Michael. *Internal Colonialism: The Celtic Fringe in British National Development.* New Brunswick, N.J.: Transaction, 1999.

Hemenway, Robert. *Zora Neale Hurston: A Literary Biography.* Urbana: University of Illinois Press, 1977.

"John Hemmer." *New York Times*, 8 Oct. 1981, B10.

Hess, Karen. *The Carolina Rice Kitchen: The African Connection.* Columbia: University of South Carolina Press, 1992.

Hickeringill, Edmund. *Jamaica Viewed: with All the Ports, Harbours, and their Several Soundings, Towns, and Settlements.* London: John Williams, 1661.

———. *The mushroom, or, A satyr against libelling Tories and prelatical tantivies in answer to a satyr against sedition called The meddal, by the author of Absalom and Achitophel.* London: Fra. Smith, 1682. Accessed 1 July 2007 via Early English Books Online, http://eebo.chadwyck.com/home.

———. *The works of the Reverend Mr. Edm. Hickeringill, late rector of All-Saints, Colchester.* 2 vols. London: B. Bragge, 1709.

Hill, Christopher. *The Century of Revolution, 1603–1714.* London: Routledge, 2002.

———. *Reformation to Industrial Revolution: A Social and Economic History of Britain 1530–1780.* London: Weidenfeld and Nicolson, 1967.

Hillhouse, William. "Notes on the Indians of British Guiana." *Journal of the Royal Geographic Society* 2 (1832): 230.

Hinderaker, Eric. "The 'Four Indian Kings' and the Imaginative Construction of the First British Empire." *William and Mary Quarterly* 3, no. 3 (1996): 487–526.

Hobsbawm, Eric. "Introduction: Inventing Tradition." In Hobsbawm and Ranger, *Invention of Tradition*, 1–14.

———. "Mass-Producing Traditions: Europe, 1870–1914." In Hobsbawm and Ranger, *Invention of Tradition*, 263–307.

Hobsbawm, Eric, and Terence Ranger, eds. *The Invention of Tradition.* London: Cambridge University Press, 1983, 2005.

Hofstadter, Richard. "The Paranoid Style in American Politics." In *The Paranoid Style in American Politics and Other Essays*, 3–40. London: Jonathan Cape, 1966.

Hudson, Charles. "The Hernando de Soto Expedition." In *The Forgotten Centuries: Indians and Europeans in the American South*, edited by Charles Hudson and Carmen Chaves Tesser, 74–103. Athens: University of Georgia Press, 1994.

Hulme, Peter. *Colonial Encounters: Europe and the Native Caribbean 1492–1797.* London: Routledge, 1992.

Hulme, Peter, and Neil L. Whitehead, eds. *Wild Majesty: Encounters with Caribs from Columbus to the Present Day.* Oxford: Clarendon Press, 1992.

Hulton, Paul. "John White's Publisher, Theodor de Bry." In *America 1585: The Complete Drawings of John White*, edited by Paul Hulton, 17–19. Charlotte: University of North Carolina Press, 1984.

Hurston, Zora Neale. "Cudjo's Own Story of the Last African Slaver." *Journal of Negro History* 12, no. 4 (1927): 648–63.

———. *Dust Tracks on a Road: An Autobiography.* London: Virago, 1986.

———. *Tell My Horse: Voodoo and Life in Haiti and Jamaica.* New York: Harper Perennial, 1990.

———. *Their Eyes Were Watching God.* London: Virago, 1986.

———. *Zora Neale Hurston: A Life in Letters.* Edited by Carla Kaplan. New York: Doubleday, 2002.

Irving, Washington. *The Works of Washington Irving.* 12 vols. New York: Putnam, 1881.

Jackson, Andrew. *Correspondence of Andrew Jackson.* 7 vols. Edited by John S. Bassett. Washington, D.C.: Carnegie, 1926–35.

Jakle John A., and Keith A. Sculle. *Fast Food: Roadside Restaurants in the Automobile Age.* Baltimore: Johns Hopkins University Press, 1999.

James, Marquis. *Andrew Jackson: Portrait of a President.* Indianapolis: Bobbs-Merrill, 1937.

Jameson, Frederic. *Late Marxism.* London: Verso, 2007.

Jantz, Harold. "Images of America in the German Renaissance." In *First Images of America: The Impact of the New World on the Old*, edited by Michael J. B. Allen and Robert L. Benson, 91–106. Berkeley: University of California Press, 1976.

Jefferson, Thomas. *Notes on the State of Virginia*. Edited by William Peden. Chapel Hill: University of North Carolina Press, 1955.

———. *The Papers of Thomas Jefferson*. 29 vols. Edited by Julian P. Boyd, Charles T. Cullen, John Catanzariti, and Barbara B. Oberg. Princeton, N.J.: Princeton University Press, 1950.

———. *Thomas Jefferson's Garden Book, 1766–1824: With relevant extracts from his other writings*. Edited by Edwin Morris Betts. Philadelphia: American Philosophical Society, 1944.

Johnson, James H. "Versailles, Meet Les Halles: Masks, Carnival, and the French Revolution," *Representations* 73 (2001): 89–116.

Johnson, Samuel. *A Dictionary of the English Language: in which the words are deduced from their originals, and illustrated in their different significations by examples from the best writers. . . .* London: William Ball, 1838.

Jonson, Ben. *Bartholomew Fair*. In *Jonson: Four Comedies*, edited by Helen Ostovich, 537–688. London: Longman, 1997.

Key, Newton E. "The Political Culture and Political Rhetoric of County Feasts and Sermons, 1654–1714." *Journal of British Studies* 33, no. 3 (1994): 223–56.

Klein, Lawrence E. "Politeness and the Interpretation of the British Eighteenth Century." *Historical Journal* 45, no. 4 (2002): 869–98.

Kupperman, Karen. "Presentment of Civility: English Reading of American Self-Presentation in the Early Years of Colonization." *William and Mary Quarterly* 54, no. 1 (1997): 193–228.

Kurlansky, Mark. *The Basque History of the World*. London: Vintage, 2000.

———. *Cod: A Biography of the Fish That Changed the World*. London: Vintage, 1999.

Landry, Donna. *The Invention of the Countryside: Hunting, Walking, and Ecology in English Literature, 1671–1831*. New York: Palgrave, 2001.

Lanman, Charles. *Haw-ho-noo: or, Records of a tourist*. Philadelphia: Lippincott, Grambo, 1850. Accessed 1 July 2007 via Early English Books Online, http://eebo.chadwyck.com/home.

Lawson, John. *The History of Carolina; containing the exact description and natural history of that country*. London: Y. Warner, 1718. Accessed 6 July 2007 via Eighteenth Century Collections Online, http://www.gale.com/eighteenthcentury/.

Lemos, William. "Voyages of Columbus." In *Christopher Columbus and the Age of Exploration: An Encyclopedia*, edited by Silvio A. Bedini, 693–728. New York: Da Capo, 1998.

Letters of Eminent Men, addressed to Ralph Thoresby, F.R.S. 2 vols. London: Henry Colburn and Richard Bentley, 1832.

Lévi-Strauss, Claude. "The Culinary Triangle." In *Food and Culture*, edited by Carole Counihan and Penny Van Esterik, 28–35. New York: Routledge, 1997.

Lewis, M. G. *Journal of a West Indian Proprietor, 1815–1817.* Edited by Mona Wilson. London: Routledge, 1929.

Litwack, Leon F. *Trouble in Mind: Black Southerners in the Age of Jim Crow.* New York: Vintage, 1999.

Long, Edward. *The history of Jamaica: or, General survey of the antient and modern state of that island: with reflections on its situations, settlements, inhabitants, climate, products, commerce, laws, and government.* London: F. Cass, 1970.

Loomba, Ania. *Colonialism/Postcolonialism.* London: Routledge, 1998.

MacPherson, James. *The Highlander: a poem: in six cantos.* Edinburgh, U.K.: Wal Ruddiman, 1758. Accessed 1 July 2007 via Eighteenth Century Collections Online, http://www.gale.com/eighteenthcentury/.

Mancour, Terry. "North Carolina Barbecue: A Primer." Accessed 4 Jan. 2007, via http://www.northcarolina.com/stories/bbq.html.

Marambaud, Pierre. *William Byrd of Westover, 1674–1744.* Charlottesville: University Press of Virginia, 1971.

Martire d' Anghiera, Pietro. *The decades of the newe worlde or west India conteynyng the nauigations and conquestes of the Spanyardes, with the particular description of the moste ryche and large landes and ilandes lately founde in the west ocean perteynyng to the inheritaunce of the kinges of Spayne . . . Wrytten in the Latine tounge by Peter Martyr of Angleria, and translated into Englysshe by Rycharde Eden.* London: Guilhelmi Powell, 1555. Accessed 1 July 2007 via Early English Books Online, http://eebo.chadwyck.com/home.

Mather, Cotton. *Diary of Cotton Mather 1709–1724.* 2 vols. Boston: Massachusetts Historical Society Collections, 1911.

Mazumdar, Sucheta. "The Impact of New World Food Crops on the Diet and Economies of China and India, 1600–1900." In *Food in Global History*, edited by Raymond Grew, 58–78. Boulder, Colo.: Westview, 1999.

McCarthy, Cormac. *The Orchard Keeper.* London: Picador, 1994.

McLellan, James. *Joseph Story and the American Constitution: A Study in Political and Legal Thought.* Norman: University of Oklahoma, 1991.

McClendon, Muriel C. "A Moveable Feast: Saint George's Day Celebrations and Religious Change in Early Modern England." *Journal of British Studies* 38, no. 1 (1999): 1–27.

Melville, Herman. *Moby-Dick or, The Whale.* Harmondsworth, U.K.: Penguin, 1992.

Mencken, H. L. "Sound and Fury." In *The Impossible H. L. Mencken: A Selection of His Best Newspaper Stories*, edited by Marion Elizabeth Rodgers, 195–99. New York: Anchor, 1991.

Middleton, Richard. "O Brother, Let's Go Down Home: Loss, Nostalgia and the Blues." *Popular Music* 26, no. 1 (2007): 47–64.

Mintz, Sidney W. *Caribbean Transformations.* Chicago: Aldine, 1974.

———. "Enduring Substances, Trying Theories: The Caribbean Region as Oikoumene." *Journal of the Royal Anthropological Institute* 2, no. 2 (1996): 289–311.

———. "Groups, Group Boundaries and the Perception of 'Race,' Review Article." *Comparative Studies in Society and History* 13, no. 4 (1971): 437–50.

———. *Sweetness and Power: The Place of Sugar in Modern History.* New York: Penguin, 1985.

———. *Tasting Food, Tasting Freedom: Excursions into Eating, Culture, and the Past.* Boston: Beacon, 1996.

Mintz, Sidney W., and Richard Price. *The Birth of African-American Culture: An Anthropological Perspective.* Boston: Beacon, 1992.

de Miranda, Francisco. *The Diary of Francisco de Miranda, Tour of the United States, 1783–1784.* 2 vols. Edited by William Spence Robertson. New York: Hispanic Society of America, 1928.

Montagu, Mary Wortley. *The Turkish Embassy Letters.* Edited by Malcolm Jack. London: Virago, 1994.

Morgan, Edmund S. *American Slavery, American Freedom: The Ordeal of Colonial Virginia.* New York: W. W. Norton, 1975.

———. "Making Use of a New World." In *The National Experience: A History of the United States*, 2–27. Orlando, Fla.: Harcourt Brace Jocavonovich, 1989.

Morgan, Jennifer L. "'Some Could Suckle over Their Shoulder': Male Travelers, Female Bodies, and the Gendering of Racial Ideology, 1500–1770." *William and Mary Quarterly* 54, no. 1 (1997): 167–92.

Morrison, Toni. *The Bluest Eye.* London: Picador, 1999.

———. *Playing in the Dark: Whiteness and the Literary Imagination.* Cambridge, Mass.: Harvard University Press, 1992.

Mullen, Harryette. "Optic White: Blackness and the Production of Whiteness." *Diacritics* 24, no. 2 (1994), 71–89.

Nader, Helen. "Andrés Bernáldez." In *Christopher Columbus and the Age of Exploration: An Encyclopedia*, edited by Silvio A. Bedini, 64–65. New York: Da Capo, 1998.

Nugent, Lady. *Lady Nugent's Journal of Her Residence in Jamaica from 1801 to 1805.* Edited by Philip Wright. Kingston: Institute of Jamaica, 1966.

Ogg, Frederic Austin. *The Reign of Andrew Jackson: A Chronicle of the Frontier in Politics.* New Haven: Yale University Press, 1919.

O'Leary, Cecilia Elizabeth. *To Die For: The Paradox of American Patriotism.* Princeton, N.J.: Princeton University Press, 1999.

Oviedo y Valdés, Gonzalo Fernández. *Historia General y Natural de las Indias, islas y Tierra-Firme del Mar Océano.* 7 vols. Edited by José Amador de los Ríos. Asunción del Paraguay: Editorial Guaranía, 1944–45.

The Oxford Dictionary of National Biography. 60 vols. Edited by H. C. G. Matthew and Brian Harrison. Oxford: Oxford University Press, 2004.

The Oxford English Dictionary. 20 vols. Edited by J. A. Simpson and E. S. C. Weiner. Oxford: Clarendon Press, 1989.

Patterson, Orlando. "Rituals of Blood: Sacrificial Murders in the Postbellum South." *Journal of Blacks in Higher Education* 23, no. 2 (1999): 123–27.

Pearce, Roy Harvey. *Savagism and Civilization: A Study of the Indian and the American Mind.* Berkeley: University of California Press, 1988. Originally published as *The Savages of America* (1953).

Peebles-Wilkins, Wilma. "Reactions of Segments of the Black Community to the North Carolina Pearsall Plan, 1954–1966." *Phylon* 48, no. 2 (1987): 112–21.

Petersen, James B. "Taino, Island Carib, and Prehistoric Amerindian Economies in the West Indies: Tropical Forest Adaptations to Island Environments." In *The Indigenous People of the Caribbean*, edited by Samuel M. Wilson, 118–30. Gainesville: University Press of Florida, 1997.

Philbrick, Nathaniel, *Mayflower: A Voyage to War.* London: Harper Press, 2006.

Pleck, Elizabeth. "The Making of the Domestic Occasion: The History of Thanksgiving in the United States." *Journal of Social History* 32, no. 4 (1999): 773–89.

Pliny the Elder. *The Elder Pliny on the Human Animal: Natural history, Book Seven.* Edited and translated by Mary Beagon. Oxford: Clarendon Press, 2005.

Poe, Tracey N. "The Origins of Soul Food in Black Urban Identity: Chicago, 1915–1947." In *Food in the USA: A Reader*, edited by Carole M. Counihan, 91–108. New York: Routledge, 2002.

Pope, Alexander. *The Works of Alexander Pope, Esq.* 6 vols. Edinburgh, U.K.: J. Balfour, 1764. Accessed 6 July 2007 via Eighteenth Century Collections Online, http://www.gale.com/eighteenthcentury/.

Porter, Roy. *Enlightenment: Britain and the Creation of the Modern World.* London: Penguin, 2001.

———. *Flesh in the Age of Reason.* New York: Allen Lane, 2003.

Preston, Diana, and Michael Preston. *A Pirate of Exquisite Mind: The Life of William Dampier: Explorer, Naturalist, and Buccaneer.* London: Corgi, 2005.

Purchas, Samuel. *Purchas his pilgrims: In fiue bookes . . .* London: William Stansby, 1625. Accessed 1 July 2007 via Early English Books Online, http://eebo.chadwyck.com/home.

Remini, Robert S. *Andrew Jackson and the Course of American Freedom, 1822–1832.* New York: Harper and Row, 1981.

Reed, John Shelton. "Barbecue Sociology: The Meat of the Matter." In Elie, *Cornbread Nation 2*, 78–87.

Roberts, Hugh D. *Downhearth to Bar Grate: An Illustrated Account of the Evolution in Cooking due to the Use of Coal instead of Wood.* Avebury, U.K.: Wiltshire Folk Life Society, 1981.

Roberts, John W. "'Hidden Right out in the Open': The Field of Folklore and the Problem of Invisibility." *Journal of American Folklore* 112, no. 444 (1999): 119–39.

de Rochefort, César. *The history of the Caribby-islands, viz, Barbados, St Christophers, St Vincents, Martinico, Dominico, Barbouthos, Monserrat, Mevis, Antego, &c in all XXVIII in two books: the first containing the natural, the second, the moral history of those islands: illustrated with several pieces of sculpture representing the most considerable rarities therein described: with a Caribbian vocabulary.* Translated by John Davies. London: Thomas Dring and John Starkey, 1666.

Accessed 1 July 2007 via Early English Books Online, http://eebo.chadwyck
.com/home.

Rogers, Pat. *Grub Street: Studies in a Subculture.* London: Methuen, 1972.

Rogin, Michael Paul. *Fathers and Children: Andrew Jackson and the Subjugation of the American Indian.* New Brunswick, N.J.: Transaction, 2000.

Rouse, Irving. *The Tainos: Rise and Decline of the People Who Greeted Columbus.* New Haven: Yale University Press, 1992.

Ryves, Bruno. *Mercurius Rusticus or, The countries complaint of the barbarous out-rages committed by the sectaries of this late flourishing kingdome. Together with a briefe chronologie of the battails, sieges, conflicts, and other most remarkable passages from the beginning of this unnaturall warre, to the 25. of March, 1646.* London: Oxford, 1646.

Said, Edward W. *Culture and Imperialism.* London: Vintage, 1994.

———. *Orientalism.* London: Penguin, 1991.

Sambrook, James. "Ward, Edward [Ned] (1667–1731)" in *Oxford Dictionary of National Biography.* Online version accessed 11 April 2006, http://www.oxforddnb .com.

Sayre, Gordon M. *Les Sauvages Américains: Representations of Native Americans in French and English Colonial Literature.* Chapel Hill: University of North Carolina Press, 1997.

Scarborough, Dorothy. *On the Trail of Negro Folk-songs.* Cambridge, Mass.: Harvard University Press, 1925.

Schneider, Bethany Ridgway. "Reading for Indian Resistance." In Castillo and Schweitzer, *Companion to the Literatures of Colonial America,* 159–73.

Shakespeare, William. *The Tempest.* Edited by David Lindley. Cambridge: Cambridge University Press, 2002.

Shange, Ntozake. *If I Can Cook, You Know God Can.* Boston: Beacon, 1998.

Shubert, Adrian. *Death and Money in the Afternoon: A History of the Spanish Bullfight.* New York: Oxford University Press, 1999.

Slotkin, Richard. *The Fatal Environment: The Myth of the Frontier in the Age of Industrialization, 1800–1890.* New York: Harper Perennial, 1994.

Smith, Captain John. *The Generall Historiee of Virginia, New-England, and the Summer Isles.* In *The Complete Works of Captain John Smith,* edited by Philip L. Barbour, 2:27–487. Chapel Hill: University of North Carolina, 1986.

Smith, Stephen. "The Rhetoric of Barbecue." In Elie, *Cornbread Nation 2,* 61–68.

Smith-Rosenberg, Carroll. "Davey Crockett as Trickster: Pornography, Liminality and Symbolic Inversion in Victorian America." *Journal of Contemporary History* 17, no. 2 (1982): 325–50.

Sollors, Werner. "Introduction: The Invention of Ethnicity." In *The Invention of Ethnicity,* edited by Werner Sollors, ix–xx. New York: Oxford University Press, 1989.

Spang, Rebecca. *The Invention of the Restaurant: Paris and Modern Gastronomic Culture.* Basingstoke, U.K.: Palgrave, 1992.

Stade, Hans. *The Captivity of Hans Stade of Hesse, in A.D. 1547–1555, among the Wild Tribes of Eastern Brazil.* Translated by Albert Tootal and edited by Richard F. Burton. London: Hakluyt Society, 1874.

Starkey, Armstrong. *European and Native American Warfare, 1675–1815.* London: UCL Press, 1998.

Staten, Vince. "Real Barbecue Revisited." In Elie, *Cornbread Nation 2*, 138–40.

Steingarten, Jeffrey. "Going Whole Hog." In *The Man Who Ate Everything: And Other Gastronomic Feats, Disputes, and Pleasurable Pursuits*, 260–75. London: Headline, 1997.

Stedman, John Gabriel. *Narrative, of a five years' expedition; against the revolted negroes of Surinam, in Guiana, on the wild coast of South America; from the year 1772, to 1777.* 2 vols. London: J. Johnson and J. Edwards, 1796. Accessed 6 July 2007 via Eighteenth Century Collections Online, http://www.gale.com/eighteenth century/.

Stevenson, Robert Louis. *Treasure Island.* Edited by John Seelye. London: Penguin, 1999.

Swift, Jonathan. *Major Works.* Edited by Angus Ross and David Woolley. Oxford: Oxford University Press, 2003.

Sydnor, Charles S. *Gentlemen Freeholders: Political Practices in Washington's Virginia.* Chapel Hill: University of North Carolina Press, 1952.

Thomas, G. Scott. *The Pursuit of the White House: A Handbook of Presidential Election Statistics and History.* New York Greenwood, 1987.

Thompson, Andrew C. "Popery, Politics, and Private Judgement in Early Hanoverian Britain." *Historical Journal* 45, no. 2 (2002): 333–56.

Tylor, Edward B. *Anahuac: or, Mexico and the Mexicans, Ancient and Modern.* London: Longman, Green, Longman and Roberts, 1861. Accessed 1 July 2007 via Google Book Search, http://books.google.co.uk/.

———. *Researches into the Early History of Mankind and the Development of Civilization.* London: Murray, 1878.

Van Buren, Martin. *Papers of Martin Van Buren.* Accessed 5 Feb. 2007 via Library of Congress Digital Collections, http://memory.loc.gov/.

Vaughn, Alden T. *Roots of American Racism: Essays on the Colonial Experience.* New York: Oxford University Press, 1995.

Walcott, Derek. "The Muse of History." In *What the Twilight Says: Essays*, 36–63. London: Faber and Faber, 1998.

Walker, Alice. *The Color Purple.* London: Virago, 1983.

———. "Zora Neale Hurston—A Cautionary Tale and a Partisan View." In *In Search of Our Mothers' Gardens: Womanist Prose*, 83–92. London: Women's Press, 1984.

Wallace, David. *Premodern Places: Calais to Surinam, Chaucer to Aphra Behn.* Malden, Mass.: Blackwell, 2004.

Walvin, James. *Fruits of Empire: Exotic Produce and British Taste, 1660–1800.* London: Macmillan, 1997.

Ward, Edward [Ned]. *The Barbacue Feast: or, the Three Pigs of Peckham, Broil'd under an Apple Tree.* London: B. Bragge, 1707. Accessed 6 July 2007 via Eighteenth Century Collections Online, http://www.gale.com/eighteenthcentury/.

————. *A Collection of the Writings of Mr. Edward Ward.* 2 vols. London: A. Bettesworth, 1717. Accessed 6 July 2007 via Eighteenth Century Collections Online, http://www.gale.com/eighteenthcentury/.

————. *A frolick to Horn-fair with a walk from Cuckold's-point thro' Deptford and Greenwich.* London: I. How, 1700. Accessed 6 July 2007 via Eighteenth Century Collections Online, http://www.gale.com/eighteenthcentury/.

————. *The History of the London Clubs, or, the Citizens' Pastime. Particularly the Lying Club, . . . the Broken Shopkeepers Club, the Basket Womans Club. With a sermon preach'd to a gang of high-way-men.* Part 1. London: J. Bagnall, 1709. Accessed 6 July 2007 via Eighteenth Century Collections Online, http://www.gale.com/eighteenthcentury/.

————. *The London Spy Compleat, in Eighteen Parts.* London: Casanova Society, 1924.

————. *Secret history of clubs: particularly the Kit-Cat, Beef-Stake, Vertuosos, Quacks, Knights of the Golden-Fleece, Florists, Beaus, &c. With their original, and the characters of the most noted members thereof.* London: Booksellers, 1709.

Ward, Geoffrey. *Jazz: A History of America's Music.* London: Pimlico, 2001.

Ware, Vron, and Les Back. *Out of Whiteness: Color, Politics, and Culture.* Chicago: University of Chicago Press, 2002.

Warnes, Andrew. "Guantánamo, Eatonville, Accompong: Barbecue and the Diaspora in the Writings of Zora Neale Hurston." *Journal of American Studies* 40, no. 2 (2006): 367–89.

————. *Hunger Overcome? Food and Resistance in Twentieth-Century African American Literature.* Athens: University of Georgia Press, 2004.

Warren, Robert Penn. *Segregation: The Inner Conflict in the South.* New York: Random House, 1956.

Watkins, Floyd C. "James Kirke Paulding and the South." *American Quarterly* 5, no. 3 (1953): 219–30.

Webster, Daniel. *The Papers of Daniel Webster.* 7 vols. Edited by Charles M. Wiltse and Harold. D. Moser. Hanover, N.H.: University Press of New England, 1974–99.

Webster's Third New International Dictionary of the English Language. 2 vols. Edited by Philip Babcock Gove. London: Bell, 1961.

Weinreb, Ben, and Christopher Hibbert, eds. *The London Encyclopaedia.* London: PaperMac, 1993.

Whitman, Walt. *A Choice of Whitman's Verse.* London: Faber and Faber, 1968.

Wills, Garry. *Cincinnatus: George Washington and the Enlightenment.* Garden City, N.Y.: Doubleday, 1984.

Wilson, C. Anne. "Ideal Meals and their Menus from the Middle Ages to the Georgian Era." In *The Appetite and the Eye: Visual Aspects of Food and Its Presentation within Their Historic Context*, edited by C. Anne Wilson, 98–122. Edinburgh, U.K.: Edinburgh University Press, 1991.

Winstanley, Gerrard. "An Appeal to the House of Commons." In Gerrard Winstanley, *The Law of Freedom and Other Writings*, edited by Christopher Hill, 109–24. Cambridge: Cambridge University Press, 1973.

———. "The True Levellers' Standard Advanced." In Winstanley, *The Law of Freedom and Other Writings*, 75–95.

Wister, Owen. *The Virginian: A Horseman of the Plains.* London: Macmillan, 1930.

Witt, Doris. *Black Hunger: Food and the Politics of U.S. Identity.* New York: Oxford University Press, 1999.

Wodrow, Robert. *The Correspondence of the Rev. Robert Wodrow, Minister of Eastwood, and Author of the History of the Sufferings of the Church of Scotland.* 3 vols. Edited by Thomas McCrie. Edinburgh, U.K.: Wodrow Society, 1842–1843.

Wood, Gordon S. *The Radicalism of the Ameican Revolution.* New York: Vintage, 1991.

Wyeth, John Allan. *With Sabre and Scalpel: The Autobiography of a Soldier and Surgeon.* New York: Harper and Brothers, 1914. Accessed 1 July 2007 via Documenting the South, http://docsouth.unc.edu/.

Zibart, Eve. "The Caribbean Islands." In *The Unofficial Guide to Ethnic Cuisine and Dining in America*, edited by Eve Zibart, Muriel Stevens, and Terrell Vermont, 333–44. New York: Macmillan, 1995.

INDEX

Adair, James, 30, 114
Adams, John Quincy, 156, 160, 166, 171
Addison, Joseph: *Cato*, 58; *The Spectator*, 54, 83
Africa, 9, 47, 78, 83, 107, 114, 130
African Americans, 8, 163, 171; and barbecue, 92–95, 98–99, 115–31, 133, 135; and Black Family Reunion Celebration, 2–3, 88; culture of, 9, 50–52, 84, 103, 107; and Harlem, 50; and Harlem Renaissance, 134; and hip-hop, 88
Africans: in American colonies, 56, 62, 64, 112–13; in *The Barbacue Feast*, 79–80, 112; in London, 67; in Surinam, 30. *See also* diaspora
agrarianism, 5, 106–14, 122, 177n38; and pastoral ideal, 80. *See also* Jeffersonian vision
Algonquian, 30–31, 37–45, 64, 80, 114
American Indians. *See* Native Americans
American Revolution, 55, 85, 109–10, 162–64, 179n70
Amerindians. *See* Native Americans
Andalusia, 12–14, 20
apples, 73, 176n16
Arawaks, 6, 23–24, 37
Armada, Spanish, 27
Armstrong, Louis, 116
Arne, Thomas, 83
Asia, 20, 47, 49, 83, 138, 139, 140, 177n34. *See also* India

atrocity: in English Civil War, 34; in Florida, 25–28; in Guyana, 33; in Ireland, 34; in North Carolina, 147–52; in Tennessee, 157–58; in Virginia, 34–35

Bailey, Nathan, *Dictionarium Domesticum*, 85–86
barbacoa, 3, 7–8, 21–25, 26–28, 30, 31, 32, 48, 174n24
Barbados, 48, 55, 78
barbarism myth, 68, 80, 89–90, 99–101, 104, 112, 134, 141–42, 171–72; and Africans and African Americans, 67, 95, 171; and Asia, 137; and barbecue etymology, 6–7, 122; and Europeans and European Americans, 20, 34–35, 63–64; and Native Americans, 3, 17, 21, 25–31, 35–45, 49, 62, 64, 68, 79–84, 144–53, 158. *See also* savage myth
Basques, 12–13, 17, 20
BBQ and Bar B Q signs, 2–3, 7–9, 97, 102
Behn, Aphra, 56, 77, 141, 142; *The Feign'd Curtizans*, 58; *Oroonoko*, 61, 64; *The Widdow Ranter*, 57–64, 81, 83, 87, 109
Benin, 130
Bermondsey, 177n34
Bérnaldez, Andreas, 16–20, 36, 79
Beverley, Robert, 30–31, 82, 114

Bible, the, 34, 144; Jeremiah, 149, 182n12; Matthew, 179n45
biscuit, 16
Black Americans. *See* African Americans
Black Family Reunion Celebration, 2–3, 88
Boston baked beans, 90
bouillabaisse, 90, 105
Brazil, 39, 47. *See also* Tupinambá
bread, 93, 126, 129; chapatti, 53–54
Brickell, John, *Natural History of North Carolina*, 114
Brown, Sterling A., 50
bullfighting, 28
Byrd, William, II, 141, 152–53, 182n17

cannibalism, 7, 10, 49, 53, 73, 80–87, 175n50, 182n8; and classical myth, 147, 153, 182n19; and conquest, 22, 28, 31–36, 39–46, 56, 61–64; etymology of, 25, 174–75n36; and frontier, 142–47, 151–59, 171–72, 183n22. *See also* Caribs; Tupinambá
canoes, 8, 31, 33
Caribs, 19, 32–33, 174–75n36
Catholicism, Spanish, 16; prejudice against, 57–58, 80, 178n40
Chanca, Diégo Alvarez, 16
chapatti, 53–54
cheese, 12, 69, 90, 155
chili, 1, 2, 13, 20, 25, 93, 173n7, 177n34
Christian calendar: Christmas Day, 4, 5, 6; nativity of John the Baptist, 177n34; and Protestant reform, 178–79n44; Shrove Tuesday, 71, 178n39
civilizing process, 6, 7, 19–20, 29, 40–42, 68–69, 83, 112–13; barbecue as a rejection of, 5–6, 49, 74–75, 89–91, 103–7, 111, 127–29, 134, 141–42, 165
Civil War, British, 34, 84–85
Civil War, U.S., 86; aftermath of, 86–87
clam chowder, 1, 90

coleslaw, 93
Colombia, 23, 30
colonialism: British, 34–36; in Caribbean, 12–26, 29–30, 32–35; cultural basis of, 19, 48–49, 52, 137–39; in Florida, 26–28; imperatives of, 29–31, 48; in Ireland, 34. *See also* imperialism
Columbus, Christopher, 12–20, 25, 27, 46, 48, 82, 102
corn pupusa, 1
Creek, 156
Crockett, Davy, 155, 183n22
Cromwell, Oliver, 34
Cruikshank, Robert, 167–68
Cuba, Guantánamo Bay, 15–18, 19–20, 44, 48, 54, 82
cuisine, 1–2, 89–106
cutlery, 49, 64, 72–74, 89–91, 96, 101, 110, 129, 161

Dampier, William, 21, 22, 23, 25, 30, 31, 34
Davis, Rebecca Harding, 113
de Bry, Theodor, 64, 70, 144; *Great Voyages*, 35–46, 61–62
Defoe, Daniel, 83; *Moll Flanders*, 62; *Robinson Crusoe*, 29
Delaware, 2
Deptford, 68–69, 177n33, 177n34
de Soto, Hernando, 25–28, 62
Devil, the, 34, 35, 67–74, 139, 152, 153, 177n34, 179n45
diaspora, 50, 117–24, 133. *See also* Africa; African Americans; Africans
Dickens, Charles, *Oliver Twist*, 178n39
Diggers, 75–76
Disney, Walt, 175n50
Dixon, Thomas, 87
drovers, 71–81, 177n36
DuBois, W. E. B., 87, 164, 180n72

Edinburgh, 85

Ellison, Ralph: *Invisible Man*, 50–57, 85–86, 159; "A Party down at the Square," 182n19
empire. *See* colonialism; imperialism
Eurocentrism, 24, 85, 117, 123, 130, 138

Fanon, Frantz, 137, 139, 159
fast food, 90, 92–102; hamburgers, 92–93, 96, 98, 99; McDonald's, 92, 180n6
Faulkner, William, 175n50
Federmann, Nikolas, 23, 30
fish, 15, 82, 105, 174n17; Algonquian preparation of, 39–42, 44, 45, 114
—types of: salmon, 1; salt cod, 12–13, 16; salted herring, 12; salted whale, 12
Florida, 25–28, 48, 120, 121–22, 134
Fourth of July, 5
Frankfurt, 35
frontier, 5, 6, 143–44, 155, 161; and Jacksonian politics, 156–57, 159; mythology of, 106–7, 113–15, 117, 139, 149, 154
fugitive slaves. *See* maroon settlements

Gentleman of Elvas, the, 25–28, 30, 79
Georgia, 96, 102–4, 110, 124
Goethe, Johanna Wolfgang von, 36
gold, 14, 15, 16, 169, 170
Graffenried, Christoph de, 144–51
Greenwich, 68, 177n34
gumbo, 2

Haiti, 21, 117–21, 124, 130–31
Hakluyt, Richard, 25–28, 30, 36, 49
hamburgers, 92–93, 96, 98, 99. *See also* fast food
Hamilton, James H., 169–71
hammocks, 32, 33
Hammons, David, 116
Hardaway, J. C., 93–96, 98, 99, 102, 104, 115, 117, 130
Harlem, New York, 50, 134, 159

Harris, Joel Chandler, 87, 175n50
Hazlitt, William, 50
Hemmer, John, 124–30, 154
Hickeringill, Edmund, 25, 49, 55–56, 141; *The Ceremony Monger*, 176n8; *Jamaica Viewed*, 7, 21, 22, 32–35, 36, 53, 61, 114, 142, 152, 171
Hispaniola, 14, 15, 19, 22–24. *See also* Haiti
hoggards. *See* drovers
hunger, 12–13, 20, 35, 174n17
Hurston, Zora Neale, 116–36; *Dust Tracks on a Road*, 116, 134–36; *Moses, Man of the Mountain*, 116; *Their Eyes Were Watching God*, 116–23
hybridity, 18–19, 53, 84, 86, 122, 131–34

iguana, 17–18
imperialism: British, 55–57, 59, 77–87, 123; U.S., 138, 140, 156–72
Incas, 37
India, 20, 84; chapatti, 53–54
Indians. *See* Native Americans
invented tradition: of barbecue, 10, 53, 57, 70, 82–84, 102, 107, 114–16, 122, 131, 134, 155, 162, 171; of Election Day, 160–61; etymological, 12–50; as a historical concept, 4–7, 31; and national cuisines, 91–92; and racial identities, 139, 144; and St. George, 178–79n44
Iroquois, 54, 79
Irving, Washington, 174n12

Jackson, Andrew, 155–61, 164, 166–71
Jacksonian politics, 7, 87, 140–42, 154–55, 162–64, 167, 168–72, 183n22
Jamaica, 7, 21, 22, 32–36, 53–56, 61, 67, 70–71, 74; Maroons of, 116, 119–21, 123–24, 130
jazz, 9–10
Jefferson, Thomas, 107–13, 115, 166
Jeffersonian vision, 106, 113–15, 116, 122

Jewish peoples, in London, 73
Jonson, Ben, *Bartholomew Fair*, 178n39

Kill-Devil. *See* rum (Kill-Devil)
Ku Klux Klan, 9

Las Casas, Bartholomew de, 27
Lawson, John, 144–51; *The History of Carolina*, 146–47, 149–51
Lincoln, Abraham, 4
London, 6, 10, 33, 53–64, 82–87, 104, 111, 149, 172
—places in: Fleet Ditch, 65–66; Grub Street, 66; St. Giles, 67; St. Paul's Cathedral, 66; Smithfield meat market, 177n36, 178n39
Louisiana, 97, 102
lynching, 140, 175n40, 178n39; and barbecue parallel, 154, 182n19

Macpherson, James, *The Highlander*, 57
maroon settlements: in Jamaica, 116, 119–21, 123–24, 130; in Surinam, 30
masculinity, 6, 7, 68, 69, 72, 121, 157, 171; and militarism, 124, 150
Mather, Cotton, 34, 141, 152–54
Mayflower, 177n34
McCarthy, Cormac, 106, 175n50
Melville, Herman, *Moby Dick*, 46, 175n50
Memphis, 91–95, 100, 104
Mencken, H. L., 21, 154
Mexico, 1, 16
mirrors, 64, 67
Mohocks, 54, 83–84, 177n34
Morrison, Toni, 50, 51–52
Murray, Albert, 116
Murrell, John, *A New Book of Cookerie*, 83

National Museum of the America Indian, 1–4, 7
Native Americans: and face painting,

179n46; and noble savage myth, 29, 63, 113; shared cuisine of, 1–2, 23; shared cultures of, 4, 7, 9; unidentified groups of, 13, 14, 16, 26–28. *See also* Mohocks; savage myth; *and individual tribal groups*
Nazism, 52, 53, 54, 131
Nicaragua, 30; Moskito coast of, 23, 48
Nigeria, 130
North Carolina, 96, 100, 103, 105, 109, 116; colony of, 114–15, 143–54, 157; and segregation, 124–31

offal, 13
Oklahoma, 113
oranges, 29–30
Orient, 12, 19, 20, 177n34
Orientalism, 36, 78–80, 83–84, 94, 137–42, 151, 177n34
Ottawa (tribe). *See* Pontiac (Ottawa leader)
Oviedo y Valdés, Gonzalo Fernández de, 22–23, 30, 33, 34
Oxford English Dictionary (OED), 21–25, 114

paella, 90
Panama, 22, 49
Parkman, Francis, 143
pastoral ideal, 80. *See also* agrarianism
Pearsall, Thomas J., 124–28
Peckham, 54, 69–75, 76–87, 91, 104, 109, 177n36, 179n45
pepper, 25, 177n34
pigs: and de Soto, 62; in England, 69–70, 71–73, 76–84, 177n38, 178n39, 178n40, 178n42, 178n43, 179n43; and pit barbecue culture, 97–99, 125–29; rhizomatic, 134; Virginia, 60–62; wild boar (in Jamaica), 118–20
Pinzón, Martín Alonso, 14–15
Piscataway, 2

plantation, 53, 55–56, 78, 107, 124–30, 132, 143, 154; and cooking 84; and labor, 62, 113. *See also* slavery

Pliny the Elder, 147, 153, 182n8

Polynesia, 175n50

Pontiac (Ottawa leader), 143

Pope, Alexander, 58, 65, 67, 83

Portugal, 27–28

primitivism, 3–4, 6–8, 31, 95, 104, 131, 154, 164–65, 171–72. *See also* barbarism myth; savage myth

Protestantism, 32–35, 58, 60, 63, 74, 178–79n44

punch, 70, 177n34

Purchas, Samuel, 25, 178n41

revolutionary politics: in America, 55, 85, 109–10, 162–64, 179n70; and Diggers, 75–76; in England, 59–60, 64, 77–78, 84. *See also* Jefferson, Thomas; Jacksonian politics

Ringmann, Matthias, 46–49

Rotherhithe, 70, 177n34

rum (Kill-Devil), 70–71, 177n34

Ryves, Bruno, 34

salted whale, 12

sausage, 13

savage myth, 30, 36, 49, 69–70, 72–74, 89, 103–4, 114, 139–40, 142, 157–60, 165–68; and the Caribbean, 16, 19–20, 24–25; and Florida, 27–28; and North Carolina, 144–55; and Virginia, 43–46, 63–64

segregation, 3; defense of, 124–31; resistance to, 95, 103

Shakespeare, William, *The Tempest*, 12

signs, barbecue. *See* BBQ and Bar B Q signs

slavery, 27, 36, 130–32, 139; and British Empire, 78–87; of Caribs, 32; in colonial Virginia, 59, 61, 62, 111; and English cultural life, 55–57,

64–65; in Jamaica, 67, 124; in Surinam, 30, 64; in the United States, 50, 52, 106–9, 112–17, 143–49, 154–61, 163–66

Smith, John, 29, 34–35, 178n41

Smithsonian Institute, 2, 3, 10, 11

smoke cookery, 2, 9, 81–82; of the Algonquian, 38–42; and native Caribbean cuisine, 16–19, 25, 30, 36, 174n17

Sorkin, Aaron, 8–9

soul food, 176n27

South Carolina, 169, 171

Spain, 16–18, 27, 23–28, 30, 32

Spectator, The (Addison and Steele), 54, 83

Stade, Hans, 44, 175n48

Stedman, John Gabriel, 30

Steele, Richard, 83–84

Stevenson, Robert Louis, *Treasure Island*, 46, 175n50

Story, Joseph, 166–67

Strachey, William, 179n46

Surinam, 30, 64

Surrey, 69–74, 75, 177n36

Sussex, 177n36

Swift, Jonathan, 65–66

tacos, 1

Taino, 13, 14, 18, 25, 31

Tennessee, 93, 156–57, 167. *See also* Memphis

Texas, 96–100, 182n19

Thanksgiving, 4, 5

Toomer, Jean, 116

Tupinambá, 37–46, 64, 144, 175n48

turnip tops, 66

Tuscarora, 147–54

Tylor, E. B., 21, 22–24

Valencia, 90

Van Buren, Martin, 169–70, 171

vegetarianism, 75–76

Venezuela, 47

Vespucci, Amerigo, 46–48

Virginia, 57, 82, 108–16, 132, 146, 152–53, 176n16; and the Algonquian, 30–31, 37–42, 58–64; and Bacon's Rebellion, 58–64; Jamestown, 19, 34–35

Walcott, Derek, 29

Walker, Alice, 116

Wallace, William, 178n39

Walton, John, 113

Ward, Ned, 55–57, 109, 112, 141, 142, 149, 154

—works of: *The Barbacue Feast*, 54, 69–75, 76–87, 91, 102, 104, 177n33; *The Delights of the Bottle*, 65; *A Frolick to Horn Fair*, 68–70, 72; *The London Spy*, 66; *Secret history of clubs*, 177n33; *Sot's Paradise*, 65; *A Trip to Jamaica*, 67, 70

Washington, D.C., 1–3, 54, 88–89, 167–72

Webster, Daniel, 167, 171

West Wing, The, 8–10

White, John, 37–44, 80

Whitman, Walt, 88, 140

wild boar, in Jamaica, 118–20. *See also* pigs

Winstanley, Gerrard, 75–77, 81

Wister, Owen, 113

Wright, Richard, 95